MW01009036

AWAKENING OF A
JEHOVAH'S WITNESS

AWAKENING OF A

JEHOVAH'S WITNESS

Escape from the Watchtower Society

DIANE WILSON

Prometheus Books

59 John Glenn Drive
Amherst, New York 14228-2197

Published 2002 by Prometheus Books

Inquiries should be addressed to
Prometheus Books
59 John Glenn Drive
Amherst, New York 14228–2197
VOICE: 716–691–0133, ext. 207
FAX: 716–564–2711
WWW.PROMETHEUSBOOKS.COM

09 08 07 06 05   8 7 6 5 4

Library of Congress Cataloging-in-Publication Data

Wilson, Diane.
    Awakening of a Jehovah's Witness : escape from Watchtower Society / Diane Wilson ; foreword by Jerry Bergman.
        p. cm.
    ISBN 1–57392–942–5 (alk. paper)
    1. Jehovah's Witnesses—Controversial literature. 2. Wilson, Diane. 3. Jehovah's Witnesses—United States—Biography. I. Title.

BX8526.5 .W55 2002
289.9'2'092—dc21
[B]   2001048435

Printed in the United States of America on acid-free paper

Dedicated to Jeff

with gratitude for seeing me through

CONTENTS

ENDORSEMENTS

Diane Wilson, former longtime member of the Watchtower organization, has written a veritable "spiritual thriller," describing her dramatic journey to psychological freedom. She explores with frankness and passion her unfortunate servitude to the Watchtower Bible and Tract Society, an organization which views itself as the sole possessor of all religious truth. The fascinated reader will be swept along emotionally as Diane details her odyssey to freedom from what most former Jehovah's Witnesses describe as a mind-control cult.

Diane spells out her initial vulnerability to the unique claims of the Watchtower Society and her fierce struggle to disengage herself from such powerfully persuasive people; in short, she reveals the dark side of Watchtower worship.

As a former high-ranking member of the Watchtower Society, I can personally vouch for the veracity of her analysis of Watchtower methods and policies. In my twenty-two years as one of Jehovah's Witnesses, I had attained the position of "Traveling Overseer" both in the United States and Brazil. I am a graduate of the Watchtower Bible School, "Gilead," and have spent tens of thousands of hours attending meetings, studying their literature, going from door-to-door with the Watchtower message, and giving sermons in hundreds of Kingdom Halls (Witness churches).

Diane's description of life in the Watchtower Society is painfully accurate. If the reader has friends or neighbors or loved ones in that organization, Diane's moving autobiography will poignantly underscore the tragic position these individuals are in. The reader will put down Diane's book (and I'm sure most will read it in a single sitting) with a greatly enlarged understanding of what life in the Watchtower cult is all about. And, perhaps

9

more importantly, with deeper sympathy for those unfortunate people known as Jehovah's Witnesses.

Donald Nelson
Former Watchtower missionary in Brazil

This is the powerful, vividly expressed story of a young woman who was persuaded to join the organization of Jehovah's Witnesses, from which, after many years of disillusionment, she had to struggle to free herself.

Diane Wilson presents her experiences and her inner thoughts in a most effective manner. Incidents that occurred while she was in the Watchtower organization are clearly and accurately described. The reader will quickly perceive her growing feelings of dismay, confusion, and trauma.

This is not a testimony of personal conversion to Christ; it is an impressive account of involvement with and escape from a cult.

Awakening of a Jehovah's Witness is both accurate and revealing. I'm sure that thousands of former Jehovah's Witness women will be able to personally relate to many of Diane's experiences and emotions. Her story makes compelling and believable reading.

Rev. Peter D. Barnes, D. Div.

Rev. Barnes was an active Jehovah's Witness for thirty years, including several years as a circuit overseer, and was responsible for sixteen Kingdom Halls. He is now an ordained Baptist minister with a support outreach for former Jehovah's Witnesses.

FOREWORD

Everyday thousands of people leave the Watchtower; and although some return, a total of about a million people have left for good. Each one of these has his or her own story to tell, and each in its own way is a fascinating history of the struggle of a person's attempt to serve God and learn the truth about the universe and its creator. A few of those people are gifted writers who have exceptional stories to tell—Diane Wilson is one of these. A thorough researcher, yet an expert storyteller, she has combined these two skills to produce a lively account of her experience in the Watchtower.

Many books on the Watchtower are theological treaties; this book, however, is a story of a real person who recounts her struggles in dealing with the turmoil the Watchtower creates in the lives of millions of people. No doubt many readers will identify with Diane's story; also, no doubt, this story will help many readers deal with their struggles about the Watchtower—both those who elect to leave, and those struggling with the current Watchtower leadership.

In any industry, failures are of critical importance to learn why the failure occurred. Those people who leave the Watchtower are the Watchtower's failures, and why these occur are critically important in understanding the Watchtower movement and its strength and shortcomings. Reading this work helps a person to know another fellow traveler and hopefully learn from the experience. Experience may be the best teacher, but it is not always the most economical one. Learning from the experiences of others can be critically important in a person's growth to avoid repeating the mistakes of others.

This work will appeal to anyone who has an interest in the Watchtower,

11

former Witnesses, and the many people who have made it their lives' avocation to understand this important religious movement. Diane's goal is not so much to convince, as to enlighten and inform to help the reader understand. If understanding is achieved, the author's effort in this work will have been more than worthwhile.

—Jerry Bergman, Ph.D., MSBS, L.P.C.C.

Dr. Bergman has extensively studied the Jehovah's Witnesses faith for thirty years. He is now the leading American expert on the psychology of Jehovah's Witnesses. He has authored over 400 articles in the field of psychology, sociology, and science, and has written over twenty-five books, book chapters, and monographs. He is listed in Who's Who in America, *and* Who's Who in Science and Religion.

PREFACE

N o one is immune to influence from the persuasive, seductive cultlike religious group known as Jehovah's Witnesses under leadership of the Watchtower Society. The public needs to be warned. The public needs to be alerted to the lures that this group uses to ensnare innocent people. The public needs to be protected against wasting many years of precious life following the alluring promises about the future world government under the Watchtower Society that Jehovah's Witnesses dance in front of their wondering eyes.

Many have fallen victim to the deceptions of this organization; the nightmare that these millions of people entered could have been avoided if they had been aware of the deceitful, entrapping, manipulative ways of the Watchtower Society.

This work is not a doctrinal treatise about Jehovah's Witnesses; instead, it is an issues-oriented human interest story that reveals inside information about twenty-five years of my adult life in this Christian sect. It deals with many women's issues as seen through the colored lens of the Watchtower Society. It spells out my vulnerability to the enticements that the Witnesses use, the many abuses I suffered while I was in the group, the horrendous psychological struggles I experienced while trying to escape their mind-control methods and induced phobias, and how a psychologist finally helped me to succeed in breaking free from their grasp.

My hope is that readers will take away with them an increased understanding of how extremely difficult leaving a legalistic, controlling group like Jehovah's Witnesses can be—even when a person *desperately wants* to leave. Telling my story was an important part of my healing process.

As part of my endeavor to make this work easy to read, I have dealt with my references to Watchtower literature in a special way; i.e., immediately after quoting from the Watchtower Society's magazines, I have indicated in parentheses the name of the magazine by using the abbreviation "WT" to represent the *Watchtower* magazine, and "AW" to represent the *Awake!* magazine, its date of publication, and the page numbers from which the quote was taken. Immediately after quoting from a Watchtower book, I have indicated in parentheses the name of the book, the year in which it was published, and the page numbers from which the quote was taken. I have used this method instead of footnoting these references in order to spare the reader having to repeatedly go to the end of each chapter to look up the corresponding footnote in order to ascertain from which text the quote came. I have provided a glossary at the back of the book to explain the meanings of special Watchtower terminology included in my text as well as a List of Periodicals that gives details about each of the references I have cited.

The part of this work that relates to my psychotherapy experience quotes my therapist as making various statements; these quotes are drawn from my therapy journal notes and my remembrances of my therapy experience, and thus may or may not be precise quotes of what was actually said.

ACKNOWLEDGMENTS

I wish to thank my brother, Bruce, for originating the idea which led to the title of this work; my friends Carolyn, Debbie, and Margie, for reading my first draft and giving me invaluable feedback; Don and Peter, for their constructive criticism and suggestions; Dr. Jerry Bergman for encouraging me to tell my story, his guidance during this project, and for contributing the Foreword and Appendices for this work; my daughter, Stephanie, for her emotional support, and most especially for her courage, which was the catalyst for my change; and my therapist, Jeff, for his endless patience, gentleness, compassion, and wisdom, without which making this transition in my life would have been much more difficult.

ONE

GROOMED TO BE A VICTIM

"I'm going to kill you! *I'm going to kill you!*" my mother shrieked, chasing me through the house, waving her torn and tattered flyswatter furiously. The filthy wire mesh flyswatter, with its broken sharp strands protruding menacingly from its surface, was an object to be feared when in the flailing hand of my crazed mother. "I must have done something wrong!" I thought. I felt confused and frightened; where could I hide to escape my mother's burning anger and the stinging swipes of her flyswatter?

My mother's state of mind was inconsistent and unpredictable; I was the victim of her erratic mood swings, as her depression frequently and without warning gave way to episodes of violent outbursts of uncontrolled anger. She would behave lovingly toward me one moment but would blaze with rage against me the next. Often my ears would ring in the aftermath of the frenzied eruption of profanities she directed at me. I was forced to do whatever she said to do, as I was beaten, mistreated, or punished if I questioned or criticized anything she said or did.

As a young child, I loved to rollerskate outdoors; at times, however, I would trip and fall, scraping my knees on the rough macadam sidewalk. My mother would laugh as she scrubbed my bleeding wounds with a stiff brush while pouring burning antiseptic over them. My screams were met with a stinging slap which often left the imprint of her hand as a red welt on my face.

A small red rocking chair became one of my favorite places of refuge; I found solace and comfort in its rhythmic movement and felt protected as I snuggled in its strong cushioned frame. The chair, however, provided but an illusion of safety, for it could not shield me from my mother's wrath. Acting upon arbitrary whims, she would drag me out of the chair to the bathroom down the hallway, violating my body by forcing enemas on me unnecessarily, striking me repeatedly to quell my resistance. My cries of protest resulted in her thrusting a bar of soap into my mouth, grating it on my teeth if I clenched them shut to avoid its acrid taste.

She abused me emotionally and physically in other ways as well throughout my childhood and adolescence. As a result of my mother's arbitrary moods and degrading behavior, I felt uncertain of myself and my ability "to see things right." I learned at an early age that the world was not a safe place, and that I was powerless, helpless, and vulnerable in the face of authority.

I grew up feeling rejected and worthless: the feeling of rejection led to a compulsive desire to please others, hoping to win their approval; the feeling of worthlessness led to my thinking that I had nothing valuable to say, thus developing a dependency on the leadership of others. Because my mother treated me like a child throughout my adolescent years, part of me emotionally stayed childlike; consequently, I developed an impaired capacity to question critically anything I was told. As a result of my mother's unstable behavior, I developed a need for absolute answers, order, stability, and rules in my life in order to feel safe and secure.

The sting of my mother's flyswatter was later replaced by the sting of her words: "I can't wait until you find a boyfriend, so you can leave!" Her inferred message of, "You can't take care of yourself; you need someone to take care of you," left its impression on my mind as deeply as if it were seared there by a branding iron. I found escape in fantasies, fanciful daydreams, and fairytale books. I envied the "magic" with which the characters' lives were played out, for no matter how bad things became, there was always a rescuer who would come and save the "damsel in distress." I believed that one day, I would be "magically" rescued, too.

I learned much later in my life that it was not by chance that I became one of Jehovah's Witnesses. The desire to belong, lack of self-confidence, the inability to express criticism or doubt, gullibility, naïve idealism, and a low tolerance for ambiguity—all of which I developed while I was growing up—are the same predisposing factors that experts[1] say can cause a person to be more vulnerable to being seduced into a cultlike group. My abusive childhood experiences, together with my ignorance of how groups can manipulate individuals, were also key factors leading to my involvement with the Watchtower Society.

NOTE

1. Madeleine L. Tobias and Janja Lalich, *Captive Hearts, Captive Minds* (Alameda, Calif.: Hunter House, 1994), pp. 27–28.

TWO

HOOKED

A bout of severe hepatitis in 1966 during my senior year in high school left me hospitalized, physically weak, and emotionally vulnerable. Desperate to get away from my abusive mother and unable to support myself, I fell prey to the attention and flattery of a young man who worked at the hospital; we were married a few months later.

Within a short time, I became unhappy with my marriage. My world seemed small, stale, and stagnant; thus I was inclined to listen when my sister-in-law started telling me about something exciting that she had been learning through a home Bible study with Jehovah's Witnesses—Armageddon! She exclaimed that the battle of Armageddon will be the time when God's heavenly forces will act to destroy all evil and wicked people.

She proclaimed that we were now living in an unprecedented time in history: "the last days" which will directly precede Armageddon!

She emphasized that my very life was at stake. She explained that since Jehovah's Witnesses are the only true religion, only they would be spared destruction at Armageddon. As the weeks went by, the more I thought about our conversation, the more my initial intrigue turned to fear; the possibility that this cataclysmic event might really happen began to frighten me. Thoughts of Armageddon loomed large in my mind and began to haunt me. My sister-in-law had moved far away, leaving me stranded with my fears; thus, during the summer of 1968, I contacted Jehovah's Witnesses from a number I found in the telephone directory in order to obtain more information.

Arrangements were made for a couple from the local congregation to visit me to answer my questions and discuss the issues that were causing me so much distress. The friendly couple were slightly older than me, with a baby the same age as mine. I liked them immediately. Smiling easily, with a ready sense of humor, they quickly gained my trust. I respected the depth of knowledge they possessed about life, religion, and the Bible, and I found their enthusiasm contagious.

While the babies played gleefully on the floor, the couple conducted a home Bible study with me, utilizing a new publication by the Watchtower Society called *The Truth That Leads to Eternal Life* (1968). They used this book as a guide in understanding the Bible; it described God's "new system of things" on the Earth, a paradise in which sickness, pain, and death would not exist. They explained how everyone would enjoy perfect health and happiness forever; children would grow older, and older persons would grow younger, until they reached the prime of life. All would have their own house and land, and delicious food would grow easily and in abundance in the fertile land that God would bless. Boredom would be a thing of the past, as all would derive deep satisfaction from interesting work and would enjoy the fruits of their own labor. No one would live in fear, as lawbreakers would cease to exist; the world would be filled only with loving and kind people. Weather conditions that wreak havoc all over the world would be subdued; even all the wild animals of the Earth would become instantly tame! All humankind would be at peace, speaking one language, united under God's world government as administered through the earthly organization of the Watchtower Society.

They showed me pictures in Watchtower literature of people of various nationalities all living together peacefully, in order to impress upon me that the Witnesses are gathering people from all walks of life to walk down the road leading to everlasting life on Earth. My teachers encouraged me to talk about all the things I had ever wanted to do, just to let my imagination soar with fantasies of adventures and possessions; they assured me that all my dreams would be realized in God's new system, when living eternally would provide all the time needed to fulfill my every desire. They taught me that even the sting of death would be removed as we welcome back our loved ones who had died, when Jehovah God brings them back to live on Earth during the resurrection. The intense desire for this religion to be the truth started burning within me.

My teacher gave me an eye-catching issue of the Society's *Awake!* magazine, entitled "Is It Later Than You Think?" The answer to that thought-provoking question could be found within its pages: "It is much later for this world than you may think! Indeed, it has only a few more years of existence left!" (*AW* 10-8-68, p. 4) This magazine pictured the world's present system of things as a train speeding downhill since 1914 toward its destruction, imminently to crash during Armageddon; a timeline established the autumn of 1975 as the date this crash would likely occur (*AW* 10-8-68, pp. 5, 14, 15).

By combining various Scriptures from the Bible, my teacher demonstrated how the Society calculated that the year 1975 was to mark the onset of Armageddon. I was amazed and excited as he showed me that in just seven years God's heavenly forces would act to annihilate all wickedness and usher in His peaceful paradise on Earth. He contrasted this new system of things with present world conditions, explaining that all of the world's ills—crime, violence, food shortages, sicknesses, earthquakes and other natural disasters—were in direct fulfillment of the Bible at Matthew 24:3–14, and were a "composite sign" marking our present generation as the one that would experience Armageddon.

He presented the world as a scary, dangerous place—full of bogeymen, so to speak—a chaotic world under Satan's control. Since I had grown up in the midst of chaos, I needed little to convince me that the world was a scary place, and that I was in need of protection from it. He told me that such protection could be found in association with the Watchtower Society's organization of Jehovah's Witnesses. My interest was immediately piqued as I grasped the seriousness and the immediacy of the situation at hand. They were sounding the warning that only "the marked generation" would hear.

The Witness couple taught me what the Bible said about an array of subjects, using their publication as a guide to a variety of Scriptures on a given topic; these Scriptures were likened to pieces of a jigsaw puzzle which, when put together, were said to form a clear picture of God's view of a matter and would represent the truth. Linking Scriptures together in this manner led to a set of beliefs that were very different than those of other Christian religions. The Witnesses pride themselves that their belief system, taken as a total package, is unique unto itself—thus they commonly refer to it as "The Truth." Having been raised as a Methodist, I could readily see that the doctrines I was now learning were different in almost every way from those with which I had been brought up. The reasonableness and the urgency with which these beliefs were presented, the appeal of these doctrines, along with the fact that only Jehovah's Witnesses were teaching them—caused me to think this religion was special.

My teachers explained that all the marvelous "truths" I was learning from them were due to the extraordinary "light of understanding" that Jehovah God transmits to the Governing Body of Jehovah's Witnesses residing at the Watchtower Society's world headquarters in New York City. A group varying between eleven and seventeen men, the Governing Body represented the figurative "faithful and discreet slave" of Matthew 24:45, "Who really is the faithful and discreet slave whom his master appointed over his domestics, to give them their food at the proper time?" (New World Translation) This Governing Body, "the slave," provides "food at the proper time" by making these truths known to the world through their literature, particularly their semimonthly magazines, the *Watchtower and Awake!* The Witnesses were encouraged to read the *Watchtower as* though it were a letter from God.[1]

After about nine months of study, my teacher informed me that speakers at a recent international convention of Jehovah's Witnesses announced the Society's decision to put a limit on the amount of time Witnesses were to spend teaching their students, so as not to waste the precious time remaining before Armageddon. Students who were not progressing quickly enough in making the necessary changes in themselves to conform to the Society's requirements and in accepting Witness doctrine after six months of study were to be dropped.

Fear gripped my heart. If my study were stopped, I would not be able to become a Witness—thus the lives of my son and I would not be spared during God's rapidly approaching battle of Armageddon.

My teacher explained that I would be required to attend the meetings at the Kingdom Hall in order for my study to continue. He spoke with such authority and conviction about the seriousness of the times in which we were living that I never questioned or doubted what he said.

Frightened and feeling that my life was at stake in the spring of 1969, I started attending the Kingdom Hall every Sunday; there the brothers (the leaders of the congregation) gave frequent exhortation to "Come to the 'ark of salvation'! Come to Jehovah's organization, which will preserve you alive through Armageddon into God's righteous new system of things on the Earth!" The Watchtower Society's organization of Jehovah's Witnesses was likened to Noah's ark of ancient times, the only means by which humankind survived when God destroyed the wicked by causing a global flood; similarly, Witnesses view taking refuge in the organization, the modern-day ark, as the only means by which humankind will survive when God destroys the wicked during His war of Armageddon.

At the Kingdom Hall, I heard a talk that stressed the important role that angels play in directing Jehovah's Witnesses to sincere people who desire to know the Truth. A tingling feeling came over me as I learned that Jehovah had sent an angel to the Witnesses to lead them to me! I was thrilled to learn that Jehovah had seen fit to extend *me* the invitation to be included among His people!

I liked the idea of God having a visible organization on Earth, knowing the answers to life's most complex and perplexing problems. The Witnesses seemed so wise. They had answers for even the deepest questions about life—answers no one else had. Associating with them provided me with a sense of safety, security, and protection—a "spiritual paradise" right now! What a euphoric feeling, to be among this elite group! Becoming one of Jehovah's Witnesses would mean having the security of knowing that I would never have to worry about making wrong choices in life—I would only have to obey the Society to have the assurance that things would always work out in the best way. The idea that there was a clear road to follow that would lead to everlasting life in paradise on Earth was very alluring and enticing.

And the thought that I would no longer have to just sit by and helplessly groan with the world's suffering masses was very appealing; I could help people by showing them God's splendid promises, and how they could be a part of it. Knowing this work of gathering God's people out from the sea of humanity was an exceptional and extraordinary time in all of history—and that I could participate in it—was very exciting and exhilarating.

I felt in grave need of a rescuer. My mother was hospitalized, suffering from incapacitating mental illness, all my friends were involved in their own lives away at college, and my husband would not accept the authority of the organization or the lifestyle of its followers—our marriage ended in divorce, and he refused to accept any financial responsibility for our son. I was left totally on my own with a demanding young child, a stressful job that did not provide enough income to cover even the most basic necessities, a desperate struggle with the county's welfare system, and the scars of an emotionally abusive marriage. Depressed and insecure, I clung to the organization and its promises about the future for comfort and hope.

The Witnesses warned me, however: "Watch out! Satan will cause people to discourage you from studying with us!" When friends, relatives, and acquaintances met my new beliefs with skepticism and ridicule, the fulfillment of this Witness "prophecy" was the culminating evidence that convinced me that the Watchtower Society was God's organization, and that they alone possessed unique knowledge about life, the future, and salvation.

Note

1. "It should be expected that the Lord would have a means of communication to his people on the Earth, and he has clearly shown that the magazine called *The Watchtower* is used for that purpose." (1939 *Yearbook of Jehovah's Witnesses*, p. 85)

THREE

ABUSIVE LOVE

M y Bible study teachers subsequently moved far away. The overseer informed me that since I had moved to a neighboring town, the Kingdom Hall that I had been attending was now located outside the boundaries of the "territory" (the geographical area assigned to each congregation to cover in the house-to-house preaching work) in which I lived, and that organizational policy was for both Witnesses and interested persons to attend the Kingdom Hall *in* the territory assigned to that Hall. He said a Witness from the Kingdom Hall in whose territory I now lived would be sent to carry on my home Bible study.

Reluctant to go to meetings at a Kingdom Hall where I knew no one, I went to the next meeting at the Hall that I had been accustomed to attending; I was shocked at the reception I received there. I was chastised with, "What are *you* doing here?" The Witnesses I was acquainted with had become aware that I had received counsel from the overseer to attend the Kingdom Hall in my own territory; my presence meant I had ignored the overseer's counsel—thus I was considered disobedient and therefore not a desirable person with whom to associate. Learning my lesson from this experience, I started attending the designated Kingdom Hall the following week.

The Witnesses at this Kingdom Hall near my home took more of an interest in me. Some of the women even volunteered to baby-sit my son for free so that I could continue to work. What a burden was lifted off of me! With this new "family" providing me with assistance and emotional support, I was finally able to cope with life's pressures.

26

A few weeks later during my home Bible study I exclaimed to my new teacher how excited I was about the prospect of soon living in the new system. He paused as he looked at me squarely, and then with deadly seriousness he spoke: "You might not be there." His words pierced my heart. He said that since I attended the meetings at the Kingdom Hall only one day each week, I was not showing proper appreciation for Jehovah's many "spiritual feasts"—the bounty of spiritual food and wealth of information presented at the other meetings, all of which was needed to survive Armageddon. He warned that my life and that of my two-year-old son were in peril, and that we might not survive Armageddon unless I showed respect for Jehovah's congregational arrangements by attending *all* the meetings. Frightened and fearing Jehovah's anger, I immediately started going to all five of the meetings weekly, my son in tow.

Four of the hour-long meetings ran conjointly on two different days, making them each two hours long without any breaks, and were difficult even for adults to endure. The Society counseled parents to refrain from bringing toys to the Kingdom Hall to help their young children remain quiet, but advised them instead to do everything they could to make sure their children paid attention to the instruction at the meetings. I often noticed children falling asleep, and I frequently observed parents pinching them to wake them up or to remind them to pay attention to the speakers. I felt it was unreasonable to expect young children to sit still and be quiet for two hours of an adult meeting that they could not possibly understand, but the Society made no provisions for children to be taught in small classes at their own level, as many churches do. Instead, the Society insisted that the Bible puts the responsibility on parents to instruct their own children about God—which they interpreted to mean that parents must bring their children to the Kingdom Hall meetings with them right from infancy, so that they would come under the protection of their parents' righteous works at Armageddon. The overseer told me that I was to make it more pleasant for my son to be *inside* the Kingdom Hall than to be outside of it; I was soon to learn the meaning of his statement.

An older Witness woman was assigned to sit with me during the meetings in order to instruct me how to properly discipline my two-year-old son; whenever he made any sound whatsoever, she immediately escorted us outside the Kingdom Hall. She instructed me to strike my son's bare leg repeatedly with a stick, while chastising him to be quiet inside the Kingdom Hall. She stood right next to me to make sure that I did as she directed, even helping me to pick out the "right" stick to use from those that had fallen from a large tree in the parking lot outside the Kingdom Hall. Despite the old adage of "spare the rod, and spoil the child," I disagreed that inflicting pain on my toddler with a switch was proper discipline for his failing to be totally quiet during the meeting; however, she told me that Jehovah knew best, and that my obedience to this command would mean I loved my son, whereas refusing to beat him when he made noise in the Kingdom Hall would mean I hated him, as his failure to learn obedience now would cause his death at Armageddon—a death for which Jehovah would hold me accountable.

The Society based this form of discipline on the Bible at Proverbs 23:13–14:

> Do not hold back discipline from the mere boy. In case you beat him with the rod, he will not die. With the rod you yourself should beat him, that you may deliver his very soul from Sheol [death] itself. (*New World Translation of the Holy Scriptures*)

Though I was not one to take issue with Jehovah over this matter, watching children being literally dragged down the aisle of the Kingdom Hall repeatedly—kicking and screaming in anticipation of their "discipline"—continually distressed me. The intensity and frequency of these beatings grew to such proportions that the neighbor across the street from the Kingdom Hall called the brothers and threatened to notify the police if they did not cease. Consequently, an announcement was made at the next meeting that parents should discipline their children in the Kingdom Hall library instead of outside in public view.

The theme of "We are the Truth, and there is nowhere else to go" was emphasized constantly at all the meetings. The world outside was pictured as a big black hole under Satan the Devil's control and that we would be sucked into it if we let our guard down for even an instant. The Society claimed that Satan was "the god of this system of things," and symbolically portrayed the world's organizations and people as marionettes, controlled by Satan as the puppeteer. The only way to avoid getting tangled in his strings was to stay active in every aspect of organizational activities.

My teacher soon told me that I needed to do more, as admonished in the Bible:

> Strip off the old personality with its practices, and clothe yourself with the new [personality], which through accurate knowledge is being made new. (Colossians 3:9-10, *New World Translation*)

"Accurate knowledge" meant the Watchtower Society's interpretations of the Bible; "the new personality" meant accepting those interpretations and conforming my life to them, making them an integral part of my personality. This "new personality" was to be the identifying mark for salvation at the time of Armageddon.

One aspect of this identifying mark required Witnesses to "keep separate from the world"; this included limiting their friendships to only other Jehovah's Witnesses. Instructions were given to impending converts to preach the Kingdom message to any friends they may have; if their friends failed to agree to accept a home Bible study with Jehovah's Witnesses, before they could be baptized into the organization, then the relationship must end. Failure to do so brought severe counsel and ostracism from the overseer and the congregation members. This requirement created an aura of aloofness among the Witnesses and an air of superiority toward all who were outside the organization. The Society viewed their prohibition of socializing with anyone outside the organization as a form of protection for the group. It was a deterrent to being influenced by others; thus, it helped to ensure that the Witnesses would stay within the safe confines of the organization. My world thus narrowed to include only Jehovah's Witnesses and a few relatives who I visited only occasionally.[1]

Another aspect of this identifying mark was abstinence from voting in any political election, or from commemorating any holiday declared to be such by the government—i.e., Thanksgiving, Independence Day, Memorial Day, and days set aside to honor various presidents—because the Society believes that the Devil controls the governments (*Reasoning from the Scriptures* [1985], pp. 182, 365; *You Can Live Forever in Paradise on Earth* [1982], pp. 17, 20–21). A further aspect was strict adherence to the Society's views of all other holidays as well. Celebrating birthdays was not appropriate, as Witnesses are taught that the Bible mentions only pagan people celebrating them, and that such observations idolize humans—as do Mother's Day and Father's Day—which is contrary to Bible principles. Valentine's Day was objectionable because Witnesses are taught that its origin is linked to an ancient Roman festival called Lupercalia which honors Juno, the Roman goddess of women and marriage. New Year's Eve parties were considered occasions of revelry and drunkenness, and therefore were deemed improper for Witnesses to celebrate. Observance of Easter was impermissible, as the Society said it was laden with pagan practices and honored the goddess Astarte. "Consider . . . the Christian festival of Easter, in which the ancient fertility rites of the spring equinox are today cunningly disguised as chickies, eggies, and bunnies. Indeed, the very name Easter is a corruption of the name of the great Near Eastern Earth mother goddess, Astarte." (AW 4-22-75, p. 29) Astarte is the Greek name given to the goddess Ashtoreth, who is thought to be another manifestation of the ancient Babylonian mother goddess of fertility. I remembered as a child how much fun I had with my brother at Easter time, dipping eggs into swirling pots of bubbling colors for Easter egg hunts. The Society, however, condemns this activity, claiming the origin of this custom is linked to celebrations of the spring equinox, the colors of the eggs representing the rays of the returning sun. I was amazed that the Witnesses do not celebrate the resurrection of Christ. Celebration of Christmas was not allowed because the Society said its date and customs are of pagan origin and are patterned after the Roman feast of the Saturnalia. Purportedly the favorite festival of the Romans, the Saturnalia was marked by feasting and gift giving. It took place at the time of the winter solstice; according to the ancient Julian calendar, that day was December 25. Participation in Halloween festivities was forbidden due to its association with ghosts, goblins, witches, the Devil, and the like. Additionally, Witnesses avoid Halloween because the Society teaches that it is a festival that propagates false ideas about life after death. (*School and Jehovah's Witnesses,* [1983], p. 20)

Obeying the Society's mandate regarding Halloween presented practical problems when costumed children came knocking on my door expecting me to give them candy. I prepared in advance—not by buying treats, but by photocopying articles from the Society's literature that explained why God does not approve of celebrating Halloween—and dropping one of these pages into their trick-or-treat bags instead. I found that rather than educating the children, this practice only made them angry, which caused me to worry that they might feel justified in "playing a trick" since they didn't get a treat, and do some damage to my house or property. Thereafter, I solved the dilemma by turning out the front porch light, as well as all of the house lights that could be seen from the street, and quietly hid out in the back of the house for the evening. Fortunately, the trick-or-treaters assumed no one was home and would simply pass on by to the next house.

The bottom line about holiday celebrations was that the Society felt that since the Bible commands Christians to be no part of the world of unbelievers, they likewise are not to share in any of its festivities. One by one, all holiday celebrations were eliminated from my life. A sense of self-righteousness replaced the sense of loss; a feeling of pride welled up within me, as I comforted myself that I was more pleasing to Jehovah than were people of the world who were still relishing in their pagan celebrations.

Christmas was the one holiday I mourned losing. Beloved carols I had sung all my life wafted through the air at shopping malls during Christmastime; often I found myself unconsciously humming along with the strains of cherished melodies. When I became aware of what I was doing, I felt so guilty that I found it necessary to avoid the malls altogether during that time of year in order to avoid sinning against Jehovah. The Christmas carols tugged at my heart and proved to be too much of a temptation to resist. I sorely missed the scent of the Christmas tree filling my house, and the enchanting, bubbling colored lights glowing amidst its branches. I felt sad, and I missed the warmth of the family gathered together to decorate the tree, sharing love and laughter. I came to cherish my memories of Christmas—trudging through the snow, the silence of the night broken only by the sound of the snow crunching beneath my feet as it glistened in the moonlight, while I walked to the midnight service at church on Christmas Eve—and of the sweet refrains of *O Holy Night* floating down from the balcony overhead.

Yielding to the Society's prerequisite to stop celebrating the holidays represented a drastic change for me—yet it was really just the tip of the iceberg, for many more were yet to come, and were introduced to me gradually as I became further enmeshed in the organization.

I soon found that even offering a toast, or participating in a group toast to someone, was forbidden. I felt that to abstain from a toast would be insulting to the person being honored, so I asked a long-time Witness how she gracefully handled this situation. She responded by explaining that she respectfully listens to the warm wishes the person offering the toast is conveying to the one being esteemed; however, when the time comes for the others in attendance to clink their champagne glasses together in symbol of agreement, she suddenly feigns a coughing or sneezing spell, from which she rapidly recovers after everyone has sipped their champagne. Thus she is spared the embarrassment of having to explain why she can't participate in the toast.

As time went on, I experienced additional pressure to give further evidence that I had put on the "new personality." My teacher told me that I needed to volunteer answers at the congregation's *Watchtower* Study in response to the overseer's questions. Giving answers in my own words, instead of just reading the answers from the pages of the *Watchtower*, would give evidence to the congregation that I had truly accepted the doctrines—

and so, wanting to be accepted by the congregation, I tried to comply.

Formulating answers in my own words was no easy task, for it meant that I had to first assimilate the material in the *Watchtower* study article in order to find another way to express the same thought back to the study conductor. Often I could not bring myself to raise my hand, as I disagreed with some of the information in the paragraphs—for example, the Society's insistence that certain events in the history of the Watchtower Society fulfill prophecy in Revelation, it has some of the signs and symbols of Revelation represent specific books that they have written and published. Usually I could find at least some parts of the article that I agreed with, and I would enthusiastically comment on those in order to avoid suspicious jabbing little remarks by others after the meeting.

Before I could be considered for baptism, however, I was also required to participate in the witnessing work, which involved distributing the Society's literature house-to-house and proclaiming the uplifting message of "The good news of God's Kingdom Government which will transform the Earth into paradise within our generation." The witnessing work was also known as "the separating work," i.e., the work of separating the "sheep" (those who respond positively to the Witness message) from the "goats" (those who respond negatively to the Witness message). That this vital work be completed prior to Armageddon was imperative. We were often told that if we did not make our very best effort to gather all the sheeplike ones together into the organization, not only would Jehovah hold us accountable, but He would also cause the rocks to cry out His message instead. At times the brothers, in an effort to keep the congregation members duly humble, would comment: "Whenever you start thinking you are important, just remember—you could be replaced by a rock!"

Jehovah's Witnesses also carry a message of doom. Witnesses believe that during Armageddon, God will destroy all who do not respond positively to their preaching efforts. Groups of Witnesses regularly met together briefly before engaging in the witnessing activity; one brother would often sternly admonish the group: "Remember, our work is twofold; if the people don't want to hear our message of good news, we must then sound the warning of impending destruction upon them." From my experience, though, few Witnesses made this proclamation of doom; doing so usually brought quite an antagonistic response, leaving the householder angry and with a negative view of Jehovah's Witnesses, which would likely be taken out on the next Witness to call on that house a month or so later.

I realized that my salvation at Armageddon hinged on my doing all I could to help others see the urgency of the times; thus I began participating in this witnessing work. I was surprised to find that engaging in the witnessing work cost one not only time, but money as well. Each Witness and Witness-in-training had to purchase her own bookbag, and stock it at her own expense with Watchtower literature. Householders would be asked for a stipulated but modest donation to cover the cost of the books and magazines, thus helping the Witnesses recoup their initial outlay. If the magazines were not placed with interested ones by the date printed on them, they were given away for free. This arrangement worked a hardship on me, since making ends meet financially was already a struggle for me. One time a brother, who likewise was having economic difficulties, was quite enterprising when the householder expressed interest in having some literature but said he had no money to give him for it. The brother unabashedly started bartering with the man, asking him for a bar of soap in exchange for the book! Although this was not a common practice among the Witnesses in my congregation, I did hear that it does happen frequently in more rural areas.

I accompanied experienced Witnesses into the "field service," i.e., the house-to-house preaching activity. I was teamed with a mature, capable older sister my first time out; I observed her for a while as she spoke easily with the various householders, but then came the dreaded moment: "It's your turn," she announced.

I felt queasy as I rang the doorbell. I didn't feel prepared to deal with the unknown entity on the other side of the door. I prayed for no one to answer. Just as I was thanking Jehovah and breathing a sigh of relief that no one was home, the door creaked open, and there stood a very large, intimidating woman. Her earrings, laden with beads and baubles which dangled down to her shoulders, bounced and swung about wildly as she tossed her head with an air of aloofness. Her raucous, gaudy dress was decorated with golden threads that glinted sharply in the morning sun. Her jet black hair was pulled back severely into a tight bun on the top of her head, accentuating her fierce-looking eyes—dark, glaring eyes which were thickly rimmed with the blackest of black eye pencil, the outside corner of which extended all the way up to her highly arched eyebrows. Her very presence frightened me. My voice quaked with fear as I introduced myself as one of Jehovah's Witnesses. Then she raised her arms, covered to her elbows with bright and shiny bangle bracelets; towering over me, her voice booming, she declared: "And I am a Baha'i!" She was so boisterous that brothers working the opposite side of the street two blocks away came racing to my aid. The sister, assuring them that I was not in danger, chuckled as she said, "I guess

Diane has been initiated!" This taste of the witnessing work had been enough for me; however, the brothers reminded me that it was Jehovah's requirement for us all to continue preaching until Armageddon, and assured me that the angels would always be watching over me—and so I began my long and arduous career in the door-to-door witnessing work.

Going from door-to-door was oftentimes dull and uneventful, save for the occasional doors that were slammed abruptly in our faces. One day proved especially adventuresome, as the man who answered the door at one of the houses I visited brought out a rifle, swearing mightily while aiming the barrel at me in a very threatening manner. Witnesses spend much time during their meetings practicing how to overcome householders' objections. Needless to say, this was one householder whose objection I was not about to try to overcome! Other days brought opportunity to use the Bible, "the sword of the Spirit" (Eph. 6:17), in reasoning with various householders. One brother was particularly adept at his skill to wield the sword; like a foil in the hands of an experienced fencer, he could pierce through any householder's arguments, shredding them into pieces. Though the elders counseled that this might not be the most effective way to win converts, he nonetheless brought some excitement to many a boring day.

Other days brought comical moments, as was true the day I accompanied an experienced brother out into the field service. This brother's weakness was an inappropriate preoccupation with talking about sex at every opportunity. I often avoided him at the Kingdom Hall, as he had a habit of cornering some of the sisters with embarrassing personal questions. One summer day he rapped authoritatively on a householder's door. I will never forget the look of astonishment on his face as the door opened, for there stood an attractive young woman clad only in skimpy shorts. Staring in awe, his mouth gaped open; this was the first time I had ever seen him speechless in the presence of a beautiful woman. Instead of excusing himself and immediately leaving, as Witness protocol would demand, he attempted to ignore the situation by endeavoring to present the biblical message. I could hardly contain myself from laughing as he floundered about until he finally stammered "I'm having a hard time keeping my mind on the Bible, ma'am."

Preaching in poorer neighborhoods was always preferable, since we found more hearing ears there than in the wealthier areas; Witnesses often remarked to each other that those in the more affluent areas already had their paradise and didn't need what we had to offer them, i.e., Jehovah's worldwide paradise in the new system.

The preaching work was difficult for me to do, in part because I just could not believe that God would really destroy good people and their inno-cent children merely because they disagreed with some aspects of Watch-tower doctrine; however, my teacher firmly and emphatically admonished, "Unless you do all you possibly can to share the Society's lifesaving mes-sage, Jehovah will hold *you* bloodguilty (responsible) for those who die at Armageddon!" Alarmed, I started engaging in the witnessing work every Saturday, and soon thereafter on Sundays as well. I was led to believe that fulfilling the ten hour "quota" of time spent in the ministry work each month would increase the possibility of winning Jehovah's favor at the rapidly approaching Armageddon. The quota was later dropped, however, and was replaced by great pressure from the congregation servants (the overseer and his assistants), and in time much social pressure from the other Witnesses, to exceed the former ten-hour quota requirement.

Since walking from house to house for hours on end was so exhausting, especially in very warm or very cold weather, many Witnesses became quite creative in finding other ways to put in their time in the preaching work; one popular way was to develop a "magazine route." This was accomplished by making a list of persons who regularly had accepted the *Watchtower* and *Awake!* magazines in the door-to-door work; then the Witnesses could spare their aching feet by driving to these houses, delivering the latest magazines to these people. I appreciated the relief this afforded, because pounding the pavement hour after hour caused excruciating pain in my feet. Our elders did not permit Witnesses to wear athletic walking shoes while in the field service. Sisters were instructed to dress as they would for a job interview; as a result, most of the sisters wore high-heeled dress shoes for hours at a time while doing this witnessing work, and silently endured the severe pain that often resulted.

One elder regularly visited a man on his magazine route for many years, even though this man never showed more than a passing interest in the Wit-ness message. When I asked him why he keeps going there when the man has obviously not been responsive to his efforts, he replied, "Just to count the time." I was shocked that he continued to make these visits only so he could have more time to write down on his monthly Field Service Report, regardless of the fact that the time was spent fruitlessly.

Deaths in the community brought Witnesses to the doors of the bereaved; some Witnesses I knew poked through the obituary columns of newspapers to locate families who were grieving, as they felt the loss of a loved one to be an ideal time to interest people in the message of the res-urrection and eternal life on a paradise Earth. I found, however, that most of these people did not derive comfort from hearing Witnesses tell them that their loved one is *not* in heaven; such calls seemed to aggravate the already distraught mourner; consequently, some Witnesses wrote letters instead to these persons as a way of increasing their witnessing hours.

Other Witnesses regularly frequented the laundromats in our territory, leaving piles of old *Watchtower* and *Awake!* magazines there; they used to brag how that was such an easy way to count time and to report an impressive number of magazine placements. For many Witnesses, the preaching work became little more than a game of how to get the highest number of hours and literature placements to put down on their monthly service report, instead of a sincere effort to search out people to warn about this doomed system of things.

The monthly Field Service Report was the principal way that one's spirituality was measured. Although purportedly used only by the Society headquarters for the purpose of keeping track of how the witnessing work is going, the elders used these reports also as a gauge of "how well one was doing in the Truth." When a Witness starts to drift away because of having doubts, often the first sign will be a reduction in the number of hours that the person spends proselytizing. Although the Field Service Report was ostensibly for the elders' eyes only, an elder broke confidentiality by privately warning me to keep a distance socially from a particular sister because "her hours have been low." The Field Service Report was especially significant for Witness men, because it was the brothers with the highest number of hours and literature placements that were recommended for "higher privileges of service," that is, for positions of leadership in the organization. Sisters are barred from serving in positions of ledership based on 1 Tim. 2:11–13, "Let a woman learn in silence with full submissiveness. I do not permit a woman to teach, or to exercise authority over a man, but to be in silence. For Adam was formed first, then Eve" [*New World Translation*], and 1 Cor. 11:3, "The head of every man is the Christ; in turn the head of a woman is the man . . ." [*New World Translation*]. The Society interprets these scriptures to mean that woman was created for the sake of man, and therefore she is always to be in subjection to them and not usurp their authority; and further, that women are not to teach men in the congregation, nor can she exercise authority over them (*Aid to Bible Understanding* [1969], p. 726).

The conductor of the Theocratic Ministry School—the congregation meeting which teaches Witnesses how to be more effective in their witnessing work—soon counseled me regarding the necessity of my joining the school. I would be required to prepare and give short talks to the congregation every few weeks. My reluctance to join the school was met with shaming comments from the school conductor, indicating that I was not showing proper appreciation for Jehovah's educational provisions. He reminded me that sisters did not always have the privilege of participating in the school—that only since 1959 has Jehovah seen fit to allow them to take part—therefore, I should show appreciation for this opportunity to hone my witnessing skills by joining the school. With the responsibilities of a full-time job, as well of those of a mother of a young child, I felt I was struggling just to attend the evening meetings, let alone participate in the school. My son's restlessness during the meetings took all my energy and most of my attention to keep him from disrupting the congregation; I felt I simply had no energy left to give to participating in the school.

I felt so guilty that I did join the school eventually, but preparing talks on subjects I knew little about, and the tension of delivering them in front of the congregation, caused me extreme stress. The anxiety that developed as a result of trying to fulfill the responsibilities of a mother *and* a Witness was becoming unbearable. I was exhausted trying to keep up the pace; the organization was controlling all of my time and every aspect of my life. The brothers told me if I tired out, my son and I would lose our lives eternally at Armageddon. I felt anger and resentment toward this God I was trying to please, Who didn't seem to know or care how overwhelmed I felt with the responsibility of providing for my young son, while trying to minister to the ever-increasing demands of His organization. Instead of finding comfort and peace-of-mind in a relationship with God, I felt constant fear and agitation because of the possibility of His judging me adversely for not doing enough, thus not meriting His protection at the impending Armageddon. I kept on, though, for to give up in defeat would be a victory for the Devil; giving up would also mean opening myself up to be overtaken by Satan and his cohorts, a terrorizing possibility.

The organization also instilled in me a terror of demons. The Witnesses I knew spent much time talking among themselves about Satan and the earthly activities of his invisible wicked spirit followers, the demons. One evening I was at a social gathering with other Witnesses, some of whom told of persons who were studying with Jehovah's Witnesses being attacked by demons who wanted to keep them in Satan's realm and out of the Truth. I was assured, though, that if I were ever assaulted by demons, shouting the name "Jehovah!" repeatedly would frighten them away.

That night I laid in bed awake, my blankets pulled up to my chin, worrying if demons would ever come after me. At least now I know how to protect myself, I thought, trying to comfort myself. Just then, as if some unseen existence could read my mind, I heard a noise. I felt the presence of something under my bed. It moved. It skittered across the slick waxed hardwood floor and bumped into the wall. I was terrified—surely it must be demons! I shouted, "Jehovah! Jehovah!" but I was so frightened that I could barely utter a sound; my words were but a faint whisper. Then I heard the noise again, coming from the opposite direction this time—the sound of fingernails scraping against the wood floor. Something slid underneath my bed, slamming into the wall with a thud. I was paralyzed with fear, yet I managed to call out, "Jehovah! Jehovah!" with fervent determination. Yet still I felt something in the room with me. A chill went up and down my spine as the invisible presence now came from several directions at once, colliding with one another, then scattering in diffused directions about my room. Then I heard a loud knocking sound coming from the inside of my closet. Petrified from this unseen attack, I screamed, "Jehovah! Jehovah! *Jehovah!*" What was wrong? I was calling on the name of Jehovah—I just couldn't understand why the demons weren't frightened away.

The activity persisted for what seemed like an eternity. Suddenly I recalled a Witness telling me that demons love darkness, but hate light. If only I could reach up and turn the lamp on, I reasoned, the demons might flee. Trembling with great fear, my fingers groped for the lamp switch; finally locating it, the room was at once illuminated, and I found myself face to face with the "demons"—a horde of mice!

Some Witnesses were so fearful that they even left *Watchtower* magazines strewn about their homes, hoping to ward off demon attacks. Even Witnesses' daily conversations were liberally sprinkled with the name "Jehovah" to keep the demons at bay. When the brothers prayed audibly for the congregation, many used the name "Jehovah" repeatedly, almost superstitiously, throughout their prayer.

During assemblies, brothers often told stories about demons attacking Witnesses who left the organization, as they were then outside the realm of Jehovah's protection. Demons were said to cause them to go crazy, to become depressed, or to lead debauched, meaningless, poverty-stricken lives full of misery and sorrow. The Society reinforced this belief at nearly every sssembly by featuring the testimony of a person who had either left the organization, or had been "disfellowshipped"[2] (ousted from the organization) and had now been reinstated. Invariably, they would tell of how horrible life outside the organization had been, and how Satan had influenced them to become prostitutes, drug addicts, or to do all manner of immoral or illegal things. They would always emphasize that returning to the organization had been the only way to straighten out their lives and obtain relief from the demons. Watchtower Society literature at times even described how their missionaries in remote foreign countries were the only missionaries able to stay alive despite deadly curses put on them by tribal witch doctors.

Telling demon stories was a favorite past-time at Witnesses' social gatherings. One sister exclaimed a demon once grabbed her while she was in the kitchen cooking dinner, and had spun her around in circles. Another said that the beautiful sofa her sister gave her was demonized, as everyone who sat on it developed an impulsive urge to kill someone. Yet another told of her Bible student who owned a blanket possessed by demons; whenever she would beckon it to cover her, it would creep up her body and snuggle itself up around her neck. All such stories were told in hushed undertones, for fear the demons would overhear. The Witnesses believed that anyone showing too much interest or curiosity about the demons would be the demons' next target. The Witnesses lived in obvious fear of demons; these stories always ended with the group agreeing how thankful they were to be Jehovah's Witnesses, as Jehovah would always protect them from these invisible adversaries. Telling and listening to these stories served to reinforce the need to stay closely involved in all organizational activities as a protection against these evil, invisible demonic forces. Hearing such stories about demons contributed towards my developing a phobia of ever leaving the organization.

I noticed the Witnesses' obsessive fear of demons also manifesting itself while in the house-to-house preaching work. Occasionally a householder would want to give the Witness a religious pamphlet from her own church; while often the Witness would refuse to accept it on the basis that she already had the Truth, at other times another Witness might accept it. However, as soon as we were out of sight of the householder, the pamphlet became like the proverbial "hot potato"—the Witness couldn't get rid of it fast enough! Some Witnesses feared that even touching the pamphlet could cause a demon to transfer itself from the pamphlet to themselves. This fear stemmed from their belief that Jehovah's Witnesses represent the only true religion, thus all other religions are false and under the control of the Devil and the demons; consequently, they believe all literature from another religion to be contaminated with demonic forces. While some Witnesses insisted that burning the pamphlets was the only safe way to dispose of them in order to avoid demon attacks, others seemed relieved to simply drop them into the nearest trashcan. I found it odd that Witnesses, who claimed to be representatives of God in doing His work, would be so frightened of a mere pamphlet.

I observed many Witnesses become nervous and abruptly scurry away from talking to a householder who talked too much about Jesus, exclaiming: "Did you notice his *eyes*? He is obviously demonized!" Witnesses often frequented garage sales, as most Witnesses were not well off financially, in large part due to the brothers urging them to work only part-time so as to have more time for the witnessing work. I noticed that Witnesses were fanatical about the articles they found at these sales, worrying that demons might have attached themselves to the items; bringing such things home would be an open invitation to demon attack. Often I watched as Witnesses, before buying something at a garage sale, peered into the eyes of the people selling the desired objects to see if they had the "special look" individuals who were demonized were thought to have. If they did, the Witness would immediately put the items down in order to avoid likewise becoming demonized, and would breathlessly beat a hasty retreat.

If a Witness ever showed symptoms of "spiritual sickness" (low witnessing hours, sporadic meeting attendance, not living in accordance with all of the Watchtower teachings), usually the elders' first course of action would be to physically go through the house of the Witness, searching for items that could have attracted demons—even helping the person to destroy any suspicious objects that they found. I puzzled over why Jehovah's Witnesses, ostensibly God's "name-people," would be so worried about demons. God was certainly more powerful than demons, and surely He could protect His people. I wondered why the Witnesses seemed to have so little confidence that He would.

After completing my study of the required book *The Truth That Leads to Eternal Life* [1968] with my teacher, I was told that I had enough knowledge of the Truth to be responsible before Jehovah God to make the decision to be baptized as one of Jehovah's Witnesses. Baptism would represent my choice to serve Jehovah, and it was a requirement in order to have even a chance of being spared during Armageddon. Although I did not understand or agree with all of the Witness doctrines, the course of action the brothers recommended for me was: "Put your questions and doubts 'on the shelf' for now. Don't worry! Later, when you become spiritually mature, you will understand everything. Don't let the fact that you don't understand some of the teachings cheat you and your son out of eternal life!" In essence, their message was: It is your lack of ability to understand that is causing you to be confused or to disagree with our doctrines. It doesn't matter if you understand or agree, just as long as you obey the Society and keep your doubts to yourself. Just trust the Society! In time, you will see that it is right.

Baptism was the symbol that would bond me to the organization, thus I would come under its protection at Armageddon. Failure to make the decision to be baptized would almost certainly mean death for my son and me at Jehovah's hand, as the Witness teaching is that minor children fall under the protective umbrella of a baptized Witness parent if they are obedient to that parent and attend the Kingdom Hall meetings; likewise they fall under the condemnatory umbrella of an unbaptized parent. If one parent is a baptized Witness but the other parent is not, a minor child would fall under the umbrella of the parent to whose influence they have been most responsive. Though the Society was promoting 1975 as the year when Armageddon would begin, an extreme urgency was felt among the Witnesses that it could occur at any moment; therefore, the risk was too great to delay getting baptized. I was terrified at the idea of Jehovah killing me and my son; so in the spring of 1970, I put my doubts and questions "on the shelf," confident that I would understand puzzling doctrines later, and requested to be baptized as one of Jehovah's Witnesses.

Deep inside, however, I was struggling to suppress the doubts I was feeling about the organization. I had the feeling that I didn't belong with this organization and this group of people. In some ways, the Witnesses seemed odd; for example, they used a peculiar "language" which had unique words that described various aspects of their special doctrines and was understood only by other Witnesses. They constantly referred to being "in the Truth" or "out of the Truth," phrases I had never heard before, which sounded very strange. They also assigned unusual meanings to ordinary words such as "placement," "pioneer," "truth," "service," "sheep," "goats," "world," "publisher," which made their conversation puzzling. Even euphemisms such as "Golly!," "Gee Whiz!," "Shoot!," "Gosh!," "Gee!," and "Jeepers!," were considered to be profanity and therefore forbidden to say; they were viewed as substitutes for swear words and therefore deemed just as bad. Particularly forbidden to use were the words "good luck" and "lucky," the latter of which was always replaced by the word "fortunate." The Society bases this prohibition on Isaiah 65:11, "You men are those leaving Jehovah . . . those setting in order a table for the god of Good Luck . . ." [*New World Translation*], which refers to the Jews superstitiously turning away from proper faith in and reliance on God.

The Society changed some of their special vocabulary every few years; Witnesses who continued to use the former terminology were looked-down upon by the other Witnesses as "spiritually weak" and were frequently the subject of gossip and were avoided socially. One of the words that underwent such a transition was the term that was used to describe the period of time after Armageddon when God's righteous government will rule over the Earth. When my children were young, it was referred to as the "new order," later evolving to the "new system," and—at the last convention I attended in 1992 before leaving the organization—I was amazed to hear the brothers delivering their talks referring to this time period as the "new world." No point was made of this change; the brothers just simply started using it in their talks at the convention as if it were nothing new at all. And really, it was not new, as I later discovered that "new world" was also the term used just prior to my involvement with the organization—which is why the Society's own Bible translation, completed in 1960, is called the *New World Translation of the Holy Scriptures.*

This "language" seemed to produce a sense of cohesiveness among the Witnesses, reinforcing their belief of being "separate from the world." I felt quite isolated from the congregation members until I learned their jargon[3]; using it myself, though, felt unnatural and caused me to feel uncomfortable, as I was experiencing a perplexing conflict within myself. I no longer felt part of the world outside the organization, but I did not feel completely a part of the world inside the organization either.

Despite my feeling divided, however, I was greatly intimidated by the threat of Armageddon—so I went ahead and began the lengthy formal questioning process with the overseer that all baptismal candidates must undergo. During this prebaptismal screening process, much emphasis was put on loyalty to Jehovah being demonstrated by loyalty and obedience to the organization. The overseer explained that all Witnesses are responsible to "keep the congregation clean"; this amounted to a system of spying that required Jehovah's Witnesses to "turn each other in" to the overseer for any infractions of the Society's rules. This ever-vigilant attitude among the Witnesses caused a pervading atmosphere of distrust, suspicion, and tension, and it caused difficulty in establishing any close friendships within the organization.

Although people sporting all styles of dress and grooming were initially enthusiastically welcomed to the Kingdom Hall, they were expected to conform to the organization's codes of dress and grooming as time passed; women were to wear dresses, and men were to don business attire. One man was denied baptism merely because he had a beard, despite the fact that the beard was short and well groomed. I couldn't understand why a beard would bar a man from belonging to God's organization and thus from having eternal life. For me to voice my disagreement with the Society's decision of not allowing men with beards to be baptized, however, would mean *my* being denied baptism. There was just too much at stake to risk that happening, so I kept my opinion to myself and proceeded with my plans to be baptized at the next assembly.

Doubts about committing myself completely to the organization came up again during the talk at my baptism when the overseer asked the group of baptismal candidates: "Will you disown yourself?" I was horrified! No one had ever mentioned that I would have to disown myself, surrender myself to the organization! I stood silent as the crowd shouted their enthusiastic affirmative response. In my silence a resounding "NO!" reverberated through my entire being. I felt shocked, stunned, and scared. What had I gotten myself into? Driven by the fear of dying at Armageddon, I was baptized on April 11, 1970, as one of Jehovah's Witnesses.

The baptism talk emphasized the position the Society believes Jehovah's Witnesses occupy in relation to the rest of the world: "Look at the people out there in the world! They don't know who they are! But we know who we are! We're Jehovah's Witnesses! We are the spectacles of the world! We are on stage, as it were, and everyone is watching us!" This attitude, together with the huge conspiracy the Society teaches that Satan and his followers on Earth wage to thwart God's organization, gave proof to me of its immense importance. Unconsciously suspending my ability for normal critical judgment in order to obtain fulfillment of my need to feel secure, I cast my doubts aside, believing I would be protected by being officially part of the "mother" organization. "If we are to walk in the light of truth we must recognize not only Jehovah God as our Father but his organization as our mother." (WT 5-1-57, p. 274)

Over time, the constant repetition of the Society's doctrines at the meetings, the mandatory reading of the abundance of Watchtower literature, the singing of the unique songs written by the Watchtower Society, participating in the meetings, socializing only with other Witnesses, teaching Watchtower doctrines, and devoting many hours each month to the preaching work—all served to cement my identity as one of Jehovah's Witnesses.

Notes

1. See Appendix B, "Community and Isolation."
2. See Appendix B, "Disfellowshipping."
3. See Appendix B, "Witness Jargon."

FOUR

THE WATCHTOWER SOCIETY PLAYS GOD

T he Witness women who were voluntarily babysitting my son as a demonstration of Christian love, kindness, and compassion for my situation soon became unwilling to continue unless I paid them. As I found out after I was baptized, special kindness is often extended to those studying with the Witnesses which is not necessarily shown to baptized Witnesses. Although I was receiving no child support payments from my ex-husband, and was nearly destitute despite working fulltime, one of the sisters demanded some of my welfare food stamps as payment. Her attitude shocked me; I wondered what happened to all the love that was shown to me when I first came to the Kingdom Hall, the love that Jehovah's Witnesses were supposed to have for one another.

Although the Witnesses called each other "brother" and "sister," I still didn't feel like part of the "family." The sisters were cliquish and didn't include me, and chatting with the married brothers was considered flirtatious and inappropriate. This attitude was primarily due to the Society's belief that because they alone are the true religion, Satan is out to tempt the Witnesses into sexual immorality—hence, they do not believe that platonic relationships between men and women are possible. I felt, though, that the Society's attitude inferred distrust of the brothers and sisters, and that it discredited them for having any personal integrity.

Several months after I was baptized, a man who worked at my place of employment showed an interest in getting to know me better; however, because he was not a Witness, dating him would mean I would be "marked" by the congregation—socially ostracized by them as a demonstration of Jehovah's disapproval of my associating with a "worldly" (non-Witness) man. A comment frequently heard among the Witnesses was: "The worst Witness is better than the best worldly person." Witnesses were allowed to go on only chaperoned dates, solely for the purpose of finding a marriage partner, and were to marry Witnesses only.

Though I did not date this man, opportunities sometimes arose during the workday for me to share some of my religious beliefs with him; his curiosity about my religion led him to visit the Kingdom Hall on several occasions. During one such visit, an older Witness brother offered to conduct a home Bible study with him in order to explain more about Witness teachings; he accepted the offer, and within seven months he had embraced the beliefs of Jehovah's Witnesses as the truth and was baptized.

Now that he was a Witness, nothing stood in the way of us getting to know each other in a more personal way; our dates consisted of visiting my mother at the hospital, participating in the house-to-house witnessing work together, and sitting together at the Kingdom Hall meetings. We were married a few months later.

Several months after our wedding, I became pregnant. Sitting still for a two-hour meeting at the Kingdom Hall twice a week wearing a dress and pantyhose became quite an ordeal as my pregnancy progressed, as pantyhose are by nature tight-fitting and uncomfortable. The sisters were required to wear nylon hose to the meetings; coming barelegged for any reason was unacceptable, and wearing socks with casual shoes was also unacceptable attire for the Kingdom Hall meetings. The situation eventually got to the point where even maternity pantyhose were too restrictive, cutting off the blood circulation in my thighs when I sat for prolonged periods of time; for this reason, I dreaded going to the meetings as my pregnancy neared its term.

The midweek congregational Book Study, a discussion based on one of the Watchtower Society's many books, met at private homes and was less formal than the meetings at the Kingdom Hall, so I decided to wear a pair of maternity slacks and blouse instead of a dress, in order to avoid the pantyhose ordeal. The slacks were far more comfortable to wear, and better for my health and that of my unborn baby; however, someone from the group made an issue out of my wearing them to the Book Study and reported me to the elders. At the next Kingdom Hall meeting, one of the elders took my husband aside and instructed him that he was not to permit me to wear slacks to any of the meetings again. From then on, I had to endure the pain of wearing the pantyhose, or stay home from the meetings—the latter of which was not considered to be an acceptable choice.

Although I had Rh-negative blood, the Rh factor did not pose a threat during my first pregnancy; however, doctors warned me that my blood may have become sensitized to Rh-positive blood as a result of that pregnancy, thus possibly posing a threat to the baby I was now carrying. That this threat is a very serious one can be seen from the Society's comments in an article entitled, "Coping with the Rh Threat in Childbirth": "Still this condition, termed erythroblastosis fetalis, is sufficiently frequent to be termed 'a major cause of fetal loss as well as of certain cases of cerebral palsy.' " (*AW* 4-8-65, p. 17) The doctor urged me to have a Rho-GAM shot—an Rh immune globuline serum injection in use since 1968—during this second pregnancy, as it offered guaranteed protection for my baby against the Rh threat of hemolytic disease. Without this shot, consequences can be severe for the unborn baby: it could develop severe anemia, which can cause fetal heart failure, or severe hemolytic disease, which could lead to the baby developing cerebral palsy, or even death. Although the Society had zigzagged back and forth over time between allowing and disallowing Witnesses to accept serum injections, they were allowing Witnesses to take serum injections in 1965; thus it was particularly amazing that an article was printed in the *Awake!* magazine during that year which announced that Rh immune globulin was objectionable on Scriptural grounds—even though it is a serum injection.

> We leave it up to the conscience of the individual to determine whether to submit to inoculation with a serum. . . . (*WT* 11-15-64, p. 682)

> Then there are reports of prevention having been realized by means of the use of Rh-positve haptens. These haptens are a blood fraction taken from Rh-positive red cells and given orally or by injection to a woman whose blood shows a high degree of immunization to the Rh factor. . . . Those using this method have reported perfect results. However, this involves the use of blood fractions, which is objectionable on Scriptural grounds. (*AW* 4-8-65, p. 18)

> [Note: That Rho-GAM is the medication being referred to here was confirmed to me through a personal letter from the Society 2-23-72].

Thus I viewed the doctor's urgings as Satan working through him to test my loyalty to Jehovah, so I staunchly refused the injection. The doctor became so incensed that he pounded his fist fiercely on the table, his face blazing. He was enraged because my religious beliefs were tying his hands, preventing him from not only protecting my unborn baby, but also from administering the major medical treatment for babies born with complications due to Rh incompatibility—namely, an exchange blood transfusion. The courts at times have overridden Witness parents' religious decisions by ordering the blood transfusion be given to the baby; the Society counseled Witness parents that if this situation is likely to arise, the course of wisdom may well be to have the baby at home, thereby preventing the blood transfusion (*AW* 4-8-65, p. 19), in spite of the fact that the baby could die. In taking this position, the Society showed that it revered blood—the biblical symbol of life—more than it revered life itself.

I subsequently wrote a letter to the Society asking for special permission to take the Rho-GAM injection; they responded with a personal letter to me on February 23, 1972, reaffirming, that "this serum makes use of blood fractions and is, therefore, objectionable on Scriptural grounds." However, they also referred me to an article they had written four months after the article disallowing the Rho-GAM shot, which pointed out that although serums injections are undesirable to Christians because of the biblical law against the use of blood, whether to accept these type of shots or not is a matter that must be decided according to one's own conscience (*AW* 8-22-65, p. 18). This article was a reiteration of the Society's policy that had been stated one year previously (*WT* 11-15-64, p. 682), namely, that serum injections are allowable. That this article did not specifically mention that the Rho-GAM serum injection was now being included along with the other allowable serum injections—as it has been specifically excluded just four months previously—is unconscionable, as there was no way to know that it was now permissable. Even the *Watchtower Publications Index* did not list this article under the "RH Factor" topic. If I had not written to the Society, I would not have known that the Rho-GAM shot was now acceptable. I wondered how many babies' suffered or died because of the Society's oversight.[1]

Although accepting or refusing the injection was ostensibly now left up to my conscience, this decision *felt* like it was really *not* up to me. The choice placed before me felt similar to the choice Adam had to make in the Garden of Eden: either Adam would follow his desire and do what he wanted to do, or he would follow the instructions that God had given him. Similarly, I experienced the choice before me as: Will I follow my desire by doing what I want to do and accept the injection to protect my baby? Or will I follow the Society's view that this injection is undesirable because of the biblical law against the use of blood and refuse it, knowing that the Watchtower Society is God's organization and that He speaks to his people through it. I was aware that mortality was the outcome for Adam's choosing to make his own decision in lieu of heeding God's instruction—in parallel fashion, I felt that death would be the outcome for me if I chose to make my own decision about having the Rho-GAM shot, in lieu of heeding the Society's view that this injection was objectionable. Thus there really was no real choice. Jehovah's Witnesses are not prohibited from accepting blood transfusions because they want to keep themselves pure (from the blood of non-Witnesses) for the final days. They are prohibited from accepting *anyone's* blood, that of witnesses or anyone else, because of the scriptural injunction (see page 185 of this volume).

Refusing the Rho-GAM shot caused me to suffer emotionally throughout my pregnancy with worry about the possibility of danger to my baby at birth; this was especially so because permitting a blood transfusion to be given to my baby would have resulted in my being disfellowshipped, ousted from the organization—this would mean I would be shunned by every Witness, and my relationship with Jehovah God would be severed until He finally killed me at Armageddon. That the Society forbade the Rho-GAM injection to protect a baby's life reminded me of Jesus' words: "You blind guides! You strain out a gnat and swallow a camel!" (Matthew 23:24, *NIV*)

I knew a Witness whose baby had been born with severe cerebral palsy that was directly attributable to problems associated with the Rh factor, which could have been prevented by the Rho-GAM shot. She had refused the injection, believing at the time that her choice was scripturally correct since it had been based on the information presented in Watchtower literature that specifically ruled out the shot for preventing the Rh factor threat (*AW* 4-8-65, pp. 17–19). She has suffered terribly with guilt for having refused the injection that would have protected her baby. She, too, felt that she had no real choice in the matter. She certainly would have safeguarded her baby and availed herself of this protective medical intervention had it not been for the Society's negative influence.[2]

My doctor informed me that he would deliver my baby by Cesarean-section, the same way my first child had been delivered. Due to the serious dangers associated with pregnancies following two C-section deliveries, added to the health problems I already had as a result of the bout of hepatitis I experienced six years previously, he warned that my life would be in grave danger if I were to become pregnant again. He urged me to have a tubal ligation—a surgical procedure involving the cutting and tying off of my Fallopian tubes—performed at the time of the Cesarean delivery to help ensure against becoming pregnant in the future. The Society allowed couples to decide for themselves what method of contraception they will use— if any—as long as the method they choose prevents the egg and sperm from uniting. Use of an IUD (intra-uterine device) was prohibited on the premise that it does not prevent conception, but rather makes the uterine lining unsuitable for a fertilized egg to attach to it. I had used an IUD after the birth of my first child; however, when Jehovah's Witnesses were conducting my home Bible study with me, they told me that I had to have the IUD removed before I could be baptized—which I subsequently did. Because other methods of contraception were either unreliable or unsuitable for me due to my various health problems, the doctor advised that a tubal ligation was the surest way to prevent another pregnancy and thus protect my life. I agreed; however, the Society did not. The Society's view was that tubal ligation is a violation of God's law.

> A dedicated Christian is under the law of loving Jehovah God with the whole heart, mind, soul and strength. The force and effect of sterilization is against this, as sterilization harmfully affects the asexualized person physically and mentally. (WT 12-1-61, p. 735)

> If a doctor claims that for a wife to have another child it would mean the death of her, then what? Then there is another way to prevent her conception, which conception might bring her life in jeopardy, than by violating the law of God, the whole tenor of which is contrary to deliberate asexualizing of a man or woman. . . . There is the need for exercising the spirit of the Lord God, one of the fruits of which is self-control. (WT 12-1-61, p. 735)

I wrote to the Society headquarters about my situation, hoping they would make an exception to their prohibition of the tubal ligation procedure due to the fact that my life was in danger; however, they responded:

> Now, let us consider your question about sterilization. . . . It is apparent from God's Word that he does not approve of the mutilation of one's reproductive powers. (Personal letter from the Society, 2-23-72)

I couldn't understand why tying my Fallopian tubes was any worse a mutilation of my reproductive powers than was the mutilation caused to my womb by two C-sections, nor could I understand how protecting my procreative powers was more important than protecting my life. My procreative powers were going to be useless anyway, since my doctor warned me that my health problems would likely cause me to die due to the stress pregnancy causes to the body.

There was also the serious danger of womb rupture—which is generally fatal to the mother and fetus—since the doctor informed me that my womb had been severely scarred and thus weakened from the first C-section, and it would be even more frail after the second one. Consequently, I felt that having the tubal ligation would be showing respect for God's gift of life by protecting my own life, which I believed stood above God's gift of procreative powers. Several Witness women I knew had had hysterectomies because of suffering from bleeding fibroid tumors or cancer of the uterus; the Society did not object to removal of the womb in these situations where the woman's life was in danger, as long as it was performed without a blood transfusion—I could not see how my situation was any different. Their objection to my having the tubal ligation surgery was clearly inconsistent and did not make sense. Although I was enraged, I felt that I had no choice but to be a victim of the Society's ignorant and irrational thinking because I believed The Watchtower Society was God's organization.

Though the Society ended their letter by saying: ". . . the decision you make is a personal one that must be made according to your own conscience," the reality was: The decision was *not* left up to my conscience *without repercussions*. Instead, it was manipulated by several factors.

1. The Society's attitude toward its members: You are free to believe, say, and do whatever you want, as long as it agrees with what the Bible says—but we will decide what the Bible says! This attitude gives the Society virtually complete control over what Jehovah's Witnesses believe, say, and do.

2. The Society's claim: "It is vital that we . . . respond to the directions of the 'slave' [The Watchtower Society] as we would to the voice of God . . ." (*WT* 6-15-57, p. 370) This claim ensures that Witnesses view the Society's opinions as tantamount to the opinions of God.

3. The Society's claim: "Would not a failure to respond to direction from God through his organization really indicate a rejection of divine rulership?" (*WT* 2-15-76, p. 124) This claim ensures that Witnesses equate rejection of the Society's rules, policies, viewpoints. and directions with rejection of God.

The overseer arrangement in the congregations had changed over the years to that of a body of elders, who then met and selected three elders to serve as a judicial committee with me and my husband to discuss the tubal ligation issue. Every Kingdom Hall would in this way formulate their own judicial committees to deal with infractions of the Society's rules. They said that if we made a decision contrary to the opinion of the Society by going ahead with this surgery, there would be grave consequences; and that the decision would have a definite impact on my husband's future career in the organization, in that they would not recommend him for positions of responsibility in the congregation. Having such a position was very important to my husband; therefore, the stand the judicial committee took brought a lot of pressure on me to comply with the Society's negative view of this surgery. The committee quoted the Bible at Deuteronomy 23:1 that "No man castrated by crushing his testicles . . . may come into the congregation of Jehovah." The committee then applied that Scripture to my situation, that *I* could not come into the congregation of Jehovah if I had the tubal ligation surgery performed. Believing that no one outside the congregation would survive Armageddon left me no choice in making my decision about the surgery.

The committee's opinion was that I would be better off to die faithfully obeying the Society than to have the surgery done. I left the committee meeting knowing that if I had the tubal ligation performed, my husband and I would not be fully accepted in the congregation, and that Jehovah would likely abandon me now until He finally killed me at Armageddon.

As I lay on the hospital operating table during the C-section delivery of my daughter, the doctors urged me to allow them to perform the tubal ligation. Through gritted teeth I told the doctors no, but my decision was one borne of pressure and fear. I was furious with the organization for instilling in me the belief that if I chose to protect my life through having this procedure, I was thereby also choosing to lose my life eternally; I was enraged for being forced into accepting their unreasonable position. I disagreed with the Society's limiting opinion, and I was indignant over their senselessly rigid, illogical, uncompassionate, and hurtful view—and how dramatically it would affect my life—and how powerless I felt to do anything about it. I hated the organization and the God whose organization this was.

Fortunately, my daughter was born with Rh-negative blood and so suffered no ill effects of my having refused the Rho-GAM injection. Following the birth of my daughter in 1972, I developed a further health problem. My doctor warned me that if I should become pregnant, this would compound the health problems that had previously put my life at risk, making it likely that I would die during the pregnancy. Not allowing a tubal ligation to be performed to prevent a life-threatening pregnancy was an especially serious matter because the Society does not permit abortions, except in the case of a tubal ectopic pregnancy where a medical certainty exists that the baby cannot continue to term, and the pregnancy puts the life of the mother at great risk (*WT* 3-15-75, p. 191). A normal pregnancy is not permitted to be terminated, even if a doctor tells a woman that due to her health problems she will die unless she has an abortion. This makes little sense, since if the mother dies during the pregnancy, the fetus will most likely die as well. The Society does not accept the reasoning that an abortion in the very earliest stages of pregnancy in such cases shows respect for the life of the mother— instead, respect for the life of the embryo is held in greater esteem. Inconsistency in Watchtower policy is evident, however, because while not allowing for the choice to be made between mother and child in favor of the mother *during* the pregnancy, it does allow for that choice should it be necessary at the time of childbirth. "If *at the time of childbirth* a choice must be made between the life of the mother and that of the child, it is up to the individuals concerned to make that choice." (*Reasoning from the Scriptures* [1985], p. 26)

I decided to talk to the elders about this new development in my health, hoping it would sway them to allow me to have the tubal ligation surgery. I was appalled that knowledge of this new complication in my health did not change the their position. They responded by telling me that only total abstinence from sexual relations would provide a sure guarantee of avoiding a pregnancy, but that such abstinence does not harmonize with the Bible's direction for married couples. If I didn't have sexual relations with my husband, Jehovah would be displeased and thus I might die at Armageddon; however, having sexual relations with my husband could result in a pregnancy from which I might die. I became very angry with Jehovah for allowing me no way out of this situation. I was terrified that I might conceive again, as I observed various sisters in the congregation becoming pregnant who were using the same contraceptive methods that were available to me. Constantly worried that a life-threatening pregnancy might result, I could never just relax and enjoy loving marital relations; the intense stress of the situation caused a terrible strain on my marriage and on my physical and emotional well-being.

Three years later, the Society changed their view regarding tubal ligation. They published an article in the *Watchtower* magazine, now *permitting* tubal ligation if a pregnancy would put the woman's life at risk (*WT* 3-1-75, p. 159). This article presented exactly the same arguments that I had used previously, which the Society and the elders had rejected. I was enraged! I told the elders that since Jehovah accepts my having this surgery performed *now*, surely He would have accepted my having had it done three years ago. I could have thereby avoided all the severe emotional distress and endangerment to my life that obeying the mandate of the Society had caused. I was astounded as I heard their reply: "It wasn't Jehovah's time to change the Society's view three years ago."

Their reasoning did not make sense to me; I could not possibly believe that God had been behind the Society's error. I was furious—I could have died because of the Society's ignorance! One of the elders told me that I had a bad attitude; he said I should get down on my knees and thank Jehovah for changing His mind about the tubal ligation surgery, and be grateful for the blessing of this more compassionate view. The suggestion that I should thank Jehovah God for changing His mind was repugnant to me. God had not changed His mind! It was clear to me that the Watchtower Society had changed its own mind, and cleverly escaped taking responsibility for that change by attributing it to God.

The Society attributes to God their changes in doctrine through the following claims:

- *The Society is the channel of communication between God and humankind.*

Jehovah poured out his spirit upon them and assigned them the responsibility of serving as his sole visible channel, through whom alone spiritual instruction was to come. Those who recognize Jehovah's visible theocratic organization, therefore, must recognize and accept this appointment of the "faithful and discreet slave" and be submissive to it. Today those thus charged with this grand privilege and responsibility are called Jehovah's witnesses . . . (*WT* 10-1-67, p. 590)

- *The Society is God's mouthpiece.*

He has appointed his "faithful and wise servant," who is his visible mouthpiece. . . . (*WT* 7-1-43, p. 205)

- *God speaks through the Bible or through His organization.*

When our heavenly Father, Jehovah God, speaks, whether through his Word, the Bible, or through his earthly organization, it is all the more important for us to listen and obey. . . . (*WT* 4-1-88, p. 31)

- *Their organization is the only organization in all the Earth directed by God's Holy Spirit.*

Consider, too, the fact that Jehovah's organization alone, in all the Earth, is directed by God's holy spirit or active force. . . . To it alone God's Sacred Word, the Bible, is not a sealed book. (*WT* 7-1-73, p. 402)

- *God reveals knowledge through the Society.*

Through the columns of *The Watchtower* comes increased light on God's Word as Jehovah makes it known. (*WT* 8-1-72, p. 460).

- *The Watchtower Society has divine authority.*

Jehovah's organization is theocratic. That means that it is ruled by the direct administration of God. . . . (*Qualified to Be Ministers* [1967], p. 380)

As a consequence to the above indoctrination, the minds of the Witnesses are "programmed" to accept anything the Society says as coming from God. In view of the lofty claims the Society makes for itself, when the Society changes its mind on an issue, a Witness automatically reasons that it must be because God has changed His mind, and the Society is simply passing that information along to the rest of us. I wondered how many Witness women had died because of refusing to have a tubal ligation, based on the Society's decision that God did not approve of it. Though they thought they had sacrificed their lives to God, they had really sacrificed their lives on "the altar of the Watchtower."[3]

And what of the suffering of all the children who had lost their mothers, and husbands who lost their wives, over this issue? In situations like this, Witnesses are taught to feel, "It doesn't matter if people die because of the Society's errors; Jehovah will resurrect them into the paradise on Earth and everything will be OK." *But everything will not be OK*—lives have been irreparably changed. Even the Society's doctrine of the resurrection could not heal this hurt. The Society teaches that death severs the marriage bond, and that resurrected persons will not marry in the new system. The Society quotes Jesus as saying, "The children of this system of things marry and are given in marriage, but those who have been counted worthy of gaining that system of things and the resurrection from the dead neither marry nor are given in marriage . . ." (Luke 20:34–35). Then in a subheading entitled

"Why Resurrection Holds Forth No Promise of Marriage," the Society goes on to say, "But what about those who are brought back from the dead to live on Earth? Will they be reunited with former marriage mates? No statement in the Bible indicates that this will be the case. The Scriptures definitely show that death dissolves the marriage." (*Is This Life All There Is?* [1974], pp. 178–79) Thus, according to this Watchtower doctrine, families have that lost a wife or a mother due to the Society's error will never be reunited as a family unit. Mothers who died during childbirth as a result of pregnancies that their bodies could not handle will never see their child grow up, and those babies will grow up without experiencing their own mother's love.

Several months after the release of the March 1, 1975, *WT* magazine which contained the Society's decision to allow tubal ligation under certain circumstances, a representative of the Society came from headquarters in New York to speak at the local Assembly Hall of Jehovah's Witnesses. Looking for help in resolving my anger with the Society over the tubal ligation issue, I approached him after his talk, confronting him with the fact that the Society had put me in grave physical danger and years of constant emotional upset with its erroneous view of tubal ligation. Ignoring the validity of my concern, he offered no apology, or explanation, or comforting words. With aloofness, he coolly replied, "Now, sister, you weren't *really* hurt, were you? Excuse me, I have others to speak to." His callous attitude spoke to a feeling I had deep inside, that this teaching had come from mere humans, not from God.

NOTES

1. Of interest is that the *WatchtowerPublications Index 1930–1985* deceptively hides the fact that they once disallowed the Rh immune globulin serum injection by not listing the *AW* 4-8-65, p. 18 under the heading, "Rh Factor: serum injection." They list only the magazine articles that followed years later that allowed for this injection.

2. Two years after I had received the Society's 1972 letter, they printed an article in the *Watchtower* stating that although they refrained from endorsing any use of blood outside the body of the animal or person to whom it naturally belonged, they specifically mentioned that accepting the specialized serum injection for Rh incompatibilty problems is a decision that Witness women can make for themselves because it involves only a minute blood fraction. (*WT* 6-1-74, pp. 351–52) This change came too late to save the son of the Witness woman I knew; his disabilities permanently remain as a stabbing reminder of the consequences of the Society's error.

Four years later, the Society confessed that accepting or rejecting the injection to fight against Rh incompatibility is a "gray area" as far as the Scriptures are concerned, and that Witness women are free to make up their own minds about it. (*WT* 6-15-78, pp. 30-31) The babies born handicapped because of the Society's influence suffer needlessly. The babies who died because of the Society's influence died needless deaths.

The Society made an astonishing turnabout when it suggested in 1990 that because "a pregnant woman has an active mechanism by which some immune globulin moves from the mother's blood to the fetus,'" Witnesses' decisions to accept or reject the Rh immune globulin injection might rest primarily *on whether they were willing to accept any health risks* involved because the serum is made from the blood of others. (WT 6-1-90, p. 31) No mention was made of all the babies whose lives were sacrificed due to refusal of this injection on the basis of religious grounds.

In 1994, the Society even seemed to be encouraging Witness women to accept the Rh immune globulin injection, by warning that those who choose not to have the shot "when medically indicated" would need to be "willing to accept the risk of having a future child seriously affected by an illness that could possibly have been prevented." (*AW* 12-8-94, p. 27)

3. In 1985, after the change that allowed a tubal ligation if the woman's life was at risk, the Society further changed its ruling regarding the permissibility of tubal ligation, going from the extreme of not allowing Witness women to have a tubal ligation, *even when a pregnancy would jeopardize their lives*, to the extreme of allowing Witness women to have this procedure merely for birth control, even when their lives were not endangered. (*WT* 5-1-85, p. 31)

YOU SHALL KNOW MY DISCIPLES BY THE LOVE THEY SHOW

Shortly after the birth of our daughter in 1972, I became extremely depressed, fatigued, and developed an insatiable craving for sweets; eating something to satisfy this craving produced momentary relief, but after a short time I felt worse than before. The elders advised that my symptoms were probably a reflection of a problem with my spirituality, likely due to not studying the Watchtower Society's publications enough. They said I needed to stop thinking so much about myself, and counseled me to become more involved in the door-to-door preaching work as a way to start thinking more about others.

The elders' cookie-cutter counsel angered me. I knew from experience that the elders frequently counseled depressed Witnesses in this manner. I once overheard one elder speaking to another about a depressed brother he went to visit who had called him for help because he felt suicidal. The other elder, with a look of complete disdain, callously replied, "Why do you waste your time with him? I've talked to him before, and he still doesn't come to the Kingdom Hall meetings regularly."

At the elders' suggestion, I started praying for more self-control, and I taped Bible verses on the walls all over the house as constant reminders; when that didn't bring relief, I blamed myself for my debilitating condition. I eventually received help from a medical doctor who explained that I was suffering from hypoglycemia, i.e., low blood sugar; with proper medical treatment, my health improved quickly and dramatically, and the cravings stopped. Even after being informed of the real cause of my symptoms, the elders never offered an apology for having erroneously blamed me for what turned out to be a medical condition.

The Society put continual emphasis on the close proximity of Armageddon, thus all available time was to be used in the house-to-house preaching work. Time spent working was to be kept to a minimum, to provide for only the absolute necessities of life; as a result, we owned few possessions. The Society constantly hammered all of the congregation members—through articles in the *Watchtower* and *Awake!* magazines, public talks at the Kingdom Halls, assemblies, and conventions—about the dangers of "materialism," i.e., an interest in owning material possessions. I noticed, however, that some of the elders enjoyed large sprawling homes that were lavishly decorated and meticulously landscaped, some complete with swimming pools and spas. An elder excused these during a public talk by exclaiming that the poorer brothers are more materialistic than the wealthier brothers, because they are constantly wishing and desiring to own more or better things; whereas the wealthier brothers don't focus on material things because they can easily afford them, therefore they don't crowd out spiritual interests in the pursuit of material interests as a poorer brother might do.[1]

My husband and I furnished our bedroom by rescuing some discarded pieces of furniture from a junk pile at a sister's house during the city's annual "clean-up week." The chest of drawers and nightstands—with their worn-out, broken drawers that fit crookedly into their distressed cabinets— looked like treasures compared to the frail orange crates we had been using. As time went on, however, I found the furniture's shabby appearance depressing. I was thrilled, therefore, when I came across an article in a women's magazine that described how odd pieces of furniture could be made into a bright and cheerful matching set by first painting them a light color, and then hand-painting Pennsylvania Dutch folk art designs on the front of the drawers and the sides of each cabinet. The magazine even contained the patterns for these colorful designs. For weeks thereafter, I laid in bed at night, dreaming of how much fun it would be to decorate our dingy nightstands and dresser in this way, how beautiful they would look, and how uplifted I would feel whenever I looked at them.

Guilt, however, soon began to torment my conscience for even thinking of undertaking this frivolous activity. My mind was besieged with thoughts of how many people would die at Armageddon because I took time to paint my furniture, instead of using it to knock on people's doors to warn them of God's impending war. Distraught, I started to rationalize, "If I spent the morning doing the preaching work, then maybe Jehovah wouldn't be angry with me if I spent the afternoon painting my furniture."

Giddy with the thought that I could at last have something pretty in my house, I bought a can of white enamel and several tubes of colorful acrylic paints. Being no artist, hand-painting the detailed designs onto the furniture pieces was painstaking work, but the result was well worth my effort as the dingy old chest and nightstands took on a life of their own. I took great pride in my work, as the colorful designs of hearts, flowers, vases, and birds that I had meticulously painted on the furniture brightened our bedroom, and my depressed mood lifted.

Excited over the successful outcome of my project, I enthusiastically pointed out my showpieces to a Witness couple who stopped by to visit. Shortly thereafter, one of the elders unexpectedly came to our home, asking to see the furniture I had painted. He said that although he could appreciate how much effort I had put into creating these decorative pieces, since hearts were included in the intricate designs, I would have to sand off my artwork and repaint the furniture. The Witness couple had reported me to the elders, complaining that the shape of a decorative heart was a pagan symbol, and my having them in my house was "stumbling" them, i.e., could cause them to conclude Jehovah's Witnesses were not the true religion after all. My heart sank. I didn't know that Jehovah's Witnesses believed that the shape of a heart was an ancient pagan symbol; I certainly didn't think of it that way when I looked at the heart designs. I associated hearts with feelings of love, kindness, and caring; but regardless of what they meant to me, because painting the hearts on my bedroom furniture offended the conscience of this couple, the elders left me no choice but to remove the artwork I had labored to produce.

Some weeks later, my husband and I stopped by this same couple's house for a short visit. They enthusiastically showed us an old recliner that they had reupholstered and covered with new fabric. They were so proud of their handiwork! The fabric they used was covered with a tiny design which looked strangely familiar; upon close examination, I realized the design was none other than little hearts! I pointed out my discovery, and told them the elders required me to sand off the heart designs from my furniture because of their complaint. Unembarrassed, they muttered that they had not realized the design was tiny hearts, and that they were so small that it was hard to tell at a distance what they were; and besides, it had been so much work and expense to reupholster the chair that they were going to leave it as it was.

I later reported to an elder that this couple's recliner was covered in tiny hearts, and demanded to know the reason why they were allowed to decorate their home using the heart symbol, yet I was not. He answered, "Because they are new in the Truth and we don't want to do anything to stumble them out of the Truth; whereas you are mature in the Truth and can handle such things." But I couldn't just "handle such things"—the elders' having two sets of rules was totally unfair. I had to give up a lot to be obedient to the Society in all aspects, and so I felt that others should be required to do the same. I was extraordinarily angry at the elders' double standard, and at being their little pawn. But in the midst of my anger, I recalled a circuit assembly we had recently attended, during which an elder authoritatively addressed the audience and instructed: "When the Society tells you to jump, don't ask 'Why?' Ask, 'How high?' " Because I felt that Jehovah was speaking to me through that brother's directive, I readjusted my attitude and determined that I would be a good example in the congregation and obediently comply with the elder's counsel, despite what others were allowed to get away with. So I sanded the hearts off of my furniture, and painted something else in their place; although the furniture now looked like it had been altered, I took comfort in knowing that I was pleasing Jehovah by getting rid of the offensive design.[2]

About a year later I felt restless and housebound, as the Society greatly discouraged the sisters from working outside the home. At that time there was a small group of deaf Witnesses in our congregation, and watching the sign language interpreter translate the meetings fascinated me. I convinced her to teach me sign language by agreeing to help translate the Kingdom Hall meetings once I became skilled enough to do so. My husband's attitude toward my learning sign language reflected the attitude the organization had about nearly everything, that learning sign language was a waste of valuable time that could be better spent in the preaching work. He declared, "By the time you become any good at it, the new system will be here; then the deaf will be able to hear, and they won't need any interpreters!" Undaunted by his argument, however, I continued to be tutored; as a result, I interpreted the Kingdom Hall meetings for deaf Witnesses for seventeen years.

One year, I decided to improve my interpreting skills by attending a college class that focused on a specific aspect of interpreting that I felt I needed to refine; however, the Society viewed college as one of Satan's tools used to distract Jehovah's Witnesses from their lifesaving preaching and disciple-making work. The presiding elder consequently put a great deal of pressure on me to quit the class. Under duress, I finally acquiesced. The elder was greatly relieved and told me that an angel had led me by the hand to the registrar's office to withdraw from the class!

For many years I volunteered to help with the interpreting at the large yearly conventions, which always featured a Bible drama. Interpreting these dramas presented quite a challenge and required the interpreters to expend a lot of time and effort traveling considerable distances to attend the drama rehearsals so they could practice their parts. About 1985, an excellent interpreter was assigned to translate only a three-word exclamation in the drama; nevertheless, she was still required to attend *all* the many drama rehearsals. Upon commenting to the elder overseeing the deaf section that I felt this requirement was unreasonable, he chastised, "If that interpreter has the right attitude, she will consider her small part a *privilege!*"

A year later there was a problem among the deaf Witnesses at the convention. They could not understand one of the interpreters. Because they would not seek assistance from the brothers to resolve the situation, I took it upon myself to talk about it with one of the elders I knew who worked in the convention's administrative office. As I passed by his office, I heard him talking to another brother. Not wanting to interrupt their conversation, I decided to wait just outside his office door until they finished their conversation. Unaware of my presence, the elder asked the brother if he would like a drink, stating that they had had a hard day and could use it. To my astonishment, the elder opened his desk drawer and took out a bottle of hard liquor. Just as he was proceeding to open it, he noticed me standing in the doorway. He tried to shrug off the situation by a chuckle that betrayed his embarrassment. He said that he hoped my witnessing this scenario didn't stumble me, but that they just needed a little help relaxing after a taxing day at the convention. That these leaders needed alcohol in order to endure the convention—the supposed Mecca of spiritual food—was shocking to discover; yet if they had observed a brother of the "rank and file" drinking at the convention, he would be sure to face judicial action when he returned to his congregation. The hypocrisy of the situation struck me—here were brothers who sat on such judicial committees, doing the very thing they condemn others for doing, yet for them this behavior was excused and they would have to answer to no one.

Soon thereafter, the Society made the decision to dictate the style of sign language used at the conventions. Despite many complaints and pleas from the deaf group *not* to change the style of signing that we had been using to interpret the conventions, representatives of the Society stubbornly insisted that their choice was the right one. Because my interpreting skills did not include the mode of signing that the Society required, I decided not to attend the sign language auditions that year. The elder in charge found out about my decision. Ignoring my explanation, he shamed me by saying that Jehovah had taught me sign language—and now here I was refusing to use my skills to His glory. He made me feel so guilty that I went ahead and attended the auditions.

The brothers on the judging panel were merciless in their critique of my signing skills, judging my performance on the basis of a signing mode I was not even using! One deaf brother even came up to me afterwards and ridiculed me in front of others. I felt betrayed, and I left in tears without anyone caring enough to console me or apologize.

I wondered what the purpose was of insisting I go to the audition against my will, other than to unjustly humiliate me. I wondered what happened to the love that Jesus said would be the identifying mark of true Christians. With a sense of indignity, I silently vowed never to interpret at the Watchtower Society's conventions again—and I never did. How I wished I could have just as easily walked away from involvement with the entire organization.

About that same time, the Society took control of another aspect of the conventions by eliminating the live orchestra—which was comprised of volunteer Witness musicians—and substituting a prerecorded musical tape instead. The explanation they gave for doing this was to protect the members of the orchestra from "getting puffed-up with pride" because of their musical talents. The Society's attitude toward the members of the orchestra angered me, for it implied that no one would use their God-given talents purely for the worship of God, to the enjoyment and benefit of others. I saw the Society's negative attitude towards developing and using one's talents as an unreasonable squelching of creativity and enjoyment of the innocent, enriching activities of life. The Society felt, however, that there would be enough time to develop one's talents in the new system, and that Witnesses should be content to wait until then and focus their efforts on the preaching work for the present time.

The Society contends that they provide large conventions annually, and assemblies several times each year, to help fortify the Witnesses to endure this system of things faithfully and to encourage them to keep active in the organization. Although they were supposedly held to build-up our spirituality, I often found them to be disheartening. No matter how early I arrived at these functions, there was always someone who arrived ahead of me to claim large sections of the best seats in the auditorium for their friends and relatives who would be arriving later on, either by literally roping off the seats, or by placing *Watchtower* or *Awake!* magazines on rows and rows of seats. In the case of the conventions that were held at outdoor coliseums, the seats would often be held by draping blankets over large sections of the bleachers. This practice of saving seats both angered and embarrassed me, as it was such a blatant example of selfishness.

Lack of Christian love was evident in other ways as well. Some of the conventions were held at large outdoor arenas; there was little shade to be had, thus most of the attendees had no choice but to sit in the blazing hot sun. As Witnesses are instructed to bring their children with them to these conventions, there were many babies in the crowd. Many times I observed mothers putting their infants down on the concrete floor of the stadium on small blankets next to their feet, in the hope that the babies would sleep so that they could pay attention to the talks that were being given. I was greatly concerned about this practice, as many babies slept for long periods of time with little protection from the searing rays of the hot sun. A concerned sister approached one of the brothers who was in charge of the public address system, asking him to make an announcement warning mothers of the possible peril to which they were exposing their babies by allowing them to be exposed to the direct sun and heat—the danger of sunburn, heat exhaustion, and sunstroke. The brother curtly replied that the Society does not allow their public address system to be used to make personal announcements. Later that day, I saw an ambulance come and take one baby to the hospital; I later heard that the baby suffered a heat-induced aliment—yet the brothers still refused to announce this warning to the multitude of young mothers present with their infants.

At a convention in 1978, I refused to sit in the sun, due to the fact that doing so aggravated one of my health problems, making me feel ill and faint. I crossed over to the opposite side of the stadium where there was a small overhang which provided a minimal amount of shade, and stood in the wide aisle there. A brother approached me and chastised me for "wandering around" instead of being in my seat paying attention to the talk being given. I explained that I was not strolling about socializing with others, but that I needed to be out of the sun for medical reasons; nevertheless, he informed me that my standing in the aisle was not acceptable. I replied that he was leaving me no choice but to go home; he just shrugged his shoulders and stood his ground, making sure I got the message to move on.

Jehovah's Witnesses claim to be the only true Christians on the Earth, emulating Christ; but I just couldn't imagine Jesus acting in such an unconcerned manner about people as I was experiencing the brothers at this convention behaving. I wondered how the officials of the only true religion could be so un-Christlike—but I chalked it up to the reason the brothers constantly drummed into our heads: "The organization as God's organization is perfect, but it is made up of imperfect people."

Another reason these meetings were so disheartening was due to the Society's frequent reminders of how worthless we all really were. The speakers' favorite metaphor used to make this point at the assemblies was:

> Thrust your fist into a bucket of water, then pull your fist out. Look into the bucket. The size of the hole that is left in the water is what you're worth!

Ostensibly, the purpose of this metaphor was to keep us humble and protect us from the sin of thinking too much of ourselves, but I experienced it as a manipulation to keep us all in subjection to the organization and from thinking for ourselves. I also felt their demeaning attitude was an insult to the God who created us. Because the Society repeatedly indoctrinated us with this feeling of worthlessness, we accepted the devalued position they put us in; thus we looked to them as the "go-between," the filter, between God and us. We had little confidence in ourselves since Jehovah was given the credit for all of our successes, but we had to shoulder the blame for all of our failures.

One of the speakers at a circuit assembly went so far as to tell us to accept corrective counsel from the elders, even if we did not say or do anything that merited getting it! "Just accept the counsel! It will make-up for all the times you needed it but didn't get any!" As Witnesses, we were so conditioned to blaming ourselves instead of ever criticizing the organization, that many Witnesses responded *gratefully* to disciplinary counsel from the elders, *even when they had done nothing to deserve it!*

Counsel was given at the assemblies about even very private matters. One assembly featured a skit of an older Witness man counseling a teenage Witness boy about the dangers of masturbation, and labeled this practice "self-abuse." Counsel was given to the entire audience on how to deal with the urge to engage in sexual self-stimulation: if one felt in danger of becoming overcome in the middle of the night with this drive, for example, then one must immediately force oneself to get out of bed, stand up, and read the Bible out loud until the urge passes. If the impulse does not go away, the speaker explained, one was to stand up and read from the Bible the entire night if necessary, in order to avoid the sin of masturbation. A single Witness woman in her twenties, who I knew was having an especially difficult time controlling this desire, told me that she confessed this weakness to the elders; they instructed her to call one of the elders on the telephone every time she experienced this urge, and to talk with him until the impulse subsides. One time when she found that even this did not curb her desire, she called the elder back and informed him of her dilemma. As a result, several of the elders went over to her house, and talked and prayed with her for several hours until she was able to gain control of herself.

At another assembly, a speaker threatened, "If you're not pioneering, (putting in 90–100 hours per month in the preaching work), you better be able to tell Jehovah *why!*" He implied that if we did not constantly work toward the goal of pioneering, we could not expect Jehovah's protection at Armageddon; however, we were constantly reminded: "Only the righteous will be saved, *and that with difficulty*." Such admonitions were extremely depressing to me and made the tremendous effort to pioneer seem futile; even the obligatory house-to-house preaching work required a lot of energy to carry out.

One day while in the witnessing work, I met an elderly German lady named Anna. It was readily apparent that she spoke no English; I had studied the German language in high school, but my German skills were quite rusty at this point. I felt the urgency of the times—Armageddon was looming near, so it was imperative that Anna be afforded the opportunity to hear the Witness message and be given the chance to respond favorably to it in order to be spared from the coming destruction—and there was no Witness fluent in German available to speak to her. Knowing this responsibility now rested upon me, I summoned up what little German I could remember, and was able to present to her the basic lifesaving Witness message in German.

She told me that she faithfully attended a very small German church that was within walking distance from her house. Because the Witness belief is that all churches are part of "Babylon the Great," the world empire of false religion, I felt a keen duty to extricate her from this church and get her to attend the Kingdom Hall instead—then there would be a greater possibility of her being spared when Jehovah soon destroyed all of the churches. I consequently took upon myself the obligation that I was taught was mine as one of Jehovah's Witnesses—to meet with this woman weekly to teach her the Truth and give her the chance to choose between it and her religion.

In order to meet this challenge, I had to study my German textbooks for several hours each week to refresh my memory of the German language. I obtained a copy of the *New World Translation of the Holy Scriptures*, the Bible translation of the Watchtower Society—which Witnesses believe to be the most accurate translation available—and the current Watchtower Bible study aid in German, and diligently prepared for hours every week for this visit with Anna. Making sure I could understand and explain Witness doctrine and the cited Scriptures in German was enormously time-consuming, and required a great deal of sacrifice on my part to accomplish.

As I gradually realized that Anna suffered from senility and was not capable of understanding the points that I was trying to teach her, I became very frustrated. I spoke with the circuit overseer, a traveling elder who visited the congregations twice a year, about my dilemma with Anna. I explained that I felt my time would be better used in seeking out others to warn, instead of continuing to spend so much time and energy with her. Showing no sensitivity to my predicament, he rebuked me for my impatience; he instructed me to continue to try to teach her for at least another six months before giving up, reminding me that if I gave up too soon Jehovah would hold me responsible for her death at Armageddon.

Continuing to meet with Anna under the circumstances was extremely stressful for me. I saw Jehovah as demanding the impossible from me and threatening me with death if I couldn't meet His demands. Witnesses are taught that they cannot hope to be saved if they don't do enough. "Therefore, take steps quickly to work for survival and for eternal life in God's new order." (*AW* 10-8-68, p. 29) But even then there are no guarantees! How different we might have felt if we had had the faith that we would be saved; then, we might have wanted to do the works, instead of feeling forced into doing them in an effort to appease Jehovah.

Feeling coerced into obeying the Society's strict dictums made me feel unhappy, but I learned that voicing that unhappiness was invariably met with the shaming rebuke of, "Happy is the man whose God is Jehovah!" If a Witness was unhappy, the inference was that his God was not Jehovah; and if his God were not Jehovah, he would die at Armageddon. As a result, many Witnesses constantly wore a fake, "plastered-on" smile. One sister who most especially wore this particular counterfeit smile overheard me complaining to another sister that I hated going camping with my husband. She immediately interrupted the conversation with the reprimand of, "I hate to go backpacking, but my husband loves it and wants me to go with him to keep him company, just as your husband wants you to go camping with him. In order to please Jehovah, we women must cheerfully do as our husbands request; we must remember that the purpose God created woman was to be a companion and helpmate to the man." Her admonition reflected the Society's view of women, i.e., that they were not entitled to have a life of their own, but exist solely as a "complement" to their husband. I was seething inside, but I forced myself to restrain my anger, lest she turn me in to the elders for disagreeing with the Society. Once again I found myself in sharp conflict with the Society's teachings; I felt I had the right to develop my skills and talents and pursue my own interests, instead of living life merely as a shadow to a man. Instead of asserting myself against the Society's limiting view, though, the Witness indoctrination caused me to finally see my anger and unhappiness as rebellion against Jehovah; thus, I stifled my feelings in order not to lose out on eternal life.

Additionally, "happiness" is a confusing matter because of the elders' frequent admonishments of: "If you aren't suffering, you're doing something wrong!" and "If you aren't suffering, you're on the wrong path!" Such admonishments lead one to the conclusion that happiness equates with suffering—which, in reality, is against normal and healthy human reasoning. Witnesses believe that the people inside the organization are the ones Satan failed to win; so, Satan tries to cause them be unhappy so that they will want to leave the organization and thus become part of his realm. Unhappiness, therefore, is a very frightening feeling, as leaving the organization meant losing one's life forever. However, Witnesses *also* view unhappiness as Satan's test and thus a reason to be happy, because it is proof that the Witness is "in the Truth." This illogical and contradictory set of beliefs caused me to feel a dizzying sense of confusion.

Because expressing or even feeling unhappy was so forbidden, Witnesses often unconsciously translated this feeling of unhappiness to that of "feeling discouraged," which was an acceptable expression to voice—and for that reason was used frequently by the Witnesses. This expression was accepted by the congregation because of the organization's basic belief that they are the only true religion, thus Satan is continually waging warfare against them, using overt but also subtle methods to undermine the zeal of the Witnesses. The congregation members readily recognized this incessant struggle against Satan as a reason to "feel discouraged," and thus always responded with kind words and efforts to encourage the discouraged person.

Being unable to admit feeling unhappy contributed toward being unable to take action to relieve the unhappiness, which frequently led to depression for many Witnesses. Depression was common among the Witnesses I knew, as "feeling depressed" was seen as a more severe form of "feeling discouraged" and therefore brought expressions of sympathy and greater attention from other Witnesses. However, the attention was frequently directed at efforts to get them more involved in organizational activities, which was usually not the solution, since feeling coerced into adhering to the organization's dogmatic beliefs was often the cause of the unhappiness. If these efforts were unsuccessful in alleviating the Witness's discouraged or depressed mood, the depressed person was usually considered to be "not encouraging," and was often avoided thereafter.

In order to reduce the number of Witnesses affected by "feeling discouraged" or "feeling depressed," the Society put a lot of emphasis on the need for Witnesses to always "act encouraging" toward each other; as a result, Witnesses often pretended that everything was fine, even when things were not. This pretense often upset me, as I felt it was living a lie— and the Society taught that lying was a sin worthy of eternal death. Nevertheless, an everyday occurrence at the Kingdom Hall was the greeting, "How are you?"; if that greeting was answered with anything less than an enthusiastic "Fine!" it commonly evoked a distressed feeling on the part of the inquirer, for it usually meant the person was either discouraged or depressed. The burden was then on the Witness inquirer to help "encourage" that person, which was an exhausting task for the already exhausted Jehovah's Witness. A response of "I'm enduring" was considered quite acceptable, however, for it meant that the person was sticking with the organization despite having some personal problems. It was always met with some expression of empathy or praise from other Witnesses. That response, however, touched something deep inside of me that said life was not meant to be merely endured, but to be embraced and lived. I never told anyone I felt that way, though, because the Witness belief is that this present life is only what we struggle to get through so that we may attain the real life, i.e., life in the new system of things under Jehovah's world government on Earth.

There was also the possibility that the person was so depressed that he or she was in danger of drifting away from the organization. Trying to "encourage" this kind of person was frightening to the Witness because of the fear of being spiritually "brought down" and becoming likewise depressed and drifting away—thus losing one's life at Armageddon. This fear was so great for me that whenever I unwittingly encountered a depressed person, I quickly offered some superficial words of comfort, and then hastily found a reason to end the discussion so I could find someone "encouraging" to talk with who wouldn't pose such a danger to me.[3]

Witnesses who were very ill—but who nonetheless always came to the meetings with a smile on their face and did not complain to others about their illness—were especially held up by the elders as fine examples for others to emulate. I clearly saw in this organization that *appearances* were far more important than what one really felt.

Another example of appearance versus reality was illustrated one time by a couple of Witness women who were discussing an inactive sister. One of them exclaimed, "If only we could just *drag* her to the meetings!" Her inference was that everything would be all right if only she were physically present in the Kingdom Hall. Her exclamation just reinforced the general prevalent attitude that what one does means more than what is in one's heart.

Others the elders pointed to as models to be imitated were faithful sisters with unbelieving abusive husbands. One sister told of her husband being so angry with her for being a Witness, that he locked her out of the house; consequently, she slept in the chicken coop in her backyard for several nights. The congregation heartily applauded her behavior as that of a good Witness wife. Another time she told of her husband hitting her, and then using a hose to soak not only herself, but her Watchtower literature as well. She recounted with a chuckle how she carefully picked up all the pages and hung them out on the clothesline to dry, and then the next day she ironed all the pages flat. The congregation lauded her fine example.

The organization has a sacred ritual similar to that of "communion" in Christian churches, and is known as the "Memorial of the Lord's Evening Meal." Observed only once a year, missing this occasion is considered nearly unforgivably sinful. For years I had found it to be a rather depressing occasion, as the Witness doctrine of only 144,000 people out of all of humankind having the hope of going to heaven after they died (this number is drawn from the Society's interpretation of Rev. 14:1, 3) precluded most in attendance from partaking of the sacred bread and wine emblems, as only the remnant of this special group living today may share in doing so. The congregation sang the same sad, dreary song, accompanied by prerecorded funeral dirge type of music, during this occasion every year. The atmosphere in the Kingdom Hall was extremely somber. An elder would always deliver a very solemn talk in which he would stress the seriousness of the occasion, and would caution the congregation of the grave consequences for partaking unworthily. Death at Jehovah's Hand would be the punishment for partaking of the bread and wine emblems if one were not of the "anointed," i.e., a member of the elite, divinely selected group.

The reason all the work Jehovah's Witnesses do to be in God's favor at Armageddon could still fail is *not* because God only accepts 144,000 to save out of the billions of humans, but rather because they didn't serve God with a full heart, or they were lax in their preaching efforts and didn't do all they possibly could to warn people about the impending Armageddon, and to teach them the only way of salvation is through the Watchtower Society.

The Witness doctrine is that only 144,000 out of all humans who ever lived will inherit *heavenly* life; however, there is no limit to the number of people who will live forever in the *earthly* paradise.

As the plates of unleavened bread and goblets of wine were passed from person to person to all in attendance, curious eyes could be seen peering down the rows of chairs, hoping to catch a glimpse of one of the anointed sipping the wine or nibbling the bread. I would tremble as these emblems were passed to me, for the silent fear was, "Hurry up and pass the emblems on to the next person before Satan the Devil causes you to taste the wine or take a bite out of the bread!" The whole event was terrifying to me; I failed to see how it could be considered a celebration.

How a person knows that they are of this special "anointed" class is somewhat of a mystery; Witnesses are taught that Jehovah's Spirit will join with the spirit of a Witness whom God has chosen to be in this unique group, thus that person will have no doubt that he or she has been selected for this privileged position. If Witnesses would ever express that they were in a quandary over whether they were or were not so favored by God, that uncertainty was viewed as proof that they were not of the anointed class. It is interesting to note that while women are not allowed to be in leadership positions in the organization on the Earth, the Society teaches that both men and women make up this group to be heavenly rulers with Christ over the Earth; the reason this is so is because when the chosen women die on Earth, they are raised as spirit beings that have no gender. (*Is This Life All There Is?* [1974], p. 179)

If Witnesses are ever viewed partaking of the emblems, congregation members are taught never to question the validity of their claim to this lofty calling; however, in reality, such ones often do become the focal point of much gossip in the congregation, since the Society claims that all of the 144,000 anointed ones were selected by the year 1935—except for replacements, should any of the chosen ones sin and be disqualified. Since nearly all of the remaining members of this special group are quite elderly, it is expected that the replacements will be up in years, as well. And although the elders teach that if a Witness feels they have been chosen by God to have the heavenly hope, that is a private matter between that individual and Jehovah—my experience has been that if a person partakes who has never done so in the past, unless they are elderly, that person will promptly face a meeting with the judicial committee to be interrogated and warned of the dire consequences of their action if they are not truly of the anointed class. And although the elders teach the congregation that no one is to judge those who partake, the elders themselves do sit in judgment of that person and decide whether or not to include that individual in the count of partakers that must be reported to Watchtower headquarters. This "screening" began when the number of anointed partakers in the world increased one year, instead of decreasing annually as some of the oldest ones die off and are instantly resurrected to heavenly glory as members of this special class. Each year that this happened, the following year an elder would give a special talk just prior to the Memorial with an especially severe warning about the consequences of partaking without having received the heavenly calling.

I felt an equally important event to commemorate was Jesus' resurrection, truly an occasion meriting joyous, triumphant celebration. I could never understand why the Society did not allow the Witnesses to celebrate it, for without the victory over death through Jesus' resurrection, where would the Christian hope be? By the Society's refusal to celebrate the resurrection, I felt they were missing the whole point of Jesus' sacrifice.

Instead of experiencing joy in serving and worshipping God, I felt my life revolving around my fear of Jehovah destroying me at Armageddon, and my efforts to escape His wrath. Even the Society's book written for children, *From Paradise Lost to Paradise Regained* (1958), depicted fear-inspiring graphic descriptions of God's coming wrath:

> Soul-chilling terror will spread through the masses of people so that they will lose control of themselves; they will begin killing one another. . . . Those who escape being killed by their neighbors will be destroyed by God's heavenly armies. . . . A flesh-eating plague will destroy many. . . . Eaten up will be the tongues of those who scoffed and laughed at the warning of Armageddon! Eaten up will be the eyes of those who refused to see the sign of the 'time of the end'! Eaten up will be the flesh of those who would not learn that the living and true God is named Jehovah! Eaten up while they stand on their feet! Where can people hide from this destruction coming from God? Nowhere! (*From Paradise Lost to Paradise Regained*, [1958], p.208-209)

I felt disturbed about what kind of God I was teaching my children to believe in.

Raising our children to be Jehovah's Witnesses required our restricting their friends to only other Witnesses. For years, my children had no friends because there were not any children their age in our congregation. While there were strict rules about not allowing Witness children to have friends who were outside of the organization, no provisions were made within the organization for Witness youths to meet and make friends with those from other congregations of Jehovah's Witnesses. I felt sad watching my son enjoying his summers vicariously by absorbing himself in piles of books, reading about the adventures of others instead of experiencing adventures himself.

As a Witness parent, having children in school presented ongoing obstacles to surmount to keep them "separate from the world." In 1973, when my son was of the age to begin kindergarten, the brothers were putting a lot of pressure on parents not to send their children to school until absolutely necessary; this was encouraged in order to keep them away from the unwholesome influence of "worldly" children, i.e., those who did not have Witness parents, since Armageddon was believed to be imminent. Since attending kindergarten was not mandatory by law, I decided the best way to protect my son from worldly influences was to keep him at home and teach him myself. I worked hard to teach him the things that would be necessary for him to know in order to stay loyal to Jehovah, since I knew I would be required by law to send him to first grade the following year. One of the teachings Witness parents were to instill in their children was the necessity of refraining from the daily flag salute at school, teaching them that the flag is an idol; thus, saluting the flag would constitute an act of worship, and would be considered as an act of treason against Jehovah.

My son was raised with strict adherence to the profusion of rules that Witnesses are required to obey; this—coupled with the obligation every Witness has to tattle to the elders on Witnesses who break the rules—led to serious problems for my son when he entered school, as he carried over this Witness mindset into the playground there. The teacher instructed the children not to step over a particular painted boundary line on the blacktop play area of the school grounds; my son took it upon himself to make sure all his classmates followed this rule, and personally tattled any infractions to the playground supervisor. This led to several of the boys ganging up on him as he was walking home one afternoon, beating him up, dragging him into the street, and leaving him there. I went in search of him when he did not come home at the usual time; fortunately, I found him before a car came down the road.

I was relieved when my son developed a friendship with a boy in his class at school whose mother belonged to a Witness congregation in a nearby town; I invited the boy to stay the weekend with our family, and brought him to the Kingdom Hall meeting with us. I was bewildered and offended when an elder told me that I was bringing a bad name on my family by having this boy stay with us, due to the style of the boy's haircut.

When I pointed out that an older Witness boy, of whom I knew this elder approved, had the same haircut, the elder responded, "Well, it looks better on him!" I was furious that this elder had violated the Scriptures by judging my son's friend by his own personal preferences about a particular hair-style, instead of on the quality of the boy's character, and that the elders could wield such unreasonable control over congregation members by forcing their own preferences about such things onto them.

Witness children cannot participate in any of the holiday preparation and birthday celebrations that occur in most elementary school classrooms; this creates many problems not only for the teacher, but for the Witness parents and their child as well, as the natural inclination of the child is to want to have fun with classmates and join in the festive activities. In an effort to avoid problems such as this, at one point several Witness parents met with a Witness teacher to discuss the plausibility of starting a private school that would be open only to children whose parents were Witnesses. Over the course of time this idea became a reality, with Witness parents volunteering their time as instructors, working under the supervision and license of the teacher. For the most part, textbooks were comprised of Watchtower litera-ture. Although the school was expensive, many Witness parents chose this way to shelter their children from the negative effects of associating with non-Witness children in the public schools. Although Witness women were not to be employed outside the home, exception was made for those who did so in order to send their children to this private "Witness school."

My son had a friend who attended this school for several years. Because the Witness school offered only a "bare bones" curriculum, he wanted to transfer to a public high school in order to take some vocational classes, and to get a diploma from a recognized high school. To his shock, he learned that the public high school would not accept many of the credits from the "Wit-ness school," as its classes did not measure up to the public school's stan-dards; consequently, he had to attend several sessions of summer school in order to catch up so he could graduate from the public high school.

Another example of the unreasonable control the elders exerted over the congregation was in the area of congregational singing. Since many Wit-ness songs have a mournful quality to them, I was delighted one day when I heard a couple behind me singing in harmony, which greatly enhanced the song and gave it an uplifting tone. When I later complimented them, they told me that the elders had severely chastised them for "drawing attention to themselves." The elders forbade the couple to sing in harmony at the meetings again.

In similar fashion, a young Witness man who was a gifted pianist once accompanied the congregational singing and decided to "jazz-up" the song by playing in a lively, spirited manner, in the hopes of encouraging more people to sing. The congregation reacted by singing enthusiastically; however, the elders consequently reprimanded him for changing the tempo of the song, and he was never allowed to play the piano at the meetings again.

There came a time when feminine pantsuits became fashionable attire for businesswomen, and many women thereafter commonly wore them to church services as well. Noticing this fashion trend, a sister decided to wear a pantsuit to the Kingdom Hall meeting; the very next meeting found many sisters wearing attractive pantsuits. The elders quickly squelched this "rebellion" among the sisters by quoting Scripture (Deut. 22:5) to those in error, counseling that pants were improper attire for sisters to wear to the Kingdom Hall. An announcement was thereafter made to the congregation that sisters were not to wear slacks to any Witness meetings. Later on, an elderly sister wanted to wear slacks to the meetings to cover cumbersome and unsightly bandages that she frequently wore wrapped around her calves, due to her having a problem with chronic leg ulcers. The elders would not permit her to wear slacks to the meetings even for this medical reason. When she acquiesced and wore an ankle-length skirt instead, an elder reprimanded her, proclaiming that ankle-length skirts were a fad and therefore unacceptable to wear to the meetings. Thus she was forced into the situation where she had to wear a skirt with its hemline just below the knee, and cover her bandaged legs with a blanket.

Simiarly, an elder imposed his personal preferences on a sister who met with the group at the Kingdom Hall in preparation for the preaching work one morning. It was a bitterly cold day, and she had recently recovered from the flu; since the Society did not allow women to wear slacks while participating in the witnessing work, this sister chose to wear a beautiful wool plaid ankle-length skirt instead in order to keep warm. I was astonished when an elder refused to let her go out with the group, explaining that she was immodestly dressed because her skirt was too long! I felt extremely agitated that "Jehovah's perfect organization" was run by men who were so imperfect that I was clashing with them every time I turned around.

This issue of the sisters wearing pants into the Kingdom Hall caused the deaf Witnesses to lose their best sign language interpreter for the convention one year. The elder overseeing the deaf section at the convention disqualified the most skilled interpreter available because she showed "disrespect" by wearing slacks to the sign language audition, in spite of the fact that the audition was held in the basement of a Kingdom Hall on a Saturday afternoon, and the interpreters were not notified that they were to dress as they would for a Kingdom Hall meeting.

These experiences contrasted strikingly with the dress and grooming I observed among Witnesses in southern California; some of the haircuts and styles of dress of the pioneers (Witnesses whose preaching activity averages ninety hours a month) and servants (elders and their assistants, all of whom are exemplary members of the congregation who are in leadership positions) of one congregation would have met with discipline by the elders in my congregation. The type of dancing I observed at a Witness wedding there would have resulted in disfellowshipping at the Kingdom Hall that I attended. I could not understand this disunity among the congregations, since the organization prided itself in its congruity, boasting that unity was one of the identifying marks of the true religion. It was evident to me that not all of Jehovah's Witnesses were playing by the rules—which made me wonder why I was.

Thinking about all these experiences called the essence of Jesus' words from John 13:35 to mind, that Jesus' disciples would be known by the love they show to one another.

Notes

1. The Watchtower Society itself is quite wealthy, however (see Appendix A, "Brief History of the Watchtower"). The organization is financially supported basically in two ways. First is the money it receives from direct contribution by individual Witnesses, who are encouraged to give at least something desite their own needs. The Society often cites a biblical story known as "the widow's mite" (Mark 12:42–44), wherein the widow—although poor—gave all she had to the temple. The Society draws the parallel to modern-day Witnesses to learn from the widow's example, by giving not only what they can afford to give, but to give enough so that the Witness will have to sacrifice something he or she wants or needs (*WT* 12-1-87, p. 30). The Society recognizes that even though most donations are in relatively small amounts, when added together they add up to a significant amount. Witnesses are also regularly encouraged to remember the organization when making out their wills (*Organization for Kingdom-Preaching and Disciple-Making*, p. 148).

The second way the organization is funded is by the profits it makes on the many books it produces. New books are released at conventions annually, and every Witness—including each of their children no matter how young—are expected to have individual copies of these. Campaigns are featured during the following year to distribute these books in the house-to-house preaching work, for which contributions are made. When I came into the organization, Witnesses had to pay out-of-pocket for literature, hoping to recover these costs by placing these with householders for a specified "donation." In 1990, however, this arrangement changed. Watchtower literature was hence forward provided to Witnesses and the public on a complete voluntary donation basis, without asking or suggesting a specific price that must be paid as a precondition to their receiving an item (*Kingdom Ministry*, May 1990, p. 7). The Witness distributing the literature, however, is expected to make up the difference should the householder not make a donation adequate to cover costs.

When this new arrangement was instituted, I was relieved that I no longer had to put up my own money to receive literature that I would use in the house-to-house preaching work. Although the *Kingdom Ministry* stated that literature would also be provided to Witnesses with no fee asked, I found out the new *unspoken* rule the next time I went to the literature counter in the Kingdom Hall to pick up my supplies. There on the countertop was something new that had not been there before—a small wooden box labeled "Donations." Determined to take the Society at its word, I requested the literature that I needed. Then, smiling from ear to ear, intending to pick up my stack of books, I was startled when the literature servant placed his hand on top of them. His eyes said it all, without his uttering a word; he looked straight into my eyes in a very intimidating manner for several moments, then he looked straight at the donation box, fixing his eyes there for a few seconds. So as not to leave any room for doubt, he again made eye contact with me, and again his eyes darted to the donation box. The message was clear: Witnesses were still expected to pay for their literature—and they were to also turn in any donations received from people while out in the field ministry! I felt myself grow hot in response to feeling so tricked. I approached an elder, exclaiming how unfair that the Society should receive money twice for the same piece of literature. His response was only that I was viewing the matter wrong, and that all the money goes for "the worldwide work."

2. Four years later, the Society—who heretofore had always been avidly concerned with the origins of customs, decorations, shapes, and designs, forbidding any which had even a remote connection with false religion, idolatrous worship, or pagan ancestry—wrote an article called, "Are They Idolatrous Decorations?" (*AW* 12-22-76, p.12-15), changing their view of the decorative heart design to exactly the same view I had previously argued futilely with the elders.

> [L]et us return to the heart-shape. Though this was a religious symbol in ancient Babylon, does it now have such a meaning where you live? Most likely not. It may be nothing more than a decoration that calls to mind the human heart or, at most, suggests "love." In that case, some Christians might feel free to use the heart-shape simply as a decorative design. (*AW* 12-22-76, p. 15)

3. See Appendix B, "Why Jehovah's Witnesses Have Mental Problems."

SIX

EXCUSES, EXCUSES, EXCUSES

The Society continued to focus attention on the fall of 1975 as being a very significant time, the year that Jehovah would act to cleanse the Earth of all unrighteousness: Armageddon. In the winter of 1975, I attended a talk given at an assembly, during which a representative from the Watchtower Society proclaimed: "We're not saying the fall of 1975 will bring the end of this system of things, *but you never hear us talking about 1976, do you?*" This proclamation met with thunderous applause from the ecstatic audience. I remember thinking, I'll never have to sew another winter dress in this system! In fact, I won't have to sew another dress for a very long time! This type of thinking was encouraged by some of the elders who would frequently get carried away during congregational talks, speculating what life would be like after Armageddon; they would often talk about Witnesses being able to avail themselves of all the goods in stores, free for the taking. A favorite activity of Witnesses strolling along in beautiful, expensive neighborhoods during the door-to-door preaching work was picking out which house they wanted after Armageddon. Sometimes two sisters working together both wanted the same house, and would get into little squabbles over who saw the house first.

Although Witnesses will deny this if asked, it is taught that God will kill all who are not Jehovah's Witnesses at Armageddon. This He will do by either afflicting them with loathsome diseases, or causing natural disasters—particularly earthquakes—to take their lives. Birds will then feast on their slain bodies, until only skeletons remain. So as not to mar the beauty of the paradise, part of the responsibility of the surviving Witnesses will be to clean up the bones that are left strewn about. So while these worldly people have been destroyed, it is believed that their homes and possessions will be preserved for the Witnesses' use.

The brother's proclamation at the assembly, while said in a way that stimulated excitement in the 1975 prophecy, however, was also an example of the mixed messages the Society was starting to give as that date drew closer. Though it spoke enthusiastically to keep excitement and interest at a peak, it was also starting to subtly hedge about just what would happen in the autumn of 1975. This was in contrast to the emphasis it had been putting on that date ever since I had been associated with the organization:

- Why Are You Looking Forward to 1975? (*WT* 8-15-68, p. 494)
- Is It Later Than You Think? Is time running out for this generation? What will the 1970s bring? (*AW* 10-8-68, p. 1)
- Who Will Conquer the World in the 1970s? (Circuit Assembly Program, 12-6-70)
- Just think, brothers, there are only about ninety months left before 6,000 years of man's existence on Earth is completed. Do you remember what we learned at the assemblies last summer? The majority of people living today will probably be alive when Armageddon breaks out. (*Kingdom Ministry* 3-68, p. 4)
- How fitting it would be for God . . . to end man's misery after 6,000 years of human rule and follow it with His glorious Kingdom rule for a thousand years! This would leave only seven more years from the autumn of 1968 to complete 6,000 full years of human history. That seven-year period will evidently finish in the autumn of the year 1975. (*AW* 10-8-68, p.14)

I wondered how the Governing Body could speak out all these years regarding their dramatic expectations for 1975, since the Bible clearly states: "Concerning that day and hour, nobody knows." (Matthew 24:36) Nevertheless, strong inference was still given that 1975 would usher in Jesus' heavenly 1,000 year reign over the Earth, and excitement ran high among the Witnesses in expectation of it. One couple I knew even gave up their jobs and nearly everything they owned in order to move to a remote area to devote all their time to the preaching work in an effort to contact as many people as possible before the rapidly approaching autumn of 1975 date. Watchtower literature praised faithful followers for selling their homes in order to use the money from the sale to support themselves during the short time left before Armageddon, so that they could become fulltime preachers in these "last days." (*Kingdom Ministry*, 5-74, p. 3)

A brother whose baby had been born with a foot defect used a brace to correct the deformity so that the child would be able to walk when he got older; many Witnesses felt his using the brace betrayed lack of faith in the Society's 1975 prophecy, as the Society teaches that God will heal all deformities immediately after Armageddon in the new system. Another Witness I knew had a son whose tooth needed a root canal; she proudly related that she had refused the procedure and told her dentist to pull the tooth out instead, explaining that her son would grow a new one when the new system came in a few months. One brother bought a house for his family, and went around the congregation exclaiming to all who would listen that he never would have purchased a house this close to Armageddon, had he not been forced into the situation—but that he had no choice because he had four children and a new baby, and his apartment manager refused to let him stay there with five children.

Even I got caught up in the frenzy this prophecy caused, telling a salesman that I had no need of the cemetery plot he was selling because I was never going to die—and further, that he was soon going to be out of business because the new system, the paradise in which no one will die, is due to arrive in a matter of months. The salesman became so flustered that he didn't know what to do. He finally indignantly stammered that he was going to cross me off his list because I didn't appreciate what a great deal he was offering. As he stumbled away, little did he realize that he was going to get the same response from my Witness neighbors at the house next door!

I was criticized for expressing my desire to have a pet dog; counsel was given by the elders at the Kingdom Hall that this time so close to Armageddon was an unwise time to get a pet, for the enemy would be sure to torture it in front of the family in order to break down their integrity to Jehovah—which would cause them to lose their lives forever. Even the normal desire to have a pet was made into a life-or-death matter. During the spring of 1975, many Witnesses criticized me for planting a small strawberry patch in my backyard; they asserted that my garden represented a lack of faith in the organization's prophecy that this system would end in the fall of 1975, since my plants would not bear fruit until the following year. I responded, "If Armageddon comes this fall, great! If not, then at least I'll have strawberries!" All of these examples illustrate just how firmly convinced most Witnesses were about the fulfillment of the 1975 prophetic date.

Many talks were given at the Kingdom Hall and assemblies to prepare

Jehovah's Witnesses for the intense persecution that the world would bring against them during the imminent Great Tribulation, the time of trouble directly preceding Armageddon. These talks emphasized that we needed to fortify ourselves in order to endure it, thus proving our loyalty to Jehovah and our fitness to live in His new system. As an aid to this end, talks and literature provided detailed accounts of unspeakable tortures that Witnesses in other countries had endured for their faith. One example I heard used many times in public discourses was that of brothers in foreign countries who were imprisoned by the government because they were Jehovah's Witnesses. In an attempt to break their faith, they were lined-up outdoors in subzero temperatures—graphic descriptions were used to depict the scene as water was poured over them, leaving them to freeze to death. Such accounts were told to strengthen our faith, because these Brothers chose to die rather than to denounce Jehovah; they had just the opposite effect on me, however, filling me instead with terror, trepidation, and dread of the future. I was horrified that young children were forced to listen to such frightful accounts, especially since they were warned that they would likely be separated from their parents to face such tortures alone.

Witnesses were not given a choice about whether or not to advocate the Society's prophecy; since they were to spend most of their free time distributing and talking about Watchtower literature, it was not possible to avoid promoting the 1975 date. In fact, refusal to put faith in their prophecy would have resulted in disfellowshipping, as the Society does not tolerate disagreement with any of its teachings.

I felt relief when 1975 came and went without the advent of Armageddon. I was not surprised that the end of this system did not occur in 1975, but I did feel embarrassed about being identified with the organization that had so vigorously promoted that date, and of my participation in it. Most of all, I felt betrayed that the Society handled its embarrassment over its false prophecy *by turning against* its loyal members who had trusted the Society to dispense Bible truth!

The Society blamed the Witnesses by declaring:

> But it is not advisable for us to set our sights on a certain date, neglecting everyday things we would ordinarily care for as Christians, such as things that we and our families really need. . . . If anyone has been disappointed . . . he should now concentrate on adjusting his viewpoint, seeing that it was not the word of God that failed or deceived him and brought disappointment, but that his own understanding was based on wrong premises. (*WT* 7-15-76, p. 441)

The Society did not acknowledge that it was the source of these wrong premises! Instead, the Society shamed the Witnesses by declaring: "But they have missed the point of the Bible's warnings concerning the end of this system of things, thinking that Bible chronology reveals the specific date." (*WT* 7-15-76, p. 440) The Society did not acknowledge that it was the source of that specific date! The Society did not accept responsibility for the 1975 date, even though it was the Society's own idea that was then forced on all of Jehovah's Witnesses.

The attitude of the Society, the "Mother," reminded me of the attitude of a mentally ill mother who demands her child do something that the child doesn't want to do. Under her insistence, however, the child obeys; then, when things don't work out well, she slaps the child for doing it—and then demands that the child obey her now.

The Society shamed the Witnesses by saying: "Are you serving Jehovah only to a certain date? Or, are you committed to serving Him forever? *If so, what are you so disappointed about?*" (Watchtower Society District Convention)

The Society even used God as an excuse for its failed prophecy by declaring: "Also, just as there was a great sifting among the anointed remnant in the decade following 1914, it seems that now there is a sifting going on among some who profess to be of the 'great crowd.'" (*WT* 10-1-78, p. 13) Any who left the organization as a result of the failed prophecy were viewed as "undesirables" who Jehovah God had "sifted-out" of His organization!

Since the Society used the excuse that " . . . it must be observed that this 'faithful and discreet slave' [the Watchtower Society] was never inspired, never perfect" (*WT* 3-1-79, p. 23), I wondered why Jehovah's Witnesses must believe and obey the Society *as if it was* perfect and inspired?

The Society claimed that its blunder was for our benefit as an excuse for its failed prophecy. "Actually, any adjustments that have been made in understanding have furnished an opportunity for those being served by this 'slave' to show loyalty and love. . . ." (*WT* 3-1-79, p. 24)

The Society said its error helped us to get a more mature viewpoint as an excuse for its failed prophecy.

> However, say that you are one who counted heavily on a date, and, commendably, set your attention more strictly on the urgency of the times and the need of the people to hear. And say you now, temporarily, feel somewhat disappointed; are you really the loser? Are you really hurt? We believe you can say that you have gained and profited by taking this conscientious course. Also, you have been enabled to get a really mature, more reasonable viewpoint. (*WT* 7-15-76, p. 441)

The Society used its zeal and desire for the new system as an excuse for their failed prophecy.

> However, during these 'last days,' have erroneous views about this system's end or *telos* (Greek) been held in advance by some of Jehovah's servants? Yes, they have. Some of these views involve the length of time it would take for the end to come. Out of zeal and enthusiasm for the vindication of Jehovah's name, Word and purposes, and the desire for the new system, some of his servants have at times been premature in their expectations. (*WT* 7-1-79, p.29)

The Society used "human fallibility" as an excuse for their failed prophecy.

> "There are some who make spectacular predictions of the world's end to grab attention and a following, but others are sincerely convinced that their proclamations are true. They are voicing expectations based on their own interpretation of some scripture text or physical event. . . . Hence, in such cases when their words do not come true, they should not be viewed as false prophets. . . . In their human fallibility, they misinterpreted matters." (*AW* 3-22-93, pp. 3-4)

Obviously, every false prophet has misinterpreted matters! If God accepted "human fallibility" as an excuse for false prophecies, how would there be any false prophets for the Bible to warn about?

Any Witnesses taking issue with any of the Society's excuses were labeled as "apostate" or "causing divisions," and were therefore subject to being disfellowshipped. (*Insight on the Scriptures* [1988], p. 788; *WT* 3-15-86, p. 11) The Society's ridiculous excuses and the way it pointed its finger at everyone except itself for the failed prophecy infuriated me; but because I was caught up in the belief that it headed up God's imperfect organization, leaving was not an option. Thus, much of the anger I felt with the Watchtower Society was directed toward Jehovah instead. My only choice seemed to be to try to convince myself that I was wrong for being upset with the organization, and to try to readjust my thinking by accepting the Society's excuses.

The Society continued to take delight in calling attention to various catastrophic events in the world as evidence that Armageddon was still just around the corner, which served to keep enthusiasm high among the Witnesses. It also supported the sense that life outside the organization was horrible and frightening, thus pointing to the need to stay under its protective wing—which kept the Witnesses focused on the organization and active in it. The Society subsequently renewed its emphasis on persecution of the Witnesses in various parts of the world as continuing evidence that they are God's people. The Society also continued to focus on the part of its prophecy that stated that the "last days" of this system, which began in 1914, would span only one generation before culminating with Armageddon. Although the Society did not print a specific date, Jehovah's Witnesses knew that it had long taught that one generation equals seventy to eighty years, based on the Bible at Psalms 90:10. By adding eighty years to the 1914 date, Witnesses knew the farthest date for Armageddon to begin would be the year 1994.

SEVEN

TRUTH OR CONSEQUENCES

The Society's claim that the organization represents the truth, but that the organization is also "progressive" (*WT* 12-1-81, pp. 16, 28), led to new meanings for "truth": "present truth" (*Revelation—Its Grand Climax at Hand!* [1989], p. 8), (*WT* 6-15-22, p. 187) and thus "past truth" and "future truth."

I heard talks in which Jehovah's "progressive" organization was likened to a beam of light along a timeline that illuminated the truth as time went on. Thus, today's truth could become tomorrow's falsehood. Anyone staying in the "old light" behind the beam (by refusing to go along with the Society's changes in doctrine), or anyone who ran ahead of the light beam (by disagreeing with the Society and deciding for oneself what the truth was), were both viewed as being "in the darkness" and would be disfellowshipped. If a Witness disagreed with any aspect of the current "light," and spoke of it openly or acted upon it, that person would be expelled from the organization. If, however, the light beam progressed forward tomorrow to illuminate that person's viewpoint as really being the truth after all, the elders would not make any apology to that person, nor would any effort be made to reinstate that person back into the organization.

According to the Society's "progressive light" teaching, today's "present truth" could become tomorrow's "past truth," which could be replaced later by "future truth" or even by yesterday's "past truth"! In my opinion, that way of thinking negated the meaning of the word "truth." The whole "light beam" illustration did not make sense to me, especially since I knew that the Society often vacillated its doctrines, at times returning to its former views which it had abandoned as "old light" and falsehood; thus, at times, the Society's "light beam" would seem to flash on and off, or even go backwards to illuminate the darkness it had left behind! Whether the Society changed a doctrine with a complete turn to the opposite view, and later returned to the original doctrine, then later again reversed itself, it always cited scriptural support for whatever view it held at the moment. No matter how many times the Society would change its doctrines, it forced Jehovah's Witnesses—under pain of disfellowshipping—to believe and teach its present view to be the absolute truth. The result was that some Witnesses were forced to violate their consciences by doing things they felt were wrong, and teaching falsehood, in order to be "right" with God.

Although the Society was completely dogmatic that its doctrines represented the truth, the fact that it changed them so frequently obviously meant that it was uncertain about many of them; thus, I resented being coerced into accepting all of its twists and turns in doctrine as absolute truth from God. The Society, through its skillful and clever explanations, could make the Bible appear to support any view it had at any given moment, instead of understanding what the Bible really meant.

During their talks at the Kingdom Hall, elders would often humorously make reference to some of the Society's previous teachings, which would usually elicit much laughter from the congregation, as if to say, "We've come a long way, Baby!" However, I failed to see anything humorous about the fact that Jehovah's Witnesses are to have absolute faith that everything the Society teaches is the truth—and then later, after that "truth" changes, the Witnesses are supposed to laugh at themselves for having held that belief.

Because the Society frequently changed many of its doctrines, often returning to views previously abandoned and then changing them back again, the situation got to the point where I had difficulty keeping straight just what the current teachings were on various doctrines. I felt angry that the Society, whose members led the organization that claimed to be God's channel, was so uncertain of what the truth actually was. It claims that no one can understand the Bible without its interpretations, but I was finding the Bible impossible to understand *because* of its interpretations.

The Watchtower Society was similar to a television set that receives its messages from God. It then broadcasts these messages to the world through its literature. However, I began to wonder:

- Why was the Society's screen so fuzzy and full of static?
- Was Jehovah not capable of transmitting His messages clearly to the Society?
- Maybe the Watchtower Society's "television set" isn't even plugged in!

In 1981, the Society addressed the issue of its shifting doctrines through an article in the *Watchtower* magazine, likening itself to a sailboat tacking in the wind, arriving at the right destination eventually despite traveling a zigzagging course.

> However, it may have seemed to some as though that path has not always gone straight forward. At times explanations given by Jehovah's visible organization have shown adjustments, seemingly to previous points of view. But this has not actually been the case. This might be compared to what is known in navigational circles as "tacking."* (*WT* 12-1-81, p. 27)

Anyone who disagreed with or refused to conform to any of the changes was silenced by being thrown out of the organization. This forced belief system struck me as blind faith, despite the brothers' frequent assertion that theirs is the only religion that is not based upon blind faith.

I sat dumbfounded while I observed Witnesses parroting their answers from this article during the congregational *Watchtower* study. I was amazed at how intelligent people could accept such a flimsy excuse for years of doctrinal mistakes. Their explanation of "tacking in the wind" was the most ridiculous explanation the Society had concocted since I had been in the organization. The Society did not accept any responsibility for the people its "sailboat" ran over en route to its final destination of "truth"—that is, people who were hurt as a result of their obedience to the Society's fluctuating doctrines, many of which related to medical issues, obedience to which cost many Witnesses their lives (see chapter 18). The Society seemed oblivious to the shattered lives its "sailboat" left in its wake.

One elder said that the oscillating doctrines were proof that the Watchtower Society is God's organization, because it is the only organization God cares about enough to correct! Another elder sported a very solemn facial expression as he carefully expounded that whatever view the Society has is

---

*"By maneuvering the sails the sailors can cause a ship to go from right to left, back and forth, but all the time making progress toward their destination in spite of contrary winds" (*WT* 12-1-81, p. 27). "To pursue a zigzag course; to shift abruptly one's attitude or policy" (*Webster's New Collegiate Dictionary*).

right and truth *for that moment*; then, when the light swings in another direction or becomes brighter, that view becomes truth *for that moment*. When I challenged this viewpoint by asking how Jehovah could *ever* consider erroneous medical doctrines that cost untold numbers of Witnesses to lose their lives to be truth, he rebuked me by declaring that we cannot presume to understand Jehovah, or in what way He could consider such doctrines to be truth—that Jehovah has lofty reasons far beyond what humans can understand for causing "truth" to change. So, we are simply to accept whatever the Society says as truth—and even if the Society reverses its viewpoint on a matter 180 degrees, and then changes it back again to the original view at a future time, none of it was in error—it was all truth for the moment it was declared to be such.

In unwitting contradiction to his explanation, this same elder at another time gave me a different explanation for the shifting doctrines, i.e., when Jehovah sees His organization teaching an erroneous doctrine, He nudges the Governing Body members to change it; but, being imperfect, they might change it too much or not enough. If they don't change it enough, Jehovah will nudge them a little more; if they change it too much, Jehovah will nudge them back a little bit the other way. But no explanation was given for the reason why Jehovah would sometimes wait twenty years or more to nudge the Society to change an error in its medical doctrines, especially when obedience to those erroneous doctrines caused many Witnesses to die. I wondered how we could ever have confidence that the Society had finally gotten it right.

Another elder told me that Jehovah has a purpose in allowing the errors in doctrine to occur, and that we cannot purport to understand what that purpose is, but we should simply have faith that there is a reason that justifies His timing of changing the doctrines, even if we humans are incapable of understanding them.

Another elder piped-up with his favorite comment: "People in other religions may be sincere, but they're sincerely *wrong*!" Evidently he hadn't stopped to think about the many times the Society had been "sincerely wrong" about many of its teachings since its inception over 100 years ago; how ironic that the Society should still claim that its religion is the only one deserving to survive Armageddon! The elders' explanations were just too far-fetched for me to believe. There were other things I was puzzled about as well. I wondered:

- Since the Society admits that it is not inspired by God, how is it that God "channels" information through its members?

- Since God used imperfect men to write the Bible originally, why was He now having such a difficult time using imperfect men to interpret it?

The Society attributes changes in its doctrines to a "new light" of understanding from God (*WT* 12-1-81, p. 16); the Society refers to such changes as "meat in due season" and "spiritual food at the proper time." (*WT* 7-1-79, p. 7) The Society's pattern of flip-flopping its doctrines, however, means it actually teaches falsehood much of the time. I wondered how that could possibly be "spiritual food" from God. Surely God, who does not lie (Hebrews 6:18), would not be directing the organization to present falsehoods cloaked as "spiritual food" to be presented to the world as truth.

Instead of taking responsibility for its mistakes, the Society pushed that responsibility off onto God:

> We will realize that Jehovah knows what is going on in his organization, and if he is willing to permit it, who are we to insist it should be different? (*WT* 5-1-57, p. 284)

> During World War I God's people expected it to lead directly into Armageddon, but Jehovah prevented such a climax at that time. (*Kingdom Ministry* 1-1968, p. 5)

The Society contended that God would allow falsehoods to masquerade as truth for a time because God's people couldn't handle knowing the truth all at once:

> When Jesus was on Earth, he said to his disciples: 'I have many things yet to say to you, but you are not able to bear them at present.' (John 16:12) If he had told them all these things at once, they would have been overwhelmed. It would have been impossible for them to grasp these things and to put them into effect in their lives. (*WT* 8-15-72, p. 501)

The Society excused its wavering doctrines by alleging that God caused the Bible to be written in vague terms so that people could have something to stumble over!

> If you find that you are stumbled or are offended about something being taught in God's organization, or some adjustments being made, keep this in mind: God has put enough in the Bible to provide a complete foundation for faith. He has also left many details of various events in the Bible out of the account, enough so that one whose heart is not right, who wants

to discover an apparent fault, who wants to find an excuse for leaving the way of truth, can find it. (*WT* 8-15-72, p. 507)

The Society even propounded that God used their zigzagging doctrines as a test of loyalty:

Of course, such development of understanding, involving "tacking" as it were, has often served as a test of loyalty for those associated with the "faithful and discreet slave." (*WT* 12-1-81, p. 31)

In claiming that all its teachings are "spiritual food at the proper time" from Jehovah, the Society eludes all responsibility for injury done to its followers due to its oftentimes contradictory course. Jehovah's Witnesses must accept the Truth, or pay the consequences, but let no one forget there are also consequences to pay for accepting that Truth.

EIGHT

THE RUBBER BAND CYCLE

I was outraged! The organization's attempt to fool us with their supposedly reasonable explanation of "tacking in the wind" as an excuse for all their doctrinal errors over the years, and their continued insistence that they are "God's channel" —instead of humbly admitting that they are just a group of men who are making their best guesses at interpreting the Bible—was an indignity. The anger I had been feeling with the organization over the years crescendoed, and I was experiencing extreme difficulty continuing active in it. In 1981, my preaching time dwindled to two hours a month, just enough to keep me from being labeled "inactive," and my meeting attendance became sporadic. The elders, observing this trend, told me that I was in a dangerous position because I was giving only "token service" to Jehovah; and further, if my children followed my bad example, they would die at Armageddon—and Jehovah would hold me responsible for their deaths. The elders told me: "Your children's blood will be on your own head!"

I immediately started experiencing symptoms of acute anxiety, sleeping fitfully and having nightmares; for many weeks I woke up frequently during the night, sweating profusely, my heart pounding, and trembling inside. During the day, my mind would race with frightening thoughts that my decreased activity in the organization could jeopardize the lives of my children. I became obsessed with the horrifying thought that my doubts about the organization might cause my children to die. I felt like a rubber band stretched to its limit; I feared I would either snap apart, or snap back into the organization.

91

None of the Witnesses suspected that I was struggling with various qualms and uncertainties about the teachings of the Watchtower Society. The penalties for expressing doubts or questioning any aspect of Witness doctrine were so severe that I was forced to keep all my thoughts to myself, compelled to suppress these feelings; the stakes were too high to do otherwise. I had seen other Witness couples break up when one of them "went into disbelief"; I didn't want to risk divorce, or losing my children's affection—a frighteningly real possibility—by voicing my questions or expressing a lack of faith in the Society.

I had to be watchful not to behave in any manner that would betray my true feelings about the organization. If my reluctance to continue to buy into all the Society's ever-changing doctrines leaked out, I would be viewed as an unwholesome influence in the congregation, one to be avoided; then members of the congregation could choose individually to "mark" me (*WT* 5-15-73, pp. 318–19), i.e., stop associating with me socially. This outcome would be devastating because of the organization's strict requirement to limit all of one's friends to only Jehovah's Witnesses. If the Witnesses were to shun me socially, I would then be totally isolated, without any friends at all.

I couldn't risk confiding my questions or doubts to even my closest Witness friends or my husband, as every Witness' loyalty is first to the organization. Baptismal candidates are carefully instructed about their responsibility as a baptized Witness to "keep the congregation clean"; thus, anyone expressing doubts would immediately be reported to the elders. Any infraction of the organization's requirement of total loyalty and agreement with all of its teachings would be punished through chastisement by the elders, public humiliation by reduction in congregation "privileges," a warning to the congregation, social ostracism, or disfellowshipping.

The Society teaches that Satan looks among the Witnesses for those who find fault with the organization. Those who allow themselves to dwell on doubts, to be thus disgruntled and provoked for an extended period of time, "allow place for the Devil" (Eph. 4:27, *NWT*). Any Witness who has doubts is then viewed as being influenced or somewhat overtaken by the Devil; and it is just a matter of time before a Witness in this circumstance would be removed from the congregation.

My battle with my doubts had to stay an internal one; the turmoil that I suffered by pretending to be in agreement with all of the Watchtower teachings, when in reality I had misgivings about several of them, eventually erupted into a period of time when I suffered from acute bouts of bulimia. I found myself overtaken by eating binges, followed by violent episodes of self-induced vomiting. It was as if I were unconsciously trying to suppress my doubts symbolically by swallowing large amounts of food; then, realizing I still had the doubts, I unconsciously attempted to purge myself of them symbolically through vomiting.

There seemed to be no way out of this dilemma; my doubts about the organization were causing my entire belief system to break down, and I felt terrified. It seemed like this religion was the glue that held me together as a person and that gave stability to my life; having doubts made me feel like I was falling completely apart and going crazy. I felt like I was being swallowed up by a big black hole, that frightening world of darkness and confusion that the Society foretold would consume any who leave the organization. I feared I was falling prey to Satan. I was so frightened that my mind became obsessed with thoughts of: Perhaps the Watchtower Society *is* God's Channel! Perhaps I have no legitimate complaints against the Society. Perhaps I am being rebellious against Jehovah's arrangement. I had no confidence in myself or in my doubts about the organization; I was scared, and I desperately wanted to feel safe again. The only way I knew to gain relief was by telling the elders that I had become "spiritually sick," and by asking them to help me to recover; thus, one of the elders began having regular discussions with me. I told him of my doubts and my difficulty in establishing any rapport with Jehovah at all. To my disappointment, he just emphasized the role of the organization and the need to be obedient to it and active in it in order to have a relationship with Jehovah. He added that if I continued to have a "disgruntled attitude" toward the organization, Jehovah would remove His Spirit from me, and also possibly from the entire congregation. Once the elders felt the latter had occurred, they would disfellowship me immediately.

I experienced the elder's counsel as a threat to get me to "behave," instead of an effort to give me any genuine help. I told him that I was still upset that Jehovah would allow years to go by before He corrected the Society's errors when a medical issue was involved that caused Witnesses to suffer or even die. When I asked him why Jehovah permitted babies to die instead of "nudging" the Society sooner to change its erroneous stand regarding the Rho-GAM injection, my question was curtly deflected with his shaming words, "You are asking questions like a person who doesn't know the Truth would ask! Where is your faith?"

Shortly thereafter, the elder showed me an article in one of the Society's publications which counseled that Jehovah will provide whatever spiritual help is needed, and that whatever help is given is to be considered sufficient. I was speechless, as the help that had been given to me had *not* been sufficient! Many of my questions had never been answered; instead, they had been met with shaming retorts. The article inferred I would be complaining against Jehovah if I complained that the help I had received had not been adequate; but the elder's counsel to be obedient to the organization had *not* helped me feel closer to God—to the contrary, the organization seemed to be getting in the way of my relationship with Him.

Not only was it unacceptable for me to vocalize my disagreement with the elder, but at the next assembly, a new ruling from the Governing Body was introduced: The sisters were not to express any disagreement with the brothers, even by their facial expressions. This meant that I could not allow a doubt or disagreement to creep into my mind at all, lest it show on my face and I be chastised for it. I felt angry and resentful about being forced into this even more subservient and degraded position; however, I felt like I was being whipped back into shape for having had doubts—so despite my feeling upset about this new ruling, I accepted it as discipline from Jehovah.

As I became increasingly active in the Kingdom Hall meetings and the preaching work once again, my nightmares and panic attacks stopped. Keeping up with the pace of all the required activities of the congregation kept me too busy to even think, which brought me peace of mind; I didn't realize then that it was really a false peace of mind that I was experiencing, which resulted from not allowing myself time to entertain any of my doubts or disagreements with the organization. I had so much invested in this religion—thirteen years of my life, my husband, my two children, and the comfort I got from feeling like I knew what life was all about—that letting a doubt creep in to cast its threatening shadow on my life became intolerably frightening.

About this time, in 1982, my husband and I were conducting a home Bible study with a family. Because they were not progressing in applying the Truth in their lives, we figured they must have an object in the house that was demonized which was impeding their progress. One day, quite a spectacle was made as we sent the various family members in different directions in their house, searching for anything that the demons may be inhabiting. The daughter brought back wall switchplates that had pictures of saints on them, which we helped her to smash. The wife found a large ceramic statue of a saint. We helped her wrap it in newspaper, and then shattered it with a hammer. She stood by quaking, fearing that the demons which must be embodied in the statue would scream, escape, or come after her. The son found a ouija board; this was considered the most demon-possessed item a person could have, because through it one could directly communicate with the invisible wicked spirits. We tried to burn it, but it would not ignite—this was considered a sign of the power of the demons. We had the family douse the board with a flammable liquid, but it was still reluctant to burn. With persistence, we finally succeeded and rejoiced greatly, feeling now that this family would come right into the Truth. Such was not the case, however; much to my discouragement, they never made the required changes in their lives and so we eventually ended their study.

In spite of all my efforts to suppress any negative thoughts about the organization, though, there were still times when my mind would suddenly be seized by thoughts of, "Exactly how does going to all these meetings and knocking on all these doors make me so much more qualified to receive God's protection than sincere people who are not Witnesses, but are trying to lead Godly lives?" I thought about various people I had known of throughout my life who were deeply religious with a heartfelt connection to God, while I was in an organization just following rules with an empty heart. These kinds of thoughts greatly threatened the sense of security I felt being a Witness. Whenever they would come up, I would try to force myself to immediately dismiss them; if I wasn't able to dismiss them, I would seek out fellow believers who were "strong in the Truth" to visit, as associating with them helped my doubts disappear. Thus, I unwittingly set up a cycle whereby my doubts drove me back into the organization.

The brothers took advantage of any doubts that Witnesses had by citing them as a reason to stay in the organization, reasoning, "If you have doubts about the organization, it is because Satan is causing the doubts; however, because Satan attacks only true Christians, your having doubts proves that the organization is the truth!" Nevertheless, the Society made it very clear that Witnesses are to fight this unseen adversary by refusing to let themselves entertain any doubts or disagreements with the organization. Not wanting to be under Satan's control, I suppressed my uncertainties and objections even more vigorously. The Society's claim that finding fault with the organization is rooted with the Devil meant there were never any legitimate complaints against it; therefore, I strove to push my questions, misgivings, and criticisms of the organization out of my awareness by pretending they didn't exist. What began as playacting eventually became reality on a conscious level, until I succeeded in burying my doubts and disagreements to the point of feeling that I had none.

The Society put much emphasis on Witnesses socializing together to keep each other "built-up" and away from temptation to form non-Witness friendships. Arriving early for congregation meetings and staying afterward was expected for the purpose of fellowshipping—a term, incidentally, that Witnesses never used, because it is a term that churches frequently use, and the Society strove to make sure that its organization was different from the churches in every way possible. The Witness terminology utilized the word "associate" instead, i.e., Witnesses go to meetings early to associate together.

Congregation picnics at local parks were frequently held during the spring and summer months to further encourage bonding with the group. Food was provided by the sisters each bringing a favorite dish to share with others. The commonly used term of non-Witnesses to describe such an arrangement would be a "potluck" meal; however, because of the Witness phobia of the word "luck," they refer it as "share-a-pan." Since Witnesses always substitute the word "fortunate" for the word "luck," I am amazed that they didn't call this picnic a "pot-fortunate"!

Witnesses were required to show hospitality to other Witnesses; often this was done by inviting congregation members over to one's house for dinner. Another way to demonstrate hospitality was to invite Witness missionaries to stay at one's home when they occasionally come back from their foreign assignments to visit the congregation. One year I extended an invitation to one such couple. I was excited to have them stay with us as they were very well-mannered, and I had recently decorated a room in our house to serve as a guestroom. They graciously accepted our invitation; however, they later changed their plans and stayed with a relative instead. They had heard of a pioneer couple with young children who were taking a vacation touring the United States; because of being pioneers, however, they had little money for such a trip, so they decided they would stay with Witnesses along the way instead of staying at motels. The missionary couple knew we had our guest room presently unoccupied, and so they suggested I offer it to this family instead; however, I didn't want to offer it to this family, as I felt it was presumptuous on their part to take advantage of the brothers and sisters in that way.

I was angry that I was now cornered into housing complete strangers with children, as any balking on my part would be construed as selfishness and lack of hospitality. To avoid such tainted labels, I allowed the family to stay for the night. To my astonishment, they did not display gratitude or the Christian personality; instead, they came marching in, demanding to be shown the room and then to be left alone because they were tired and stressed from the trip. The woman was not appreciative of the hospitality they had received from other Witnesses during their trip, rudely complaining of the inadequacy of some of the accommodations they had to put up with during the trip so far.

Because my guestroom had only two beds, I provided sleeping bags for the children to sleep on the floor. The next day, as they were preparing to leave, I was shocked to discover that one of their children had a bed-wetting problem, and that our new sleeping bag was literally soaked. When I pointed out this situation to the woman, she made no offer to replace it or even to have it cleaned. Making no apology, she crudely told me to just hang the sleeping bag out in the sun to dry—and then demanded to know where the cereal was kept so they could eat and be on their way!

I was enraged at this supposedly exemplary family's lack of respect for my hospitality; but knowing the Witness teaching that anger is of the Devil, with great difficulty I contained my feelings and said nothing. Inside, however, I was furious at being so controlled by the organization.

Despite the constant whirlwind of social and organizational activities, which kept me exhausted mentally and physically, the Society gave constant counsel to do more. Warnings were given that if we were not giving our best effort to organizational activities when Armageddon struck, consequences would be dire for us. This warning was illustrated in Watchtower literature by a drawing of a man in a rowboat on a swiftly flowing river, with a huge waterfall just ahead. Rowing as hard as he could against the strong current, he was perspiring heavily and had a look of sheer terror on his face as his boat was swept toward the waterfall despite his strenuous efforts to prevent it from being carried away and crushed by the pounding force of the cascading rapids. The purpose of this illustration was ostensibly to give encouragement to Jehovah's Witnesses to "row harder"—to make even more strenuous efforts to be active in the organization, to put more time into the preaching work, to study Watchtower literature more zealously, and to keep themselves increasingly separate from the world outside the organization—in order to avoid being swept away with the unrighteous world when Jehovah destroys it at Armageddon.

The expression on the man's face in the picture depicted exactly how terrorized the organization made me feel, that I was in constant danger of being swept away despite my rowing as hard as I could. Time available for rest or recreation was already at a minimum; I felt like a hamster on a treadmill, running faster and faster but still getting nowhere with the organization's never-ending demands. Depressing and discouraging also was the fact that there was never any assurance of having an approved standing before Jehovah. An elder, addressing the congregation, would often ask:

"How do you know if Jehovah has forgiven you? You won't know until Armageddon, but we have to keep trying, or else we will truly be lost."

Though this was evidently said to spur the congregation on to greater activity, I felt even more despondent upon hearing his words. If there is no way to know if Jehovah has forgiven me for the sins all imperfect humans make everyday, then I might not even be in this "race for life"! (1 Cor. 9:24) At times I felt so tired that continuing to try to "run the race" anyway did not seem to be worth the effort. However, I believed my only chance of surviving Armageddon lie with doing as much as I could in the organization. I continued studying the Society's literature diligently, endeavoring especially to understand the difficult *Watchtower* articles assigned to the congregation study, only to be constantly frustrated by not being able to understand the Society's reasoning.

Leaving the Kingdom Hall dazed and confused, I noticed a glazed look in the eyes of many of the other Witnesses. Feeling "snowed" by the Society's wordy and complicated explanations, we all just shrugged our shoulders and agreed that the lesson was "over our heads," beyond our ability to understand at the moment. Surprisingly, this feeling of inundation caused many of us to feel secure, knowing our all-wise "Mother" did understand such deep things of God.

A circuit overseer visited our congregation and told us that he was formerly a pioneer, as he felt that doing so would ease his conscience and help him feel secure that he was doing his "all" in serving Jehovah. To his dismay, he soon felt guilty under the Society's constant admonition to "do more" and "row harder"; desiring to be free of that pressure, he decided to become a circuit overseer, devoting *all* his time to organizational activities. However, he lamented that even that did not bring him relief. Rather than feeling encouraged by his story to strive even harder in the organization, I felt defeated instead, and sad that the organization could cause good people to suffer so much emotionally.

I had long been wanting to visit Bethel, as the Watchtower headquarters and printing factory in New York City is called, to see for myself how it created such magnetism, drawing young Witness men away from a normal life into complete servitude to the organization. Bethel had the reputation of being a spiritual haven, and only the most theocratic men were invited to live and work there. Witnesses deem serving Jehovah at Bethel a great privilege. Jehovah's Spirit was said to be especially active there, as that is where the Governing Body resides, and from where the Watchtower magazine emanates. My husband and I finally made plans to go.

Upon our arrival at Bethel, we were given a tour of the facilities. We were invited to have lunch with a brother who was formerly a member of our congregation in the private cafeteria where all the Bethel workers had their meals. I was astounded at what took place: a bell rang, and the brothers started eating very rapidly, not pausing for a moment to have conversation with anyone at their table. They didn't even look up—they just focused intently on consuming the food before them. A very short time later the bell rang again, and the brothers instantly put down their forks, stood up next to their chair, arms straight at their sides, and filed quickly out of the dining hall to return to their jobs in the Watchtower printing factory. I was speechless. Lunch was over! "No wonder they are all so thin!" I thought.

On the tour of the book printing facilities, we were introduced to one of the workers. His appearance was at once striking, as he was completely devoid of body hair despite being a very young man. The tour guide informed us that he had developed this condition shortly after coming to serve at Bethel, and advised us that the Society had sent him to the best doctors, who found no medical reason for his strange condition. Although he seemed to be a happy worker, I couldn't help but wonder if his affliction was not one induced by stress, frustration, boredom, and fear.

My visit to Bethel was not a fortifying experience. I never felt God's Spirit there. Rigid control and lack of love was clearly evident. I felt even more despondent, as I found myself again doubting that this could possibly be God's organization. Upon my return home, I told a sister how horrified I had felt by what I saw take place at Bethel; she retorted that she didn't see how a visit there could possibly be anything but upbuilding, and that she planned to visit Bethel as soon as she could afford to go. She treated me indifferently after that conversation, and she never resumed our previous warm friendship thereafter.

When I related my experience about Bethel to another sister, she confided to me that when she was younger, she had been one of the few women accepted to serve there. She told me of the horrendous working conditions she had to silently endure, including being required to sit next to a boiler daily for months while she did data entry work, despite the temperature inside the building soaring to over 100°F. The sweltering heat radiating from the boiler caused the already uncomfortable working conditions to become nearly unbearable. Requests to be moved to a different location were viewed as complaints, and all complaints were viewed as of the Devil. She explained how anyone who said anything negative about the conditions at Bethel was immediately labeled a "B.A.," for "Bad Attitude," and anyone so labeled would eventually be rejected and sent back home to face the great humiliation and shame of being found a misfit at Bethel.

She told me the few sisters who were accepted by Bethel generally were given the "privilege" of being used as maids to clean the workers' rooms. Despite working five-and-a half days per week in the factory, all Bethel workers were given only a small monthly stipend to pay for toiletries and incidental expenses; however, she related that most of that modest allowance had to instead be used to buy subway tokens for transportation to the required five weekly meetings at the various congregations in New York City to which they had been assigned. There was little money left over with which to buy necessities, so they had to rely on charitable contributions from other Witnesses.

The only draw to Bethel that I could see was the high esteem in which the Witnesses held it. The way the Society depicted Bethel to Jehovah's Witnesses was much different than what I found to be true, but then the Society has long presented matters using two sets of scales, making themselves appear to be something that they are not. For example, the Society makes the statement:

> The Catholic Church occupies a very significant position in the world and claims to be the way of salvation for hundreds of millions of people. Any organization that assumes that position should be willing to submit to scrutiny and criticism. (*AW* 8-22-84, p. 28)

The Watchtower Society assumes that same position for themselves, claiming to be the only way of salvation for humankind; from the above quotation, one would infer that they are willing to submit themselves to scrutiny and criticism. However, while this may be true for those outside the organization, it is definitely not true for those *inside* of it.

THE SOCIETY'S TWO SETS OF SCALES

Although I felt angry about the unfairness of the Society's hypocritical double standards, I accepted them because the Society constantly admonished us to become as children in relation to their authority. "Unless you turn around and become as young children, you will by no means enter into the kingdom of the heavens." (Matt.18: 3) Young children have little critical thinking faculties and are dependent upon their parents to make decisions for them. The organization assumes a parental attitude toward its members, forbidding independent thinking and fostering dependency on

NON-WITNESSES	WITNESSES
"As a thinking person, however, you would do well to consider some pertinent questions." (*WT* 4-15-95, p. 5)	"Avoid independent thinking" (*WT* 1-15-83, p. 22) —Witnesses cannot be 'thinking persons'; the Society does their thinking for them.
"An Open Mind Wins God's Approval" (*AW* 11-22-84, p. 8)	"Think: Have I progressively made my mind over?" (*WT* 8-15-72, p. 505) —Witnesses are not permitted to have an open mind. They listen only to what the Society says.
"Truly it is 'intellectually dishonest' not to want any opposing views heard . . ." (AW 10-22-73, p. 7)	"Do you wisely destroy apostate material?" (*WT* 3-15-86, p. 12) —Witnesses are not allowed to consider views opposing those of the Society.
"We need to examine . . . what is taught by any religious organization with which we may be associated." *(The Truth That Leads to Eternal Life* [1968], p. 13)	". . . we shall not be suspicious, but shall, as the Bible says, 'believe all things', all the things that *The Watchtower* brings out . . ." *(Qualified to Be Ministers* [1967], p. 156) —Witness may not critically examine the Society's doctrines.
"However, *The Watchtower* . . . invites careful and critical examination of its contents . . ." (*WT* 8-15-50, p. 263)	"Does this set a precedent for regarding critically the publications . . . ? Not at all!" (*WT* 2-15-81, p. 18) —Witnesses cannot be openly critical of *The Watchtower*.

itself as the authority; by dictating the rules to live by and eliminating choice, it creates in its members a childlike dependency on itself. In time, I got to the point where I didn't want to be bothered with the Society's long-winded explanations of confusing doctrinal matters, and their use of "Scriptural gymnastics" in connecting various scattered Scriptural texts to arrive at their unique interpretations. Since I believed they were God's channel of communication, I had to accept whatever they said anyway—so I eventually started feeling that they should quit wasting what precious little time I had, and just tell me what to believe! Defending some of the Society's doctrines had long presented a problem for me anyway, because in spite of its complicated explanations, I could not always find biblical support for its conclusions and interpretations. Whenever that happened, the doubts I had worked so hard to suppress would re-emerge, and I would feel fear and panic grip me all over again. Like a rubber band being stretched out and snapping back I would go from the extreme of total acquiescence to the organization, to the opposite extreme of having severe doubts about it. Like a rubber band, I would be pulled by my doubts, and then I would repeatedly snap back out of fear again into immersion in the organization. Every time, I determined to stay safely in the "protection" of the organization; but around every corner something would happen to again cause doubts to unexpectedly flare up, and I would become frightened—and the rubber band cycle would continue.

NINE

MY STRUGGLE TO STAY IN THE ORGANIZATION

O ccasionally while I was involved in the preaching work, I would meet people who would accuse the organization of being a cult. I refused to pay attention to these accusations because the Society taught that such accusers are tools of the Devil, sent by him to deceive Jehovah's Witnesses and seduce them out of the Truth—or to use outsiders as lures to entice us into the world. Consequently, I became very cautious, suspicious, and distrustful of people on the outside; if anyone said anything against the organization, that became proof to me that Jehovah's Witnesses represented the true religion.

I held rigidly to the Society's rules; I eventually became intolerant of any Witnesses who even bent the rules, viewing them as dangerous "bad associates." I continued to diligently raise my two children in the strict Witness environment; I was determined to stay in "the race" no matter how hard it became, at least until my children were old enough to be accountable to Jehovah themselves, in order to give them the best chance I could to survive the impending Armageddon.

As time went by, living in the narrow world of Jehovah's Witnesses made me feel out of touch with the real world. Constantly repressing my true feelings, submitting to the organization, and putting up mental roadblocks to avoid death-dealing independent thinking was a lot of hard work which resulted in my feeling stripped of my own personality and little more than an automaton. In spite of obeying all the organization's rules, I still felt empty, distant from God, and unable to establish any rapport with Him at

103

all. I felt angry that all my hard work as a Witness brought only a hollow, aching feeling inside of me.

I tried to fill the emptiness and soothe the aching feeling by avidly studying the Society's literature, but to no avail. As time went by, I felt increasingly upset with the Society for frequently changing its doctrinal views without making it clear or obvious that changes were being made. The Society often wrote articles in its magazines explaining its position on a matter, as though that had been its position all along, even though at times it was a complete reversal from a former viewpoint! This deceitful and dishonest presentation angered me. The Society's habit of sneaking in changes to doctrines without calling attention to the fact that it was making them disoriented and confused me.

One day I asked an elder about a doctrinal point, to which he replied: "Notice that we haven't heard anything from the Society about that point for a while now." *What?* I felt that sickening, "crazy" feeling again—what was his comment supposed to mean? He was insinuating that we shouldn't believe that doctrine any longer simply because the magazines had not mentioned it for awhile—but, how could that be? The Society frequently made reference to articles in its older publications and had stated that past information is still valid until such time as different information is printed. The elder's inference that we were supposed to "read-into" the Society's silence that a change was brewing was confusing to me, because at other times Witnesses had been chastised for "speculating" and accused of "running ahead of the organization."

This same sort of craziness occurred in the preaching work also. Despite the many hours spent at the Kingdom Hall learning how to overcome objections that householders might express, the prevalent attitude of Witnesses regarding the preaching work was just the opposite: "Don't try to shear the horns off the 'goats'! We are looking for 'sheep-like' people only!" Similarly, circuit overseers would frequently give conflicting counsel. One of them told us, "Relax in the preaching work! If the people are 'sheep,' they will listen to you!" but another had exactly the opposite attitude and warned, "If you don't present the Society's literature correctly to the people, it will be your fault if they don't listen!" This warning was ominous because I knew that if the people didn't heed our message, they would die at Armageddon; if it were my fault that they turned a deaf ear to us, then I would die, too. Thus, the preaching work resulted in a great deal of confusion, pressure, and stress for me as I struggled to stay in the organization.

One afternoon in 1986 when I was in the house-to-house preaching work with my teenage daughter, a householder excitedly invited us to come inside for a few moments. She wanted us to listen to a few songs from her new Christian music album. Although I was leery about doing this, as most Witnesses would be, I thought our showing an interest in what she wanted to share with us might make her more receptive to the message we wanted to share with her.

The music was beautiful; my daughter commented that she liked it and wanted to know why we didn't play that kind of music at home. As I listened to the words of the songs, I found the lyrics to be very touching; I could find nothing wrong with them. I felt that the Society's labeling of such songs "demonic" simply because they did not come from themselves was unreasonable. I felt torn; however, my trained response was, "It is not from Jehovah's organization—it's from 'Christendom' (all Christian religions outside of the Watchtower)—therefore, it is demonic and unacceptable." The words I spoke to my daughter, however, were worlds apart from the words my heart spoke to me. I stifled my feelings, though, in order to present a solid Witness model for my daughter; however, the Society's stance about the music did not make sense to me. Trying to defend it was painful, as it not only put me at odds with myself, but created an invisible wall between me and my daughter as well.

The Society also had other teachings that didn't make sense to me, and I was growing weary with continuing to conceal my feelings about them. For example, the Society often ridiculed other religions for teaching the "mystery of the Trinity"; however, the Society had its own "mysteries" that it never talked about: The mystery of exactly how persons know they are of the elite "anointed class," the only ones to have the heavenly hope. And then there is the mystery of exactly how Jehovah puts into the minds of the Governing Body the information He wants printed in the *Watchtower* magazine. My letter to the Society requesting an explanation of these mysteries went unanswered, giving me yet another reason to doubt the Society's claim of its unique connection to God.

A couple of other "mysteries" bothered me also: The brothers criticized Catholics for believing that the pope is God's representative on Earth; but I couldn't see where that was any different than the Witnesses believing the organization is God's representative on Earth. The brothers criticized Christians for wearing a charm of a cross on a necklace, an outward symbol of Jesus, the source of their salvation; but I couldn't see where that was any different than the many Witness women I knew who wore a charm of a watchtower on a necklace as an outward symbol of the organization, the source of their salvation.

In spite of the internal struggles that I was having with the organization, I tried to outwardly project a manner that showed confidence in it, in order to present myself as a strong example for my children so they would not lose their lives at Armageddon because of disagreements I had with the organization. Despite my efforts, however, my daughter was having doubts of her own; this became evident in 1986 when she was fourteen years old, as she exclaimed one day, "How do you even know this religion *is* the truth?" I felt stabbed, convicted, as her question reflected my own doubts that I had denied for so long. I felt stunned as repressed emotions and feelings suddenly flooded into my awareness. How could I answer her question when I wondered the same thing? No matter how hard I worked at convincing myself that I had no doubts about the organization, they always had a way of surfacing at unexpected moments without warning.

My daughter had little way to know if Jehovah's Witnesses represented the truth or not, since aside from brief conversations with classmates, she had never been able to compare their beliefs with those of other religions. Witnesses who were born into Witness families knew only what the Society had chosen to tell them about other religions; visiting churches to investigate what they taught was a disfellowshipping offense. The Society claims that it has done all the research about various religions for us, so that we should not waste our valuable time doing research on our own. Especially forbidden was any literature that was critical of the Watchtower Society. I felt sick at heart at the thought of Jehovah refusing to spare my daughter simply because I was unable to help her due to my own doubts, and I was filled with trepidation at the thought of Jehovah destroying me at Armageddon, too.

Several months later, much to my astonishment, my daughter expressed her desire to be baptized as one of Jehovah's Witnesses. Instead of rejoicing, I was heartsick; I felt she was too young to fully understand what this commitment to the organization meant. I expressed my sincere concern to the elders, only to be severely shamed and chastised for not being encouraging to her. Nagging thoughts of what effect her commitment to the organization would have on our future relationship plagued me; what if I should ever give-way to my doubts and be unable to force myself to stay in the organization? Then she would be forbidden to ever speak to me again. The day of her baptism was one of the saddest days of my life, as I feared losing her to the organization forever. To avoid the suspicion of others, however, I had to fight my tears and feign happiness—but inside, I felt ill to the very core of my being.

Shortly after my daughter was baptized, she told the elders of her desire to serve in the congregation as a permanent "auxiliary pioneer," devoting sixty hours every month to the preaching work after school and on weekends. However, the elders concealed her request from my husband and me until her appointment was announced to the congregation. We were shocked that the elders would encourage a minor child to commit to such an exhausting schedule of activity, and that they showed disrespect for "the headship principle" (i.e., that the father, as biblical head of the family, has the right to decide what is in the best interest of his children) by not consulting us prior to making the announcement. Indignant, I immediately confronted the presiding elder about his having gone behind our backs and thereby undermining our authority as parents in this matter; he responded, "You should be thrilled!" But, I *wasn't* thrilled; I was furious that my right as a parent to decide what was in the best interest of my child had been snatched away from me by the elders, and that they met my protests about it with ridicule and shame.

More and more of the Society's doctrines and viewpoints were not making sense to me, and I was losing my desire and ability to continue to tolerate them; consequently, continuing to teach these to others in the witnessing work was becoming increasingly more difficult for me, and my field service hours dwindled as a result. Also, the Society's belief that innocent children will die at Armageddon if their parents refuse to respond positively to the Witness message caused me a great deal of heartache while participating in the house-to-house ministry. Young children would often respond to our knocks on their door, with their parents following close behind them. Many of the children were curious and wanted to listen to us; most of the parents, however, would hastily shoo them away from the door. When their parents would respond to my preaching efforts by showing disinterest or even animosity, often extremely distressing mental images of their children being slaughtered at Armageddon would pop up into my mind. Watchtower books portrayed Jesus riding on a white horse, bow and arrow or spear in hand, charging forth on a conquest to vindicate Jehovah's name by executing all who wouldn't listen to the Witnesses' warning about Armageddon (*Revelation—Its Grand Climax at Hand!* [1988], p. 91; *You Can Live Forever in Paradise on Earth* [1982], p. 119). I just couldn't understand how a righteous God could justify murdering innocent babies and children on the basis of their parents' attitudes.

At one point I was conducting a home Bible study with a woman I met during the door-to-door witnessing work. She was an intelligent, professional woman who had an interest in the Bible. Every week, however, I had more and more difficulty answering her thought-provoking questions. Her keen mind at times found inconsistencies in the Society's literature that even I had not noticed, and I repeatedly found myself in the embarrassing situation of being unable to explain them. The Society's study books have questions printed at the bottom of the page to prompt the student to mirror back the points taught in the lesson. I remember the time when she gave an incorrect answer to one of these questions; I was amazed, since this had never happened before. As I gently corrected her, she pointed to a paragraph in the book and replied, "But, that's what the book says!" I wondered if she was feeling well, since what she said did not appear in my book. Startled by her insistence that hers was the correct answer, I asked if I could see her book. Laying the books down on the table side-by-side, I could not believe my eyes. The page that we were considering was exactly the same in both of our books, with the exception of this one sentence. The Society had changed their view on this small doctrinal point, and *without* calling attention to it, reflected this change in the next printing of the book. Here I was teaching this woman that the Society is God's channel, and everything they say is truth, yet here before us was two different versions of "truth"! I was mortified. My mind became flooded with all of my previous doubts, and I wondered how long I could go on teaching people that this religion was the truth. My thoughts raced back to a similar occurrence when the Society released a book at their conventions the summer of 1975, containing commentary on a parable in Matthew 13:31. The book stated that the man in the parable who sowed the mustard grain pictures Satan the Devil (*Man's Salvation Out of World Distress At Hand!* [1975], p. 208). However, just a few months later, the *Watchtower* magazine had an article that referred to that same parable—only now the man of the parable was said to picture Jesus Christ! (*WT*, 10-1-75, p. 600) Again, the teaching had been changed without any point being made of it, nor was any explanation given for the change. I was relieved when she eventually dropped the study, but that did not erase the doubts in my mind that her questions had raised.

I was also struggling with the Watchtower Society's basic tenet that no one can understand the Bible except through itself:

> Jehovah God caused the Bible to be written in such a way that one needs to come in touch with His human channel before one can fully and accurately understand it. True, we need the help of God's holy spirit, but its help also comes to us primarily by association with the channel Jehovah God sees fit to use. (*WT* 2-15-81, p. 17)

The brothers had frequently spoken of the Bible as being "a dark book," a book that no one had been able to understand until the Watchtower Society came on the scene a little over 100 years ago; this struck me as an absurd and presumptuous claim. It seemed unlikely to me that God would go to all the trouble of causing the Bible to be written if it would be incomprehensible until modern times, especially since the Bible does not mention God raising up an organization just prior to Armageddon.

The Society's publication containing its interpretation of the Bible book of Revelation was yet another case in point; I was shocked at the impudence of the Society in making its grandiose claims that its organizational history had fulfilled many of the prophecies of Revelation. (*Revelation—The Grand Climax at Hand!*, [1988] Chap. 21-25) I felt embarrassed to be known as one of Jehovah's Witnesses.

In 1988, I experienced a personal tragedy when my father, who had never been a Witness, committed suicide in a very violent way. I felt devastated by his sudden, unexpected death. The presiding elder called me in a very perfunctory manner and briefly stated that he was sorry to hear that my father had passed away. Some of the Witnesses told me I should be glad he died at this time, as now he will have a chance to be resurrected into God's earthly paradise instead of dying eternally at Jehovah's hands during Armageddon. This is because Witness doctrine provides that non-Witnesses who die prior to Armagaddon will be resurrected to live in the new system of things on the Earth under God's rule, in order to be given a chance to learn about Jehovah and be obedient to Him, whereas those who die during Armageddon perish at Jehovah's hand because they are considered to have already had the opportunity to learn about Him and be obedient to Him, but rejected it.

My father's funeral was held at a small chapel at the cemetery. I could not attend the funeral since doing so was considered to be mixing with false religion. In order to obtain some closure for myself and my children, I asked an elder to give a memorial talk for my dad at the Kingdom Hall. One of the elders who had known my father volunteered to give the talk; however, the discourse did not prove to be comforting, as it was impersonal and seemed like just another opportunity to promote Watchtower doctrine. Only one Witness friend came to console me. I painfully recalled when my favorite uncle laid dying in the hospital several years ago; since he was not a Witness, I was discouraged from going to see him and encouraged to use my time in the preaching work instead. Regretfully, I sent him a Watchtower publication in place of making a personal visit.

Upon arriving home from the Kingdom Hall one evening, I noticed a business card had been left in our front door. This unexpected caller was the county coroner; the same coroner who had found my dad now had my mother as well: she had committed suicide just five weeks after my father had taken his life, despite the fact that they had been divorced and had not seen each other for seventeen years. I subsequently developed severe abdominal pain; my doctor explained that this was due to extreme stress because of internalizing my grief over my parents' unexpected and shocking deaths. He sent me to a psychologist to get help dealing with my emotions and working through my grief.

Meanwhile, my daughter had been actively serving in all aspects of Witness activities since her baptism three years previously. Though I sensed her silent, internal struggle—and I feared that she sensed mine— we both went on wearing our masks, acting the part, stuck in the belief that the organization held our lives in its hands. In 1989, however, my daughter broke the silence and shattered her mask by telling me that she felt something was "weird" about our religion; she announced that when she became eighteen years old, she planned to leave home and her life as a Witness as well. Much to the shock of the congregation, one year later on her eighteenth birthday, she moved out of our home and became inactive in the organization.

I felt that I had failed, that somehow my daughter had seen through my veneer and had imitated the doubts that I thought I had so carefully been guarding. Distressed and burdened with guilt, I sought consolation from one of the elders. He did not comfort me, however; instead, he made my grief unbearable by blaming me for our daughter's departure from the organization, and for having left us as well. I felt stunned, crushed, and devastated as the elder whipped me with his words.

I continued going to the Kingdom Hall in spite of my anger with the elders and with the organization because I feared it was God's "imperfect" organization—and that association with it was necessary to survive the end of this system. Forcing myself to go to the meetings, though, was like dragging myself up a steep mountain. Because my husband was an elder, there was a lot of pressure on me to offer comments and answers at every meeting; however, doing so became increasingly difficult—just raising my hand to give an answer caused my heart to race. In time, I felt a heavy pressure on my chest whenever I was called on to speak. Unable to take a breath, my words became a whisper, to the point where I could not speak to answer at all. Eventually, I experienced difficulty breathing while just sitting and listening to the meetings, feeling as if I were being literally suffocated. I frequently had to leave and walk around outside the Kingdom Hall in order to get relief.

Pretending not to have doubts was exacting its toll in another way as well. I was having increasing problems with attacks of lancinating, electric shocklike pains in my head during the meetings, which resulted in my feeling confused and unable to concentrate. Later, I often experienced hundreds of these jolting head pains during the daytime, which would make me so tired and disoriented that I was frequently unable to go to the Kingdom Hall meetings at night. These attacks became so frequent and severe that I went to a neurologist for a consultation and examination. An MRI of my brain revealed no physical cause for my symptoms. I was astounded by the doctor's startling explanation:

> This type of shocklike head pain can be caused by a chemical imbalance in your brain, which can be due to stress that is caused by living in a way that is not in agreement with the way you feel internally.

The doctor's words struck me. My body was telling me what my heart had tried to say, but that my mind had refused to believe—that deep inside, I was having severe doubts that the Watchtower Society was truly God's organization. For so many years, I had kept what I felt hidden inside of me so that I could live the life of a Witness in obedience to the organization; however, now it was evident that if I were not going to consciously acknowledge what I really felt, my body was going to do it for me.

TEN

AWAKENING

After coming to grips with my parents' deaths, I decided to stay in therapy in order to get some assistance in improving my low self-esteem, and to get a more objective view on my life, so that I could understand what was causing the undercurrent of unhappiness that I was feeling. Yet I felt guilty about doing so, since the Society had made many disparaging remarks about psychologists and psychiatrists over the years:

[W]e cannot afford to submit ourselves to the psychologists and philosophers of this world. (*Let God Be True* [1952], p. 307)

So we must shun the . . . babbling psychologists, wordy psychiatrists . . . all of which have built up such tremendous reputations as colossal failures. (*WT* 1-15-52, p. 53)

But, as a rule, for a Christian to go to a worldly psychiatrist is an admission of defeat . . . (*AW* 3-8-60, p. 27)

Being a Christian involves everything one does in life. . . . Even when deep emotional problems arise, he does not turn for counsel to men who may be highly educated in worldly psychology . . . (*WT* 2-15-63, p. 124)

[T]he failure of psychiatrists generally to know how properly to apply the best medicine for mental ills—the divine quality of love—is likely to render their treatment ineffectual. (*AW* 4-22-75, p. 18)

Then there was the psychiatrist who . . . prescribed sexual relations with himself as therapy and then charged for the "treatments." (*AW* 4-22-75, p. 18)

But is the turning of people from the clergy to the psychiatrists a healthy phenomenon? No, for it really is a case of jumping from the frying pan into the fire. They are worse off than they were before . . . (*AW* 8-22-75, p. 25)

Psychiatrists and psychologists . . . are not the ones to go to for help when one is depressed and beset with all manner of problems. . . . The blind egotistical folly of many of these professional men . . . (*AW* 8-22-75, p. 26)

Can psychology be taken seriously as science . . . ? It is . . . contradictory and high-minded pseudo-knowledge . . . (*WT* 8-1-82, p. 23)

Getting involved in therapy with a psychologist will lead you right out of the Truth. (Counsel from an elder, 1982)

Although in 1975 the Society decided that consulting a mental health professional is a personal decision left up to each Witnesses to decide for himself (*WT* 4-15-75, p. 255), choosing to see a therapist was still difficult to do with a clear conscience because not only had the Society long cast psychologists and psychiatrists in a very negative light, but it continued to do so even after this decision. From time to time, the Society warned of the risks involved in seeking such help. Painting these professionals as being without moral principles, the Society warned that they may encourage their clients to act in ways contrary to Bible principles. The Society focused also on the danger that the therapist may try to persuade the Witness that his troubles are caused by his religion (*AW* 3-8-60, p. 27). The Society warned that many psychiatrists are atheists (*WT* 4-15-75, p. 255), thus one could experience a shipwreck of one's faith by opening oneself up to being influenced by them. Thus, if Witnesses do seek professional mental health counseling, while they can be open about what they say to the therapist, they usually carefully filter what counsel they will accept from him. "They [Witnesses] have to weigh seriously (or have help to weigh) counsel offered by a therapist." (AW 10-22-81, p. 25) I have even heard the suggestion that a Witness bring another Witness with her to any consultations with a therapist, as a protection to her spirituality.

While visiting a close Witness friend who lived several hundred miles away, I accompanied her to a Kingdom Hall meeting at the congregation she attended. She pointed out a brother there who was making an excellent living though his psychotherapy practice serving Witnesses only, as the brothers and sisters do not feel they are putting themselves in spiritual danger with him as they do with therapists who are not Witnesses. An odd twist, however, is that while they can listen to his counsel without fear of spiritual damage, they must be guarded about what they tell him, as he requires each Witness to sign a waiver of confidentiality[1] which frees him to reveal their confidential conversations to the Witness's elders should the Witness patient confide to the therapist any wrongdoing or breaking of the Society's rules. This waiver also provides for the therapist to end the therapy should the client be subsequently disfellowshipped by the elders. Professional therapists regard this waiver as highly unethical and not conducive to the environment needed for therapy to succeed.[2]

The Society gave much encouragement to seek out help for emotional problems from the elders instead of from an outside therapist (*AW* 9-22-71, p. 23). The problem with this advice, however, was that the elders were given no training in how to deal with mental or emotional problems.

> In my experience, the elders often do more harm than good. Putting a person (elder) who has no training, a false view of humanity and a distorted view of reality in charge of an emotionally disturbed person could well be lethal, as it sometimes has been. —letter to author from Jerry Bergman, Ph.D., MSBS, L. P. C.C.

The Watchtower magazines at times contain anecdotes of suicidal and mentally unbalanced persons being restored to health by studying the Bible with Jehovah's Witnesses (*AW* 9-22-71, p. 23) (*AW* 8-22-72, p. 23) (*AW* 4-22-75, p. 19), despite the fact that Witnesses receive absolutely no training in dealing with people with emotional or mental problems.

I disagreed with the Society's view of psychologists and of therapy—my own experience had proven them wrong. I sensed my therapist genuinely cared and sincerely wanted to help me, and indeed he had been extremely instrumental in enabling me to cope with the traumatic deaths of my parents. He had always treated me with kindness, respect, compassion, and heartfelt empathy that absorbed my pain; thus, I decided to ignore the Society's opinions and warnings about psychologists and secretly remain in therapy.

As a child, I learned that making mistakes or voicing disagreements resulted in abuse, punishment, or humiliation. The Society's strict consequences for "messing up" so precisely fit what I had learned about the way the world works, that they prevented me from acknowledging how I truly felt inside. As an adult, I had been playing a game of self-deception for so long, that much of the time I didn't even know what I really felt. Over time, my therapist often said things that struck a chord deep inside of me, crystalizing feelings and doubts that had been repressed into my unconsciousness. Through therapy, these things started to slowly move back into the realm of my awareness, where I could begin to deal with them.

I came to learn that the feelings of suffocation I had been experiencing at the Kingdom Hall were actually reflections of the suffocation I felt from allowing the authority of the organization to dictate my thoughts and feelings for the past twenty years, and from my own pretense of agreeing with the organization when I actually felt much differently. Evidently, my unconscious mind was causing my body to rebel in protest of my living my life behind a mask, living a life not true to myself. I had suppressed my true feelings because the Society taught that one's heart is the source of one's feelings, but is treacherous and is not to be trusted. Consequently, I felt that my feelings needed to be stifled in favor of strict obedience to the organization. Doing so, however, was causing me grave distress. My therapist suggested, "As much as possible, get what you feel in line with what you're thinking and saying and doing." Though I ached for inner peace, I could not see any way of achieving it. I had been angry with the organization for as long as I had been associated with it, but getting my actions in line with my anger would mean leaving the organization, an unthinkable option. I wouldn't allow my anger to cause me to die at Armageddon. Continuing to have my feelings be so inconsistent with my actions, though, was causing me ongoing, ever-increasing anguish. I heard the wisdom of my therapist's words: "Present to the world, as honestly as you can, who you are."

I was stunned with the realization that I didn't even know who I really was. For half of my life, my whole identity had been tied up with the organization as one of Jehovah's Witnesses. My having disagreements with the Society now meant losing that identity and being faced with the formidable predicament of figuring out what the truth about God and life really is—a frightening prospect, about which my therapist counseled: "What makes sense to you is what will feel like the truth; so live the truth as you feel it, and be internally consistent." He encouraged me to think more about what really makes sense to me, and what kind of life I want to have—knowing there would be a price to pay for that if I decided to leave the organization—but he reminded me that I also pay a hefty price in not being true to myself. He encouraged me to think about the price I had paid for all the compromises of myself I had made to the organization: I didn't get to feel free; I didn't get to tell people that I felt trapped and miserable. All of that really was a high price.

NOTES

1. Jerry Bergman, Ph.D., MSBS, L.P.C.C., "Witness Psychologist Requires Patients to Sign a Legal Form Allowing Them to Report Their 'Sins' to the Elders," *Free Minds Journal* (July/August 1994): 10–11.

2. See Appendix A, "Why Jehovah's Witnesses Have Mental Problems," section 3.

ELEVEN

COMPASSION

M y husband and I decided to take a trip to Hawaii in 1991 to celebrate our twentieth anniversary. As was our custom in the past
whenever we took a vacation, we paid one of the brothers from our congregation to make daily visits to our house to take care of our houseplants,
bring in our mail, water our garden, answer our telephone messages, and so
forth. We had known one responsible young man from the time he was a
child. We had complete faith in his honesty and integrity to oversee our
home in our absence. Since he had been a very close friend of our son
during their formative years, having spent many nights at our house and
having joined in many activities with us over the years, we felt like he was
part of our family. When our son had moved away and married a young Witness, our daughter remained at home; it was during this period of time,
when our daughter was still an active Witness, that the friendship between
this young man and our daughter grew close.

The elders had been trying to contact our daughter to set up a judicial
committee meeting with her, to ascertain why she had abruptly stopped
attending the Kingdom Hall meetings, why she had moved out of our home,
where she had been staying, what she had been doing, with whom she had
been associating, and so forth. She was not interested in meeting with them,
and so their attempts to meet with her had proved fruitless. Not ones to be
easily foiled, the elders pursued her relentlessly through telephone calls
and letters, insisting on meeting with her.

When all their attempts had been frustrated, they hatched a plan to

117

catch her off-guard so that they could force a confrontation with her. The elders were aware of her close friendship with the young man who was taking care of our house while we were gone. Knowing his loyalty to the organization would trump any loyalty to our daughter as his friend, they proposed a plan using him to trick her so that they could finally interrogate her. They were confident of his cooperation, as they knew his allegiance was with the organization, and with the elders as part of its administrative arm. As we later learned, the elders asked this young man to call our daughter and fabricate a reason to get her to come over to the house. Under the guise of "theocratic warfare,"[1] lying was acceptable if it served the needs of the organization. Consequently, the truthfulness of the reason he gave her to get her to agree to meet him at the house was insignificant. He feigned helplessness about some aspect of taking care of things at the house, asking her to meet him there at a specified time so she could help him out. Trusting that he would never betray her, she agreed.

The day arrived for this plan to be carried out. Under veil of darkness, the elders showed up at our house before the designated time for our daughter to arrive. They split up, one elder hiding behind the front fence that divided our house from the house next door, another hiding behind a bush in our front yard, and yet another concealing himself behind a large tree near the street in front of our house. Positioned and poised for action, they laid in wait for her arrival.

At the specified time, our daughter's car pulled up in front of the house. As the elders saw a young female get out of the car and walk up the pathway leading to our front door, they suddenly rushed out from their hiding places and surrounded her, thus forcing a confrontation. The young woman they had accosted, however, was not our daughter—much to their frustration and cha-grin—as being quite intuitive, she sensed that something was awry and had sent a friend in her place. When we arrived home from our trip, the young man reported to us all of what had taken place.

My husband and I did not hear from our daughter for many weeks. Then one Saturday, the elders informed us that they had decided to set up a judicial committee meeting to speak with her, and they set the date of that meeting for the following Saturday. On Tuesday evening at the Kingdom Hall, just after the regular meeting had ended, I mentioned to my husband that I had made plans to visit our daughter on Thursday, as I wanted to be sure to be able to talk with her prior to the judicial committee meeting scheduled for Saturday.

Moments later, an elder—high on a power-trip and strutting like a rooster—approached me, saying he had received a letter from our daughter.

Because the letter indicated she would not be coming to the committee meeting, they had decided to disfellowship her, *effective immediately*. In an obvious display of power, the elder said that I would not be permitted to visit my daughter on Thursday as I had planned. He had known of my desire to see her prior to their judicial committee meeting, yet he seemed to delight in using his position of power, control, and authority to deliberately intercept my visit with her. I felt as if he were armed with sharp two-edged swords, standing between me and my daughter, as anyone going against the elders' decree would themselves be disfellowshipped—shunned, ostracized by the congregation, and deemed worthy of eternal destruction. I was furious that the committee had "pulled the rug out from under me" with their spontaneous decision, about which I felt powerless to do anything. A flood of emotion crumbled my dam of restraint. Being unable to contain my rage, I angrily exclaimed to the elder, "I warned you four years ago she was too young to be baptized! And now you tell me I can never speak to my daughter again?! This would not be happening if you had listened to me then!" Defending himself, he asserted, "We elders are not responsible for this! We can't read a person's heart or mind; we just have to take people at their word when they say they want to be baptized."

I was enraged at the control the elders wielded over my life, yet I felt that I had to helplessly submit to them as leaders of God's organization. Now that my daughter was disfellowshipped, I was barred from having any normal mother-daughter contact with her. The only way the situation could be changed would be for her to return to the organization by requesting the elders to reinstate her as a Witness. Reinstatement was a tedious, lonely, and humiliating process to endure. If she wished to return, she would have to beg forgiveness of the elders, and then prove her sincerity by attending all the meetings—even though she would be completely ignored by everyone present. This ritual could last anywhere from three months to a year or more, until the elders decided she had proven herself to be truly repentant. If she never requested to be reinstated into the congregation, she would be considered "spiritually dead," and all Witnesses would be required to behave as if she did not exist, including me.

Several days later, the elders made the public announcement at the Kingdom Hall meeting that my daughter had been disfellowshipped. For a moment, my mask dissolved, and I cried openly as the congregation remained silent. A young ministerial servant immediately went up to the platform to introduce the next speaker; I was shocked at his insensitivity when he began his introduction with lighthearted joking. Suddenly, the congregation's silence was broken by their laughter. I was offended that they could dismiss the serious announcement about my daughter so quickly.

My therapist helped me to understand that the congregation's laughter did not mean that they didn't care about my daughter being disfellowshipped, but that they felt anxious and uncomfortable when they heard the somber and depressing announcement, so they eagerly followed the brother's lead and laughed to divert their attention away from their upsetting feelings. I was struck by the gentleness and compassion of my therapist's thought as he contemplated, "Isn't it better for people to share their pain and figure out a way to help themselves with it, than to hide their pain and deny having it?" I thought that would certainly be a more supportive and kindhearted way to deal with such a sensitive situation. I felt distressed that it was one so foreign to Jehovah's Witnesses.

About three weeks later, while I was driving home one afternoon, the seriousness of the situation about my daughter struck me full-force with the realization that the committee had judged her worthy of eternal death, and that I was to treat her as if she were literally dead. I started crying and my body started shaking uncontrollably. I desperately needed someone to talk to who could understand what I was going through and help me cope with it.

I was near the home of a brother, an elder in a neighboring congregation, who had been a longtime friend of our family. I decided to stop at his house, confident that he would comfort me and then I would feel better. Feeling weak and nearly hysterical, I almost collapsed as I rang his doorbell. He answered the door, surprised to see me in this extreme emotional condition. After I briefly explained what I was feeling, he reluctantly invited me to come in and sit down. He had no words of comfort for me, only words of shame and guilt. He said that the elders had acted with Jehovah's direction to disfellowship her, and that my being upset about the situation showed a lack of loyalty to Jehovah. Although I was clearly still very agitated and trembling, he said he was out of time and had to get ready to go to the Kingdom Hall meeting. Not only did he not comfort me, but his telling me that my feelings were unacceptable and displeasing to God only added to my grief.

Still in distress, I drove home and called an elder who lived in my neighborhood who had known my daughter since infancy. He was an elderly brother who, like a huge soft teddybear, had always had a big hug for my daughter and for me. I called him, confident that he would console me; I was shocked when he indignantly reproved me, asserting that we should not waste our time grieving for those who leave Jehovah. It was a brief conversation that ended with his prayer asking for Jehovah to strengthen me to accept His decision and to shun my daughter. This conversation caused me to feel as if I had violated my relationship with God by being despondent about the situation with my daughter.

My husband offered me no solace, as he was an elder and fully committed to honoring the decision of the judicial committee. Everywhere I turned, there was no relief; I felt torn between the part of me that feared this was God's organization, and that my daughter would die for having left it, and the part of me that admired her ability to sense something was wrong with the organization and to act upon what she felt by leaving it. I respected her courage, and I wished I had her inner strength.

NOTE

1. See Appendix B, "Theocratic Warfare."

TWELVE

My Struggle to Get Out of the Organization

In obedience to the organization, forcing myself to "do what is right," I shunned my daughter for three months. The elders told me that shunning her was the only way to show true love for her, the only way to show her that Jehovah was displeased with her, the only way to make her "turn around" and come back to the organization, and thus the only hope of salvation for her. However, ignoring my daughter and behaving as if she were dead did not feel like an act of love. Shunning her did not make sense to me—deep inside, it did not feel right. I feared the organization was the true religion, and thus bought into its view that my disagreements with it were rebellious and of Satan.

My confusion regarding whether or not the organization was God's organization led to constant emotional turmoil. Whenever the thought that the organization could possibly be wrong or not of God entered my mind, my brain actually started to ache. I would feel stunned and dizzy as the room seemed to spin around me, rendering me unable to think or make any decisions about my feelings regarding the organization or my daughter. In discussing my concern about such disturbing episodes with my therapist, he explained: "The emotional turmoil results in paralysis; how could you possibly act, when you feel so divided? And no matter where you turn, you're stuck because you're turning against a part of *you*."

I then realized that the only way out of this dilemma was to acknowledge my feelings and doubts about the organization that I had suppressed for so long, and what it meant that I was having them. But doing so was extremely frightening to me, because trying to face up to my doubts nine years ago only resulted in panic attacks and anguish, which ultimately drove me back into the organization. This time, though, I knew I would have to see it through, as my body would not cooperate with the charade any longer. I knew that the physical ailments which frequently rendered me unable to go to the meetings were likely emotionally induced and were unlikely to go away until I became strong enough to make the decision to stay away from the meetings, instead of falling back on being ill as an excuse not to go. Because the Society viewed a deliberate decision to stay away from the meetings as extremely sinful, I continued to force myself to go whenever possible, and to suffer the physical consequences of feeling so divided. One day while driving to the Kingdom Hall, I suddenly burst into tears, crying out, "Please, God, let this religion *not* be the truth!"

While I desperately wanted to believe that this religion was false, I was determined to force myself to stay in it if I felt it really was the only true religion. I explained to my therapist that even though I wanted to be freed from bondage to the organization, having my entire belief system turned inside-out was still a terrifying experience, to which he responded: "You feel you've been living a lie, in some respects, and now you're trying to disentangle yourself from that, and that is going to be painful. But, that doesn't mean it's not better for you, too."

I felt stunned by my therapist's words, because deep inside I knew I had been living a lie by pretending that my doubts, my anger, and my disagreements with the organization were either unfounded, unimportant, or didn't exist. My therapist helped me to see that pretending I didn't feel a certain way about the organization had caused me a lot of distress in not being able to be honest with myself, and had taken a real toll on my self-confidence. He advised that the more honest I could be with myself about what I feel, the easier it would be to make the appropriate decisions about how to handle my dilemma about my daughter and my involvement with the organization.

The internal anguish I felt as a result of years of ignoring my feelings and thoughts had become too great to ignore, yet it was difficult for me to see beyond the immediate pain that leaving the organization would cause. Thinking about breaking away from the organization struck terror in my heart. Trying to discuss it with my therapist would often result in my feeling extremely dizzy, as if I were sitting amidst a huge whirlwind. Many times I was unable to even accurately describe to my therapist the terrifying sensations I was experiencing. My thoughts seemed so jumbled that at times I couldn't even remember what my therapist had said during our discussions.

Often my therapy sessions were interrupted by me going into spontaneous "stunned mode," an emotional state characterized by "paralysis" of my brain, a kind of suspended animation of my ability to think. At times this would cause me to experience a hallucination of sorts, during which my therapist seemed to be moving physically farther and farther away from me, causing me to feel isolated and alone. Although I cognitively knew his chair remained in the same place in the consulting room, and I felt he was right there with me emotionally in trying to sort things out, still this aberration was extremely frightening to experience. I felt it as a premonition of what my life would be like if I left the organization—isolated and alone.

One day I was cleaning my house, frantically trying to make order out of the disorder that I suddenly saw everywhere I looked; everything seemed to be in disarray. My exasperation flared to anger. Unable to get a grip on my emotions, I stormed into my next therapy session exclaiming, "Nothing is in its place!"

My therapist pointed out that the depth of my anger had gone far beyond that which the situation actually provoked, and that the frustration I was feeling with the disorganization of my house was triggering the much greater frustration that I was feeling with the organization, and the general disarray in my life that my doubts and disagreements with the Society were causing. Truly nothing in my life was in its place.

In addition to anger and frustration, however, thinking about breaking away from the organization made me ache with an "empty" feeling. Through therapy, I learned that I had carried that "empty" feeling with me from my abusive childhood into my involvement with the organization. Since the organization likens itself to a parent, the "Mother," I had unwittingly developed a dependency on it in the hope that it would be a better "parent" than my own mother had been. The thought of leaving the organization caused me to experience that "empty" feeling so intensely because leaving would mean I was giving up the hope that being a Witness could ever fill this emptiness inside of me. Leaving would mean I would have to find a way to fill that "empty" feeling myself.

The chance to talk to other Witnesses about my doubts in the hope that they would be sympathetic or struggle with the same doubts themselves—and thus obtain some camaraderie and support—was remote. I had to be tight-lipped about my misgivings and disagreements with the organization and its doctrines, or else risk being betrayed by the Witness to whom I confided my reservations—and thus be forced to face judicial committee action by the elders, which would lead to chastisement, punishment, humiliation, ostracism, or disfellowshipping.

During one of the evenings that I stayed home from the Kingdom Hall meeting, I received a telephone call from one of the sisters, asking why I had not been attending the Kingdom Hall regularly. I took a bold step forward by expressing some of my complaints about the organization. These were couched in quite guarded terms, however, due to my fear of her reporting me to the elders for apostasy. To my surprise and delight, my openness led to her expressing some of her own uncertainties about the organization! Having an honest conversation—an exchange of genuine feelings and thoughts—with another Witness felt wonderful! It gave me a sense of connection that seemed to ease that "empty" feeling; it was something I had seldom felt during my involvement with the Witnesses. Although the Society forbids such conversation, for some reason she was trusting me with her true feelings. She was depressed and crying over her frustration at being unable to keep up with the Society's demands. And she was extremely distraught by the belief that Jehovah would soon kill her daughter at Armageddon because she was not a Witness.

Suddenly, in the midst of the conversation, she seemed to "wake up" as to how open she was being and abruptly exclaimed, "I can't feel this way! I have to act strong so I don't discourage others in the congregation!" Thus our conversation ended, and she avoided talking with me thereafter. Evidently, she was not ready to face the fact that she had her own disagreements with the organization. Seeing her façade, however, made me acutely aware of my own pretense of being a Witness.

My attempts at asking the elders questions, and my expressing frustration because of receiving unsatisfying answers, were met with either the shaming reply of, "It is not possible to know everything! Where is your faith?" or the avoidance reply of, "Write to the Society!" The latter was the usual response when an elder was cornered with a legitimate question about an inconsistent doctrine—but a useless one—since my letters to the Society requesting explanations to confusing doctrinal points had gone unanswered. Instead of my questions being taken "off the shelf" and answered as I "matured spiritually" in the organization, more questions continued to pile up on it, and now the shelf was breaking because of the load!

All these years in the organization, I was not permitted to disagree with the Society's doctrines openly, nor could I object to their rules. All my opinions and questions just had to stay on the fire in a pot with a lid tightly covering them—until now they were bubbling over! I suspected that other Witnesses had questions and doubts about the organization similar to mine, that were admittedly uncomfortable to have; but it seemed like the whole organization was built on denial of the discomfort, instead of dealing with it.

I brought up in my therapy session the conflict I was experiencing—that although I was angry with the Watchtower Society, I still felt unable to leave the organization. I felt burdened, as if all my unanswered questions had been taken off the shelf and put into a knapsack on my back that I carried everywhere. The load seemed so heavy that I often felt immobilized, unable to act to do anything about it. My therapist reasoned, "Not being able to take action is depressing; you get depressed because you get so paralyzed. Taking action is what you can do to stop that feeling of helplessness."

As desperate as I was to be convinced that the Society would have no effect on my destiny, at some level I still believed it was God's channel and that my life hinged on obedience to them. Unable to bring myself to take action to separate myself from the organization, the rage I felt with it turned back onto myself. One day I cried out to my therapist, "I fear this religion is the truth, and that I'm just wicked for being unable to accept it anymore!" I kept telling myself, "*You're going to die!*" There was no escaping the nagging fear that my disagreements with the Society would cause Jehovah to have nothing to do with me until He killed me at Armageddon. Feeling my pain, my therapist acknowledged, "It sounds like you're just really being *tortured* by this."

Indeed, I was in anguish. Being in the organization had come to feel like I was locked in a room that had no windows, and was surrounded on the outside by blackness and death. I felt like I was in a no-win situation, a dilemma without a solution. If I stayed in the room, I felt I would suffocate, for the organization gave no space to breathe and had no capacity to admit its errors or allow its members freedom of conscience to have their own opinions. If I left the room, I felt I would die, for the Society had implanted in its members the phobia that certain death lay outside of the organization. I felt like I was backed into a corner with no way to escape. "The organization, the place I once ran to for safety, is sucking me under!" I bewailed to my therapist. "They can take away my *family*!" Moved by my grief, my therapist observed, "It's sad that the organization is so riveting, that you can't get out of it."

He reminded me about how, as a child, I curled up into a ball when my mother hit me, and that my feeling of being "paralyzed" now was the adult parallel of that reaction. He gently helped me to understand that curling up into a ball was not my only choice at this time. I could take care of myself now that I was an adult. Yet to take control of my life by leaving the organization still felt like certain suicide. I felt condemned for hating God's organization, the only means to salvation. I desperately wanted to live, but I could no longer accept the agency through which life was offered. I was extremely frustrated, angry, and frightened as a result of feeling so trapped. Stimulating me to think, my therapist asked, "So, this religion is the only vehicle for salvation? What allows you to buy into the idea that this is the only way to look at it?"

He explained that there were psychological reasons for my vulnerability to the organization's influencing me to believe that it was the only path to God—the reasons were related to the way I grew up. Because little children don't know any better, they tend to believe that they must have done something bad to deserve being beaten, yelled at, or otherwise mistreated; consequently, they go on guard all the time for what they're doing wrong, and they carry that behavior with them into adulthood. The part of me that my mother convinced was "bad" dovetailed with the organization's warnings that independent thoughts, personal opinions, or disagreements with them were bad—so that I didn't question their authority, the ways they enforced their rules, or their claim of being God's only channel of communication to humankind. I didn't listen to my doubts about the organization because I had a crisis of faith in myself. Although my therapist empathized that the religion issue *feels* like a crisis with no solution, he assured me, "You're at the point where you're going to start turning the situation around."

Trusting him fully, his comment gave me hope even though I could not fathom how that was going to happen. Exasperated and feeling that I was on the brink of being overwhelmed one day, my emotions gave way as I broke into tears while desperately exclaiming to my therapist, "Who can fight against God, and win?" Looking at me with deepest sincerity, my therapist clarified, "You're not fighting against what God says. You're fighting against what *they* say God says." His statement marked a major turning point in my struggle to break away from the Watchtower. I felt as if a window had opened up in my mind! I experienced incredible relief upon realizing the possibility that there may be another way to look at things besides through Watchtower-colored lenses. Perhaps I had not been able to have a relationship with God because I had been having one with the organization instead. My therapist helped me to step back from the Society's twisted, distorted logic and to reason, "Wouldn't God want you to be honest with yourself? Would He really want you to fool yourself, or lie to yourself, or go against your conscience, in order to stay in the organization? So—God is going to kill you for obeying your conscience, and leaving the organization? But He won't kill you for being a hypocrite and staying in the organization? It sounds like you've been carrying this burden of feeling like a hypocrite. You hadn't let yourself think that you were just going through the motions, when you felt something different."

His comments caused me to begin thinking about the word "hypocrite," and then I realized just how confused I was about its meaning. I approached my therapist one day with the concept of "good hypocrites" and "bad hypocrites," and the thought that God would approve of a person who was a "good hypocrite." "Hypocrite" being by definition a rather negative label, he looked at me with a puzzled but curious expression. I went on to explain that a "bad hypocrite" would be the person who says he is one of Jehovah's Witnesses, but doesn't live his life in accordance with their rules and principles. A "good hypocrite" would be the person who applies all of the Witness rules and principles in her life because she believes or fears the organization is of God, but hates doing it. Guiding me to think about the matter more rationally, my therapist said, "Going to the meetings, doing the works, but not believing it all. If only you were a hypocrite, you'd be saved?"

His question made me aware of how distorted my thinking had become as a result of being in the organization for so long. Perhaps the idea of hypocrisy being the route to salvation made sense to me because my experience in the organization had been that its leaders were not very concerned with what was in one's heart, the emphasis being placed on one's physical behavior instead. I remember a sister expressing to a circuit overseer that she didn't want to go out in the house-to-house preaching work one morning, but she forced herself to get ready to come meet with the group nevertheless. She sighed as she confessed that she knew it wouldn't count with Jehovah, since her heart was not in the work. The circuit overseer, however, responded that it is a person's actions that matter; thus he insisted that her coming out in field service that morning did count with God, despite the fact that her heart was far removed from it. I had been appalled at his reasoning. In the silence of my heart I disagreed with the circuit overseer's statement, for I believed that what was in a person's heart was most important.

Cautiously and with great sensitivity, my therapist noted: "It sounds like in your heart, you've already left the organization." Jarred and taken aback by words that cut through my denial, bringing to my consciousness feelings that had been repressed, I was convicted by his observation—I now realized consciously that for a long time I had just been going through the motions of being a Witness. Since I believed that God can read the heart, what good was continuing in the organization doing me? Whenever I stayed home from the meetings, however, I felt like I was digging my own grave. I was terrified and suffered extreme anxiety from feeling as if I were sitting on death row. Sensing my anguish, my therapist responded, "The elders say that if you're not suffering, you're on the wrong road. Then, you're on the right road! Who has suffered more with this than *you* have?"

I wondered if there would ever be an end to the agony that I was going through. In great distress one day, I told my therapist that I felt as if I were symbolically caught between two gigantic icebergs, both pressing in on me—God on one side, the organization on the other—and there was nothing I could do to stop their movement. I was powerless to prevent the icebergs from colliding, crushing me between them. My therapist interpreted this image as an expression of my rage with the organization. If only my anger were hot enough to melt the icebergs, I would be able to escape and be free.

Another day, I complained to my therapist that I felt as if a heavy weight were pressing down on me, making it difficult for me to even get up from the chair that I was sitting in. As we sat in silence for a few moments, my therapist sharing in my pain, I noticed that he possessed an inner peace, a peace I wondered if I would ever experience. I expressed how terrorized I was, due to feeling like an ominously massive weight were suspended over me, poised to crash down and crush me at any moment. He asked me what the "heavy weight" was; I responded, "God." He then said, "But your sense of God is that He reads your heart. So if you're being honest now and saying, 'I don't believe the organization is of God,' isn't that somehow being in better relationship to God than when you were pretending to go through the motions and not being honest about it?" As I understood the sense of his reasoning, I felt great relief as the heavy weight disappeared.

I chuckled with amusement one day as I told my therapist of absurd statements I had read in a *Watchtower* magazine (*WT* 7-1-43, p. 205), which proclaimed that the Lord Himself had given organizational instructions to the Society for all Witnesses to participate in the preaching work at least sixty hours a month, and to call on all the homes in each congregation's territory at least four times every six months. My therapist thought for a moment, and then asked me a very thought-provoking question: "Why do you think it's ridiculous that the Society said those things, but you don't think it's ridiculous when they say you'll die if you leave the organization? Why do you suppose that would be?"

He helped me to see that the threat of death that I was feeling as a result of my disagreements with the Society had its roots in my traumatic childhood, where it literally felt like death to disobey my mother. The Society had become a substitute parent in my life; my fears of disobeying my own mother fit perfectly with the fear Witnesses have of disobeying the "Mother," i.e., the organization. Because I had all the experience in life to back up that feeling, I bought into their claim that they were the only means for staying alive. My therapist pointed out, "The organization abuses people just like an addiction does. It takes away your autonomy, your choices, and your freedom."

My dependency on the organization and my fear of it caused me to tolerate that abuse, because like an addiction, the fear of leaving it was worse than staying in it. The price was too high: withdrawal from it was too scary, too painful, and too death defying. I was at the point, however, where I needed to deal with this dilemma. I also needed to make a decision about my relationship with my daughter.

THIRTEEN

HIDING BEHIND A SCREEN

Several months of shunning my daughter had not helped her in any discernable way; however, I could see where continued and prolonged shunning could possibly cause her to return to the organization under false pretenses—not because she felt she was wrong for being out of the organization, but because she missed the love and association of her family. I could not see where my contributing to the development of that kind of dishonesty could possibly help her. As I explained to my therapist the Society's belief that "shunning is a display of love," he pulled me out of their damaging and distorted view as he asked, "What kind of love is that, to make people toe the line and lie to themselves? It's a fear-based love, and is very destructive." The contrast of this perspective with the Witness view startled me; I winced inside as I realized the warped idea of love with which I had been ingrained as a Witness. Shunning my daughter did not feel like love, and doing so was breaking my heart. My therapist asserted, "Shunning is a display of fear, rather than a display of love."

"What?" I exclaimed. My therapist was saying the exact opposite of what the Society had taught me! As I pondered the matter, my mind whirled with a jumble of thoughts. Then I realized that people with an opposing or differing viewpoint did seem to be feared. When in the witnessing work, for example, the elders would discourage us from listening to a householder's arguments. We were told not to waste our time with those who don't want to listen to us. But there was also the fear that we might be swayed by their thinking. I believed that truth is strong and would stand up to scrutiny, and that listening to opposing views should cause people to think and analyze their own beliefs, but the Society obviously did not agree. If the organization were really teaching the truth, then there should be nothing for it to fear, as truth would stand in contrast to any false ideas a dissenter might speak. Consequently, one would emerge with even stronger faith and conviction of having the truth. If, though, such analyzing of one's beliefs proved the Society's teachings to be in error, certainly that would be important to know—and evidently *that* was what the Society feared.

Thinking about the act of shunning as a display of fear triggered the memory of the day a disfellowshipped person called to speak with my husband, who was serving as an elder. Because my husband was not at home at the time, I offered to take a message; while doing so, I remember trembling with fear, as I was afraid I would be contaminated by evil just by listening to the disfellowshipped person's voice, or that Satan would travel over the telephone line and attack me! I also remember how frightened I felt whenever I had encountered disfellowshipped Witnesses in stores while I was shopping; my heart would pound as I raced out of the store in order to avoid a confrontation with them. My own experience verified that I had really shunned disassociated or disfellowshipped Witnesses out of fear, and not out of love.

The issue of shunning came up again when our daughter called to say she would be coming to our house to get her bicycle. My husband, in obedience to the Society's requirement to shun her, decided that would be most easily accomplished by his placing the bicycle in the front yard for her to pick up. He would stay in the backyard, thus avoiding the pain of having to shun her to her face. I tried to force myself to stay away from the front room window when I knew she had arrived, but I found myself instead peeking at her through the curtains. I was torn between what my mind and my heart were saying to me. My mind echoed the warning words of the elders to shun her completely, but my heart urged me to embrace my daughter. Unable to make a conscious decision what to do, my heart spontaneously won out as I found myself racing outside to hug her, confirming the part of me that knew love counts. My daughter embraced me tightly, tears streaming down our cheeks. We clung to one another for several moments, my heart surging with joy. My happiness, however, was dampened by guilt caused by the Society's prohibition of my having contact with her; I was furious that the Society had come between my daughter and me.

I was terrified that Jehovah would kill me if I had a relationship with my daughter. Although the elders assured me that it was she who had left me by leaving the organization, I was obsessed with guilt about feeling like I had abandoned her. I became filled with despair; then, I remembered that the Society had changed their doctrine twice in the past about the issue of Witnesses keeping contact with disfellowshipped relatives: banning such association (*WT* 6-1-70, pp. 351–52) then later allowing such association (*WT* 8-1-74, p. 471), and then reverting back to forbidding such association (*WT* 9-15-81, pp. 29–31). My mind raced, excitedly scheming a solution to escape the anguishing dilemma about my daughter. If the Society was again in error about this doctrine, and if the elders disfellowshipped me for having a relationship with my daughter, it would be their responsibility before Jehovah for disfellowshipping me unjustly—but I would be free!

My therapist pointed out in subsequent discussions, however, that I was searching for a way out of the organization that would enable me to leave without taking responsibility for leaving. He counseled that there would be a price to pay for doing that in terms of my self-esteem and my self-respect. A more healthy choice would be for me to face up to the fact that this was really *my* battle with the Watchtower Society, and my argument with myself about being honest with myself and living what I believe. I needed to admit to myself that I wanted to leave the organization for me, and to stop hiding behind the screen of my daughter.

Through therapy, I came to recognize that my daughter had become a symbol, a reflection of my own feelings about the organization. I had been playing a game with myself, deceiving myself about my motives for wanting out of the organization, by plotting a neat little strategy to avoid taking responsibility for making the decision to leave it. All my years in the organization, I had felt like a puppet with the Watchtower Society pulling my strings; leaving the organization would mean cutting those strings, and I feared that I would crumple to the ground, having nothing to hold me up. As much as I resented the organization, facing life on my own without it seemed frightening, for I had difficulty seeing that I could learn to pull my own strings.

My therapist suggested that getting the opinions of ministers of other religions regarding the shunning issue might help me in making a decision about the situation with my daughter. I finally decided to make an appointment with a psychologist he recommended who was also an ordained minister, as I knew I would not be disfellowshipped for going into a psychologist's office, but I could be disfellowshipped if a Witness reported seeing me going into a church to talk to a minister.

The minister explained to me that elders of any church have the right to tell someone they can't be a member of their church anymore if that person violates what the elders had decided is acceptable in that religion. But that is entirely different than saying a person is exempt from salvation, unloved by God, and their prayers are not heard—as the organization does—which he felt is not warranted by Scripture. He felt it is the prerogative of the elders to be judges of their church, but that it is not their prerogative to act in the place of God and say someone is condemned forever. He felt that taking a scriptural text and beating someone to death with it without understanding the origin of the text, the intent, the historical circumstances, or the theology, violates the text and violates the person. He warned that the Bible's message is that God's ways are not our ways, and that we should be very suspicious whenever we are becoming enslaved to men's ways. This warning struck me because life as a Witness was lived in total subjection and enslavement to the men of the Watchtower Society's Governing Body.

Regarding the situation with my daughter, he counseled that shunning her would actually be contradicting the gospel of love. He encouraged me to investigate what "shunning" meant at the time the Bible writer used that term, in order to understand the proper interpretation of what is should mean in present times. He assured me that God, who is kinder and gentler than Jehovah's Witnesses, doesn't let us close the door. He keeps on knocking.

Following that conversation, I wrestled with myself about contacting my daughter. While wanting to follow my heart by writing her a letter, I felt like I would be signing my own death warrant if I did so. The mother-child bond was very strong, however, and thus after much anguish I finally went with my heart by deciding to write to her. I assured her that I did love her, and explained how confused I had been in my own feelings about the organization. A series of emotionally charged letters were hastily exchanged between us, each of them tugging at my heart. I finally decided that I would go to see her.

I told my husband of my decision to visit our daughter. Just two days after that visit, the circuit overseer and the presiding overseer came marching up the pathway leading to our house to talk with me. I figured the purpose of their call was to give me strict warnings about breaking the Society's rules on shunning, and I feared they might even disfellowship me for my disobedience—especially because I was not sorry that I went to visit her, and therefore would show no repentance. Though I was an adult, I was still acting as a child in relation to their authority, for their intimidating presence caused me to become literally dizzy and unsure of myself and all of my reasons for disagreeing with the Society. Anticipating this possible reaction, I had prepared myself with a list of points to prompt my memory; I was determined not to let their arguments convince me I was wrong, or to let them chastise me without making a rebuttal in defense, or to miss the chance to vent my anger at the organization they represented.

The presiding overseer's face had an intense and determined expression. He was a very powerful man, widely known among Jehovah's Witnesses and feared by most of the other elders. Nearly all of the Witnesses I knew shuddered if he approached them, as he had the reputation of strictly enforcing the Society's rules to the letter. The circuit overseer, though, was an elderly and more kindly man. To my amazement, I never needed to look at my notes, for the meeting was surprisingly brief. The circuit overseer simply stated that he could understand my motherly concern for my daughter, and although shunning her was the way Jehovah wanted me to behave toward her, he could understand just how difficult that could be for a mother to do. His advice, however, utterly amazed me: "Sit in the back of a smoky restaurant when you visit with her, so no one will see you, and just don't tell anybody about it!" I was stunned both by his statement and by the hypocrisy of his advice. He had just finished telling me how Jehovah would not approve of me visiting my daughter, yet here he was giving me permission to go and see her on the sneak! The presiding overseer's reaction was priceless! His jaw hung open in apparent shock. He was speechless as he squirmed nervously in his chair. Obviously the presiding overseer, who always authoritatively exacted obedience to all of the Society's rules, had not expected his superior would counsel me as he did. I wondered if the circuit overseer was unaware of the Society's current view, which forbade Witnesses to speak to their disfellowshipped relatives, or if he was trying to show some compassion in spite of the organization's dictates—or if he just thought Jehovah couldn't see in the back of smoky restaurants!

The issue of me having contact with my daughter seemed to be settled for the moment. As long as I kept my relationship with her a secret and none of the other Witnesses found out about it, the elders would not enforce the Society's rule against visiting one's disfellowshipped relatives and would not take action to disfellowship me. While knowing that I could probably get away with visiting my daughter without discipline from the elders was a relief in one way, yet in another way it was not, for it was forcing me to face my own internal battles regarding the dictates of the organization.

The circuit overseer's decision to "look the other way" regarding my relationship with my daughter foiled my plan for the elders to "unjustly" disfellowship me, thereby giving me my freedom without having to take responsibility for declaring it myself. Now I couldn't put the responsibility for leaving the organization onto the Society by blaming its unreasonable prohibition against me seeing my daughter. The circuit overseer's decision meant I could no longer use the Society's requirement to shun my daughter as an excuse to leave the organization. If I left, the responsibility for that decision would rest solely on me, as I would be leaving for reasons having nothing to do with my daughter. The circuit overseer's decision meant I could no longer hide behind the screen of my daughter. The battle with the Watchtower Society was now *mine*.

FOURTEEN

LEAVING THE GUIDEBOOK BEHIND

W hen my husband and I took our trip to Hawaii in 1991 to celebrate our twentieth wedding anniversary, I wanted to see and do as much as possible during our short stay there. I became obsessed with using a guidebook to plan our daily schedules. I frequently became frustrated and angry upon finding that in spite of all my meticulous planning, often the guidebook was incorrect; it contained errors, and many times things were not as the book said they would be. I was extremely upset that my enjoyment of the trip was so greatly affected by feeling so angry and cheated because of being misdirected by the guidebook. In discussing this with my therapist, he offered the following suggestion: "You're angry at the organization, the 'guidebook' you depended on. You discovered that the organization is not what it promised to be. You wanted a loving community, and you gave up a lot for that in terms of self-determination and choices; and you feel cheated and misled. You followed the Society's path and you found there wasn't anything on the way." The frustration and annoyance I had felt with the guidebook in Hawaii had tapped into the much deeper feelings of disappointment and rage I had with the organization.

We arrived home in time for the circuit assembly. Although I seldom attended the regular meetings at the Kingdom Hall, I had not yet missed an assembly. I was afraid of what other Witnesses would think if I didn't attend. Even worse, I was afraid of offending Jehovah, since assemblies were considered to be among Jehovah's finest spiritual feasts, so I restrained my aggravation with the organization and went. As I sat listening to the program, I started experiencing a sensation of extreme pressure bearing down on me, pressing in on me from all sides, as if I were being compressed into a tight little box. The pressure was nearly intolerable, but it served the purpose of proving to me beyond a doubt that I could no longer endure being a part of the organization.

Upon arriving home, I collapsed onto my bedroom floor, sobbing uncontrollably. I told my husband I now knew I could never again go to another meeting of Jehovah's Witnesses. "Then, you'll be all alone in the world!" he declared. I had felt alone for years anyway, despite being in the midst of the congregation; in fact, twenty-three years in the organization had produced no genuine friendships. All Witness friendships were completely contingent on obedience to the Society; and even though I rigidly adhered to the Society's rules and doctrines all the years I was active in the organization, I still had no true friends. Being a Witness produced only an illusion of friendship. The ostentatious claim that "The brothers and sisters are there for you" was really just a fantasy. I still felt pain from losing my two favorite Witness friends, as they told me they just did not have time for our friendship anymore because they had become pioneers.

Forming friendships in the organization was difficult, as the Witnesses were so paranoid and fearful of being led astray that they were constantly on guard against even those inside the organization, causing them to be constantly judging one another, looking for any trace of an "untheocratic attitude" which had to be immediately reported to the elders. Fear of being turned-in thwarted the intimacy needed for a friendship to flourish. Witnesses claim to have intense love for one another, but I always felt this as a forced love that came out of the organizational requirement to "love one another." It produced an artificial love among the brothers and sisters that was superficial at best, and was born out of fear of dying at Armageddon rather than coming from their hearts. They didn't seem to care about one another *as people*, but only as Witnesses. Although small, friendly gatherings were held occasionally at the homes of various brothers and sisters to help foster a spirit of closeness, the elders maintained some control even over these by giving frequent reminders during the Kingdom Hall meetings to be "spiritually upbuilding" during these get-togethers. This meant that conversations should center on "theocratic" activities, i.e., sharing experiences one has in the door-to-door preaching work, expressing appreciation for recent talks given at the Kingdom Hall, explaining how one came into the Truth, and the like instead of talking about personal interests, vactions, pets, hobbies, and so forth. Putting on this front of "theocraticness" interfered with getting to know fellow Witnesses on a personal level in order for a more genuine love to develop.

The thought of being all alone in the world frightened me, but it was not enough to make me continue to put on a front and go to the meetings. Continuing to keep the mask on was intolerable; I had had enough of not having a whole part of me be accepted, and I was tired of lying to myself about what I really felt. Being a hypocrite, playing the part, wearing the mask, were all just too painful; but leaving the organization was painful, too, for it brought the feeling of death to be outside of the "protective fold." My therapist encouraged me to think and reason on this matter by asking, "The 'protective fold' was cruel to make you put on the mask. So really, how was that a protection for you? You had to give up what you really feel." It was then I realized that being in the organization had really not been the protection that my mind had been programmed to believe it was. I had to pretend to feel things I didn't feel in order to get affection and acceptance from the congregation members, but no matter what I did, I never had the feeling of "belonging" to the group. Over the years, I had often puzzled about why that was so. My therapist offered this observation: "You had to stuff so much of yourself away to be accepted by the group that you unconsciously never really committed to it completely, which caused you to always feel like an outsider looking in."

His observation took my breath away. As dedicated as I thought I had been to the organization, hearing my therapist suggest that I had never really committed to it completely shocked me. Yet his words also struck me in a profound way, for they touched a memory buried deep inside of me—the memory of the day of my baptism when I refused to disown myself to the organization. To be confronted with something I had repressed for so long was jolting, but I also felt a great sense of relief as the pieces of the puzzle started to come together, and I was able to understand why I had felt like an outcast even though I had been in the middle of the flock.

Although I never really felt a part of the organization, still the decision to become inactive in it was terrifying. Rather than feeling like I was making a definite decision, I felt the decision was out of my control—like something inside of me would not allow me to continue to go to the meetings or to be a Witness. Compounding the problem, I suffered from a constant stabbing sense that the Watchtower Society was God's organization, and that only those active in it would be spared God's wrath at Armageddon. I was still under the influence of the Witness belief that anyone not choosing "life"—which equated with choosing to be one of Jehovah's Witnesses—was thereby choosing death. Because I was unable to continue the charade of life as a Witness, I believed the Society's teaching that I was thereby "choosing death." Not wanting to die but feeling helpless to do anything about it is what so overwhelmed me the night of my emotional collapse on the bedroom floor.

I came to realize that the reason I was so worried about what the Witnesses thought about me was because I was unconsciously waiting for them to validate me and say what I felt was OK, something which they clearly are not capable of doing. They could never understand my position because their whole lives are invested in keeping their position. All my life, I had been pushed into a place of having to accept what other people said was the way things were. To pull out of that situation now incurred the displeasure and judgment of the whole congregation.

Life as a Witness had not been spiritually satisfying to me. I had not felt held and cared-for by the congregation; instead, I had felt victimized by the authority of the organization and beat up by its rules. I longed for a better way of life, yet I felt so frightened about the thought of looking elsewhere to satisfy my spiritual needs, since the Witnesses teach that demons inhabit all the churches; and I felt guilty that I was feeling so dissatisfied with Jehovah's spiritual provisions. My therapist encouraged me to see beyond the organization's illogical thinking by asking me, "How could being honest and open about what you feel, and searching for what you feel is truth, not be the right thing?"

The Society's "roadmap to life" had proved itself unreliable, and it was hurting me to continue to stay on it. It was time for me to leave the organization behind as my guidebook, and begin to search for what I felt was the truth; however, I was not yet able to break free from the Watchtower Society because I still feared its authority.

FIFTEEN

THE VISION

Through my daughter I learned that some former Witnesses lived in a nearby town. I was torn between my instincts and curiosity to go and talk with them and the Society's prohibition against speaking to anyone who had left the organization. I was lying in bed one morning, worried and feeling greatly distressed as to what I should do. As I was praying for guidance, I suddenly felt a very strong pressure pushing my shoulders to my bed, shaking me forcefully. I felt my breath and my strength ebb out from me, feeling as if an inward part of me were being drawn heavenward. Lasting perhaps less than a minute, the shaking stopped as suddenly as it had begun, and I was again able to breathe and full strength returned to me instantly.

Knowing that the Society teaches that such an experience could come only from demons, I was puzzled that I had not felt terrified; instead, I had experienced a sensation of extreme inner peace. I immediately told my husband what had happened, and asked him if he thought demons had caused this phenomena. To my amazement he answered without hesitation, "No." Though I felt confused about exactly what this experience meant, I nevertheless felt it was God's way of "waking me up" and getting my attention.

I decided to go ahead and meet with the former Witnesses. They emphasized that God had provided Jesus, not an organization, as the way to Himself. I struggled with the concepts of having a relationship with God through a personal relationship with Jesus Christ, or through the Watchtower Society.

Lying in bed awake one morning
I prayed
and
asked God if it were necessary
for me to have a personal relationship with Jesus.
Immediately,
I felt the same force pressing down on my shoulders
shaking me
more gently this time
and
as the shaking continued, there appeared before me

A Vision

of a man's hands
extending down toward me,
surrounded by a golden glow of light.
I knew without a doubt that they were Jesus' hands
and
as I observed His hands,
I felt love and kindness and caring emanating from them
and
I saw His fingers gently curl,
embracing something that I could not see
and
although I did not feel or see His hands grasp mine,
at that moment
witness was borne to me that it was my hands
He was gently embracing
and
at the moment of that realization
the shaking abruptly stopped
and
the vision vanished.

This vision gave me more confidence to leave the organization. I definitely felt it was in answer to my earnest prayer, and a positive indication that leaving the organization would be the right step to take. However, instead of continuing to be comforted by the vision, my problem of excessive self-doubt soon caused me to start questioning the reality of it. I subsequently went to see a counselor at a non-denominational church and described my experience to him. I asked him if he thought the vision was real, and if he thought it meant that Jesus was really reaching out to me. He responded without hesitation, "Absolutely!" Then I discussed the vision with my therapist, asking him if he thought it was real, or if he thought it was just a fabrication of my mind due to the stress I was experiencing in trying to leave the organization. He asked me, "What if it *was* real?" I immediately responded, "Then I would leave the organization!" He gently replied, "I wonder if that's not why you doubt the experience. You're doubting because it's hard to leave the organization. You want to doubt yourself, because doubting yourself forces you not to act, not to leave. The problem is that you don't trust yourself. It's a problem with self-esteem and self-confidence. As to the vision, the mind usually doesn't fabricate things in that way."

All the years of striving to have a relationship with Jehovah through the organization had proved to be in vain. I remember feeling closer to God when I was a teenager going to a Protestant church than I ever felt as one of Jehovah's Witnesses.

SIXTEEN

THE SHOE FITS

A Cultlike Organization

I wavered between feeling that the Society was wrong in claiming their authority was from God, and feeling something was inherently wrong with me for not being able to submit to the Society as God's authority. In discussing this with my therapist, he said, "There is something inherently *right* with you, that you need to know yourself and use your mind to critically evaluate information."

He suggested that I read a book about cults. *Cults!* The implication that I might be involved in a cultlike group alarmed me; the mere word conjured up images in my mind of satanic groups controlled by demonic forces. The organization claimed to be a haven and protection from demonic influences, so I wondered how they could possibly be a cultlike group. Though I had prayed many times that this oppressive organization not be God's organization, I still found myself dazed and disoriented at the thought that it really might not be; however, I was determined to find out the truth.

I decided to go to the library. Trembling with fear about what I might find, I combed the shelves for books about cults. Constantly looking over my shoulder to make sure no one was watching me, I finally took a book off the shelf. My heart pounded as I approached the checkout desk with it. A Witness I knew worked part-time as a clerk at the library; I felt certain he would turn me in to the elders if he saw the book I had selected. Relieved after making it through the checkout desk unnoticed, I breathlessly raced for the safety of my car, clutching the book tightly under my jacket. Anxious to see what it said, I was astonished to find that though I felt protected in the privacy of my car, I experienced a "paralyzed" feeling that rendered me unable to even open the book; it lay on my desk at home for two weeks before I was able to attempt to read it.

When at last I had the courage to open the book, the first thing I saw was a checklist of characteristics of cults. As my eyes scanned the list, I realized with horror that nine of the ten characteristics of cults listed fit the attitudes and behaviors of the Watchtower Society! Frightened, I slammed the book shut in denial. I sighed with relief as I dropped it into the book return drop at the library. Yet deep inside I knew that simply getting rid of the book did not erase what the organization really was. Facing up to the fact that I had been deceived into believing the organization was the truth, though, was a difficult thing to do.

I was surprised at my fearful reaction. I thought discovering the organization was a cultlike group would be a relief and would make leaving it easier. Having repressed the desire to leave the organization for many years, this would be the perfect reason to finally escape it. Several weeks went by, however, before I could bring myself to the point where I was ready to learn more.

I subsequently purchased books about religious addiction and toxic faith,[1] abusive churches,[2] and spiritual abuse.[3] In them, I found information that identified:

Traits of Abusive Churches and Toxic Faith Systems

1. Control-oriented, arrogantly assertive, power-posturing leadership.
2. Authoritarian and legalistic with dictatorial, dogmatic doctrines that are proclaimed to be "the Truth."
3. Claims of being the channel of communication between God and humankind; having unique knowledge that makes them special. If members do not submit to its dictatorial rule, the leaders emphasize that any waver of support to the organization or church is evidence of waver of faith in God.
3. Manipulation of members by guilt, shame, blame, and fear.
4. An "Us-versus-Them" view, a perception of being under persecution.
5. Demanding, rigid lifestyles and overwhelming service requirements. Members' lives are controlled by both spoken and unspoken rules.
6. Loss of focus on God, replaced by a complicated process of furthering the church or organization and its rules.
7. Followers "in pain," hiding real feelings that oppose or disagree with the religious system.

8. Intolerance of individual thinking, and of criticism of the religious system by its members. Fosters an unhealthy dependency by focusing on themes of submission, loyalty, and obedience to those in authority.
9. Severe discipline of members.
10. The religious system puts down other religions.
11. Leaving the religious system is painful and difficult.
12. Closed communication: Information is only valid if it comes from the top of the religious system down, and from inside the system to the outside of it.
13. Labeling: a technique used to discount a person who opposes the beliefs of the religious system, i.e., "apostates."
14. What you do is more important than who you are.
15. Love and acceptance are earned by doing certain things.
16. Scripture-twisting.
17. Scare tactics; focus on demons.
18. Threats to remove members from the group.
19. Members are misled into thinking the only safety is in the religious system.
20. A view that education is bad or unnecessary.

I was shocked that these traits were identical to those the Society possessed; however, I also felt a great sense of relief, a feeling of vindication, that I was not a "disgruntled Witness" as the brothers would have me think. I was a victim of a religiously abusive system.

> When these characteristics exist in a church or Christian family system, the result will be spiritual abuse.[4]

> . . . certain characteristics of spiritually abusive systems make it immensely difficult for people caught up in them to leave. . . . This system acts like a "spiritual magnet," pulling in people from the outside. Inside, however, the system acts like a black hole with spiritual gravity so strong it is very hard for people to get out.[5]

When I read the above, a wave of relief flooded over me. I realized what was keeping me stuck in the organization was not only my personal psychology and my weaknesses—keeping people trapped was a function of the abusive system. All the years I had been a Witness, the brothers had frequently quoted a favorite Scripture, applying it to Witness "apostates" as a way of getting the congregation to disregard any criticism of the organization:

I know that after my going away oppressive wolves will enter in among you and will not treat the flock with tenderness, and from among you yourselves men will rise and speak twisted things to draw away the disciples after themselves. (Acts 20:29–30, *New World Translation*)

Witnesses voicing complaints against the elders or any part of the organization or its doctrines were viewed as oppressive wolves to be feared, and the congregation members would quickly withdraw association from such ones. Now I realized that Scripture more aptly fit the Watchtower Society, instead. This organization had arisen from amongst Christianity, with men speaking twisted things, drawing a following after themselves, and not treating their members with tenderness.

Next I purchased a book about cults,[6] and another about recovery from cults[7] and learned about the characteristics of cultlike groups.

Characteristics of Cults and Cultlike Groups

1. Members of the group must believe the doctrines of the group are the one and only "Truth."
2. Members must follow the doctrines even if they do not understand them.
3. The doctrines form the basis for all thoughts, feelings, and actions.
4. An "Us-vs.-Them" belief that no outside group is recognized as godly.
5. No independent thinking by members is allowed.
6. Teaches that there is a huge conspiracy working to thwart the group.
7. Teaches that spirit beings are constantly observing the members, and can take possession of them if they feel or think in ways different from the group.
8. Members are made to feel elite, chosen by God to lead humankind out of darkness.
9. The group looks down on other religious groups.
10. Members are told if they don't fully perform their duties, they are failing humanity.
11. Members are required to render absolute obedience to their superiors.
12. When members leave the group, the love that was formerly shown to them turns into anger, hatred, and ridicule.
13. The group uses guilt and shame to control its members.
14. Fear is a major motivator.
15. Members feel a great sense of urgency about given tasks.
16. Many groups teach that "The Apocalypse" is just around the corner,

and have timetables for its occurrence with dates near enough to carry an emotional punch.

17. Members are kept extremely busy.
18. The future is a time when members will be rewarded because "The Great Change" has come.
19. There is never a legitimate reason for leaving the group.
20. Members are indoctrinated with the belief that if they ever leave the group, terrible consequences will befall them.
21. Members are forbidden to think negative thoughts about the group.
22. Members are forbidden to have contact with former members of the group.
23. The "truth" is changed to fit the needs of the situation.
24. Friendships in the group are shallow; the only real allegiance is to the leader.
25. There is no allowance for interpretation of or deviation from the group's doctrines.
26. The leadership systematically creates a sense of powerlessness in its members.
27. The group causes members to become extremely dependent on its compliance-oriented expressions of love and support; dread of losing the group's support.
28. "Love Bombing": members shower much attention on prospective members.
29. Members must project a façade of happiness.
30. Members must believe the group is always right, even if it contradicts itself.
31. Members spend more and more time with and under the direction of the group.
32. Those who do not conform to the group's requirements will be expelled.
33. Disagreement with or doubts about the group's teaching are always the fault of the member, due to lack of faith or lack of understanding.
34. The group is superior to and different than all other groups.
35. Members must trust the group leaders instead of themselves.
36. Members have similar odd mannerisms and modes of speech.

I was stunned as I read these characteristics of cults, since the Watchtower Society had demonstrated all these characteristics during the twenty-three years I had been in the organization. Knowing the organization exhibited cultlike characteristics, however, meant I had spent half of my life use-

lessly following the dictates of the Society. I was furious that I had been suffering all those years while serving mere men. But discovering the organization possessed many of the traits of a cult helped me to realize that the
Watchtower Society likely did not derive its authority from God. I felt
embarrassed, foolish, and stupid about having been duped by the organization. My therapist helped me deal with these feelings by clarifying, "Involvement in these types of groups has nothing to do with intelligence; it
has to do with emotional reasons for needing to be in the group."

As a Witness, the elders would tell us that the purpose of going to the
same houses year after year in the witnessing work was "in hopes of
catching householders during a time that something adverse had happened
in their lives since we saw them last, that would cause them to want to listen
to our message now." As a Witness, that is what I fully believed was true.
Now that I have knowledge of the tactics cultlike groups use, however, I can
look back and see what was *really* happening. Witnesses were unwittingly
looking for people who were experiencing difficulties in their lives that
made them particularly vulnerable to the recruiting methods the organization taught them to use.

> Most cultists were relatively normal persons experiencing an unusual
> level of stress when they encountered a cult.[8]

> People join cults, not because they make a rational, informed choice.
> They join because they are duped. The process is a seduction, not a mutu-
> ally beneficial agreement or the choice of an informed "consumer."[9]

Cultlike groups prey upon people by promising to satisfy their needs.
Anyone who is not aware of the techniques cultlike groups use to attract
new members could be vulnerable to these groups, if the timing were right.

NOTES

1. Stephen Arterburn and Jack Felton, *Toxic Faith* (Nashville, Tenn.: Oliver-
Nelson Books, 1991), pp. 163–89.

2. Ronald M. Enroth, *Churches That Abuse* (Grand Rapids, Mich.: Zondervan
Publishing House, 1992), pp. 78, 80, 103, 105, 118, 176.

3. David Johnson and Jeff VanVonderen, *The Subtle Power of Spiritual Abuse*
(Minneapolis, Minn.: Bethany House Publishers, 1991), pp. 53–79.

4. Johnson and VanVonderen, *The Subtle Power of Spiritual Abuse*, p. 79.

5. Ibid., p. 73.

6. Steve Hassan, *Combatting Cult Mind Control* (Rochester, Vt.: Park Street Press, 1990), pp. 78–84; 99; 102–104.

7. Michael D. Langone, *Recovery From Cults* (New York: W. W. Norton & Co., 1993), pp. 257–58.

8. Langone, *Recovery From Cults*, p. 6.

9. Ibid., p. 6.

SEVENTEEN

Now you see it, now you don't

False Prophecies

I had heard through my daughter about books that expose the truth about the organization, but I was afraid to go into a Christian bookstore in search of them because the Society teaches that such bookstores are inhabited by demons. This teaching stems from the organization's claim that only it represents true Christianity; the literature in Christian bookstores, being other than their own, represents false Christianity which is influenced by the Devil. Thus, going into them is viewed as opening oneself up to demon influence that would lead one out of the Truth. In discussing this fear of influence from demons with my therapist, he proposed a question to stimulate my thinking:

> If demons can make a person have insight to think another religion makes more sense, then why is it not demons that influence a person to think that the Watchtower Society is the truth? Why couldn't the thought that a person has that says the Watchtower Society is the channel of communication from God come under the same umbrella?

My therapist's questions left me awestruck. I had never thought about the possibility that the Devil and his demons could be working through the Watchtower Society to draw people away from God; I couldn't deny that, logically, it could be a possibility. Feelings of relief and hopefulness engulfed me as I realized there was a chance that the organization might *not* represent the truth.

Just as a pearl inside the shell of an oyster starts out as an irritating grain of sand that eventually becomes covered over with layers of protectant, so the false prophecies, inconsistencies, and zigzagging doctrines of the Society were irritants to me, which I covered over with the protectant of denial by shelving my doubts, accepting their excuses, buying into their blame, and convincing myself that I believed their doctrines. With my therapist's assistance, slowly those layers of protectant were peeled off in order to get at what I really felt. Now I was at the point of being able to face the real truth about the Watchtower Society.

I decided to research the organization to obtain proof beyond a shadow of a doubt that the Watchtower Society is not God's channel of communication and does not represent the truth. To begin my investigation, my daughter accompanied me to a bookstore to order a publication that one of her coworkers had learned about and had suggested she read. It was a book written by a former Witness elder exposing some of the Watchtower Society's jaded history.[1] I read it and was astonished that I could be in the organization for as long as I had been and still have no idea of the dark secrets the Society had kept hidden. My appetite whetted, I had an insatiable thirst to know more.

The ex-Witnesses I had visited told me of two countercult ministries[2] that made literature critical of the Watchtower Society available through a mail-order catalog, and suggested that some of it might aid me in my examination of the organization. Knowing that the Society views such literature to be "spiritual pornography," I was afraid to have any of it delivered to my house. My husband was an elder, and I was not prepared to accept the consequences of his finding it in my possession; thus I felt compelled to obtain a post office box so I could receive the information that I wanted discreetly.

The first time I went to the small postal substation to check my mailbox, I sat in my car for several minutes, scrutinizing the parking lot for any Witnesses who might observe me. When I felt sure no Witnesses were there, I summoned up the courage to go in. Relieved to find no one in the lobby, I excitedly opened my mailbox where I found a note indicating that a package had arrived for me. With keen anticipation, I went over to the window to pick up my box of reading materials. While I was signing for the parcel, though, I suddenly felt the presence of someone behind me. My heart began to race with anxiety. Had someone come in? What if it was a Witness that I knew? Instinctively, I clutched my clandestine package to my chest, obscuring the name of the return address stamped on the corner of the box.

Trying to convince myself that I was just suffering from paranoia at being in the organization for so long, I turned to walk through the tiny lobby toward the exit. I stared at the floor, not daring to look up. Witnesses were nosy by nature. If the person who came in had been a Witness friend, surely she would ask what was inside my box, and why was I having it delivered here instead of to my house.

I began to panic. Only one exit existed. There was no other way out. I had no choice but to squeeze by this person in order to make it out the door. As I slowly raised my eyes, I was seized by terror as I recognized the person as my former neighbor, a Witness friend of mine for many years. Although he looked at me with suspicion, I gave him no opportunity to ask about the contents of my package. I quickly brushed by him, casually acknowledging him with a hurried greeting.

The odds of such a chance encounter were so remote, I was mystified at how this could happen to me. Then I remembered that the elders used to say that angels maneuver events in order to expose anyone who is having doubts about the organization, in order to protect the congregation from that person. A shiver of fear went through my body as I entertained the thought that perhaps Jehovah's angels caused this Witness friend of mine to catch me with my box of "apostate" literature, and that maybe this incident was proof that the Watchtower Society was God's organization after all.

This episode caused me to realize just how tenuous a situation I was in. I could not afford to waste time in conducting my investigation of the organization. I wanted to make my decision to stay in it or to leave it before that decision was ripped away from me by a Witness discovering my forbidden books and turning me in to the elders.

A close encounter occurred in 1992 when I carelessly left on a countertop in the kitchen one of the forbidden books that I had obtained surreptitiously. Of all the reading materials that I had ordered, *Crisis of Conscience*—written by Ray Franz, former member of the elite Governing Body—was the cream of the crop. It is a goldmine containing a wealth of information not available elsewhere, for it contained the inside story of what really goes on behind the closed doors of the secretive meetings of the Governing Body. I had been so engrossed in reading it that I had failed to take my usual precautions to keep it hidden. My husband, arriving home earlier than usual from work, caught me offguard by strolling into the kitchen. With horror I noticed my prized book was in full view. Praying that he wouldn't see it, my hopes were dashed as he asked, "What is this you're reading?" I held my breath as he picked the book up and read its cover. He at once became enraged, shouting, "How dare you bring pornography into my house?!" His fury escalated, surpassing any display of emotion I had ever witnessed from him. His brow furrowed and his nostrils flared; he was seething with hatred. His glaring eyes, now fierce with anger, drove darts through my very being. I was terrified; for the first time in our marriage, I feared he would strike me.

And then, without any apparent cause, his rage sudddenly and spontaneously disappeared. He stood silently for a few moments in a catatoniclike state, a look of peace replacing what just momemts before had been the pinnacle of furor. Asking him what was going on, I was astonished at his reply: "Holy Spirit has come upon me, and I know that I must allow you to read that book." With that declaration, he left the room. Puzzled, knowing that this kind of talk is foreign to Jehovah's Witnesses, I followed him into the dining room. Driven to know more, I asked him to describe more fully what had just occurred. He replied only that it had been the strangest experience he had ever had, and emphatically stated that he did not want to talk about it. Further prodding a few days later only elicited the same response.[3]

My initial research focused on the prophecies that the Watchtower Society had made as God's claimed spokesman. In addition to its constant emphasis on the imminence of Armageddon since the organization's inception over one hundred years ago, I was astonished to find over twenty other prophecies, all of which had failed to come true. There was no evidence that Jehovah had corrected any of their erroneous predictions; they simply ran their course, the Society changing them when time proved them false.

FALSE PROPHECIES OF THE WATCHTOWER SOCIETY

- *The year 1872 marks 6,000 years from the creation of Adam.*

   "In this chapter we present the Bible evidence which indicates that 6,000 years from the creation of Adam were complete with A.D. 1872. . . . " (*The Time Is at Hand* [1889], p. 33)

- *The year 1975 marks 6,000 years from the creation of Adam.*

   "According to this trustworthy Bible chronology six thousand years from man's creation will end in 1975, and the seventh period of a thousand years of human history will begin in the fall of 1975 C.E." (*Life Everlasting—in Freedom of the Sons of God* [1966], p. 29)

- *The Kingdom of God will begin exercising power in 1878.*

  "Be not surprised, then, when in subsequent chapters we present proofs
  that the setting up of the Kingdom of God is already begun, that it is
  pointed out in prophecy as due to begin the exercise of power in A.D.
  1878. . . ." (*The Time Is at Hand* [1911 edition], p. 101)

- *The Kingdom of God will be fully established by the end of 1914.*

  ". . . we consider it an established truth that the final end of the kingdoms
  of this world, and the full establishment of the Kingdom of God, will be
  accomplished at the end of A.D. 1914." (*The Time Is at Hand* [1911 edi-
  tion], p. 99)

- *The Jews will be restored, and the Gentile kingdoms will be broken in
  pieces between 1874–1914.*

  "And during this forty years, [1874–1914] the kingdom of God is to be set
  up . . . the Jews are to be restored, the Gentile kingdoms broken in pieces
  'like a potter's vessel,' and the kingdoms of this world become the kingdoms of our Lord and his Christ, and the judgment age introduced."
  (*Three Worlds* [1877], p. 83)

- *Jesus' second presence began in 1874.*

  "The Scriptural proof is that the second presence of the Lord Jesus Christ
  began in 1874 A.D." (*Prophecy* [1929], pp. 64, 65)

- *Jesus' second presence began in 1914.*

  "Bible evidence shows that in the year 1914 C.E. God's time arrived for
  Christ to return and begin ruling." (*You Can Live Forever in Paradise on
  Earth* [1982], p. 147)

- *The End of This System of Things spanned from 1799 to 1914.*

  "The 'Time of the End,' a period of one hundred and fifteen (115) years,
  from A.D. 1799 to A.D. 1914, is particularly marked in the Scriptures."
  (*Thy Kingdom Come* [1891], p. 23)

- *When "the end of this system of things" did not occur by 1914, the Society changed the meaning of the 1914 date to denote the* beginning *of "the end of this system of things," instead of the* end *of it.*

    "Both in Bible chronology and in the events that were foretold to take place from 1914 onward we find confirmed beyond doubt that 1914 was the beginning of the end for this present system." (*AW* 10-8-68, p. 6)

- *World War I will not result in victory for any nation.*

    "The war will proceed and will eventuate in no glorious victory for any nation, but in the horrible mutilation and impoverishment for all. Next will follow the Armageddon of anarchy." (*New York Times*, 10-5-1914 [quoting Pastor Russell, first president of the Society])

- *Armageddon began in 1874, and will* end *in 1914*

    "The date of the close of that 'battle' is definitely marked in Scripture as October, 1914. It is already in progress, its beginning dating from October, 1874." (*WT* 1-15-1892, p. 22)

- *Armageddon will* begin *in 1914.*

    "The present great war in Europe is the beginning of the Armageddon of the Scriptures." (*Pastor Russell's Sermons* [1917], p. 676)

- *In 1940, the Society proclaimed that Armageddon is just ahead, and that God's Kingdom is already here.*

    "The Kingdom is here, the King is enthroned. Armageddon is just ahead. . . . Therefore the great climax has been reached." (*The Messenger*, 9-1940, p. 6)

- *In 1950, the Society announced that the march is on to the field of Armageddon.*

    ". . . the rulers are being irresistibly gathered by the demon-inspired mouthings of worldly systems. The march is on! Where? To the field of Armageddon for the 'war of the great day of God the Almighty'!" (*This Means Everlasting Life* [1950], p. 311)

- *The Society announced in 1968 that Armageddon would occur within a few years, at most.*

  "What does the Bible show as to the meaning of all these world events? It shows that for this unrighteous world time is running out fast! It shows that within a few years at most there will take place a climax in human affairs so gigantic that it will affect every person on Earth, every man, woman, and child. It will, without fail, affect you. What is this climax? God himself will take a direct hand in world affairs. He will use his overwhelming power to crush wickedness and wicked people. This act of God is called 'Armageddon' in some Bible versions." (*AW* 10-8-1968, p. 4)

- *Only 90 months left!*

  "Just think, brothers, there are only about ninety months left before 6,000 years of man's existence on Earth is completed. Do you remember what we learned at the assemblies last summer? The majority of people living today will probably be alive when Armageddon breaks out, and there are no resurrection hopes for those who are destroyed then." (*Kingdom Ministry*, 3-68, p. 4)

- *Armageddon—1975!*

  "According to this trustworthy Bible chronology six thousand years from man's creation will end in 1975, and the seventh period of a thousand years of human history will begin in the fall of 1975 C.E. . . . It would not be by mere chance or accident but would be according to the loving purpose of Jehovah God for the reign of Jesus Christ, the 'Lord of the sabbath', to run parallel with the seventh millennium of man's existence." (*Life Everlasting—In Freedom of the Sons of God* [1966], pp. 29–30)

  "Why Are You Looking Forward to 1975?" (*WT* 8-15-68, p. 494)

  "Many living today will have the opportunity never to die. They will survive the destruction of the present ungodly system and thereafter gradually be freed from sin and brought to human perfection." (*Is This Life All There Is?* [1974] pp. 165–66)

- *When Armageddon didn't occur in 1975, the Society clung to its prophecy that Armageddon will occur before the generation of 1914 passes away.*

"Most important, this magazine builds confidence in the Creator's promise of a peaceful and secure new world before the generation that saw the events of 1914 passes away." (Masthead of *Awake!*, 11-8-94, p. 4)

- *Christian religions will be gone by the end of 1914.*

    "And, with the end of A.D. 1914 . . . what men call Christendom, will have passed away, as already shown from prophecy." (*Thy Kingdom Come* [1891], p. 153)

- *When the Society saw that Christian religions were still going strong by the end of 1914, they changed their prophecy to the year 1918 as the year God would destroy the churches.*

    "Also, in the year 1918, when God destroys the churches wholesale and the church members by millions. . . ." (*The Finished Mystery* [1917], p. 485)

- *In 1940, the end of religion had come.*

    "The prophecies of Almighty God, the fulfillment of which now clearly appears from the physical facts, show that the end of religion has come and with its end the complete downfall of Satan's entire organization." (*Religion* [1940], p. 336)

- *Every kingdom of the Earth will pass away in 1920.*

    "Even the republics will disappear in the fall of 1920. . . . Every kingdom of Earth will pass away, be swallowed up in anarchy." (*The Finished Mystery* [1917], p. 258)

- *Millions of people alive in 1920 will never die.*

    "Then, based upon the promises set forth in the divine Word, we must reach the positive and indisputable conclusion that millions now living will never die." (*Millions Now Living Will Never Die* [1920], p. 97)

- *Totalitarian dictators, along with the Roman Catholic hierarchy, will seize control of almost all the nations.*

    "You may expect totalitarian dictators, acting with the Roman Catholic Hierarchy, to overrun the Earth, seize control of almost all the nations. . . ." (*Judge Rutherford Uncovers Fifth Column*, [1940], p. 15)

- *The end of Nazi-Fascist hierarchy rule will mark the end forever of demon rule.*

  "Thus the end for ever of Nazi-Fascist hierarchy rule will come, and that will mark the end for ever of demon rule." (*WT* 12-15-41, p. 377)

- *The Society declared in 1958 that destruction of the Anglo-American world power is imminent.*

  "All Earth is in a trouble the like of which has never been known since the Flood. With good reason this is so. Destruction of the seventh world power, the Anglo-American dual world power, is at hand." (*Your Will Be Done on Earth* [1958], p. 360)

- *In the year 1925, God will resurrect Abraham and other ancient prophets from the dead to live on the Earth.*

  "Therefore we may confidently expect that 1925 will mark the return of Abraham, Isaac, Jacob and the faithful prophets of old, particularly those named by the Apostle in Hebrews chapter eleven, to the condition of human perfection." (*Millions Now Living Will Never Die* [1920], pp. 89, 90)

- *When Abraham and the other prophets did not appear in 1925, the Society changed the date to "shortly* after *1925" for their resurrection on Earth.*

  "We should, therefore, expect shortly after 1925 to see the awakening of Abel, Enoch, Noah, Abraham, Isaac, Jacob, Melchisedec, Job, Moses, Samuel, David, Isaiah, Jeremiah, Ezekiel, Daniel, John the Baptist, and others mentioned in the eleventh chapter of Hebrews." (*The Way to Paradise* [1924], p. 224)

- *When Abraham and the ancient prophets still did not appear, the date was changed to "shortly" in 1942—and a house was built for them to live in!*

  "More than this: the Scriptural and the physical facts prove that Job is due to be resurrected shortly with those faithful men and to appear on Earth with them." (*The New World*, [1942], p. 130)

  "In this expectation the house at San Diego, California...was built, in 1930, and named 'Beth-Sarim,' meaning 'House of the Princes.' It is now held in trust for the occupancy of those princes on their return." (*The New World*, [1942], p. 104)

The words of Deuteronomy 18:22 spoke to me clearly:

> [W]hen the prophet speaks in the name of Jehovah and the word does not come true, that is the word Jehovah did not speak. With presumptuousness the prophet spoke it. You must not get frightened at him. (*New World Translation*)

I was shocked at these many prophecies that my investigation had uncovered. The Society had done such a remarkable job of guarding their past that even with all the years that I had been in the organization, I still had no clue that it had made false prophecies to such an extent; none of the older Witnesses I had chatted with over the years had ever mentioned any of them. They had been cleverly covered over or avoided in the Society's publications that had been in use since I became associated with the organization.

Ironically, the Watchtower Society's own publications advise how those who make such prophecies should be viewed:

- "How are we to know whether one is a true or a false prophet? . . . If he is a true prophet, his message will come to pass exactly as prophesied. If he is a false prophet, his prophecy will fail to come to pass." (*WT* 5-15-30, p. 154)
- "The true prophet of God *today* will be telling forth what the Bible teaches, and those things that the Bible tells us are soon to come to pass. He will not be sounding forth man-made theories or guesses, either his own or those of others." (*WT* 5-15-30, p. 155)
- "Their prophecies did not come true. Therefore they are false prophets; and the people should no longer trust them as safe guides. . . ." (*WT* 5-15-30, p. 156)

I was amazed at the contradictions within the Society's own publications, a case in point being the meaning they ascribed to the word "prophet." The *Awake!* magazine featured an article entitled, "They shall know that A PROPHET WAS AMONG THEM," and asked the question: "Who is this prophet?" The answer followed, "It was the small group of footstep followers of Jesus Christ, known at that time as International Bible Students. Today they are known as Jehovah's Christian witnesses." (*AW* 4-1-72, p. 197) In a later article, however, they also claimed, "True, the brothers preparing these publications are not infallible. Their writings are not inspired as are those of Paul and the other Bible writers." (*WT* 2-15-81, p. 19) Thus, although the Society touts itself as a prophet, it nevertheless claims to be an *uninspired prophet*. Looking further into the Society's writings, I found the word "prophet" in their Bible dictionary, which said: ". . . the use of this distinctive term shows that true prophets were no ordinary announcers but were spokesmen for God, 'men of God' with inspired messages." (*Insight From the Scriptures* [1988], p. 694) So, according to the Society's own definition, true prophets were inspired; hence, there is no such thing as an uninspired prophet who is from God—*uninspired prophets are simply false prophets!* The Society unwittingly hanged itself in an article it wrote about others:

> True, there have been those in times past who predicted an 'end to the world,' even announcing a specific date. . . . The 'end' did not come. They were guilty of false prophesying. . . . Missing from such people were God's truths and the evidence that he was guiding and using them. (*AW* 10-8-63, p. 23)

By its own mouth the Society stands condemned! I just couldn't believe that Jehovah had channeled all the erroneous prophecies that the Society had made. To the contrary, I wondered if they had been unwittingly influenced by Satan. Interestingly, I found a statement in the Society's own literature regarding its excuse for its 1925 prophetic failure that seemed to point to that conclusion:

> It is to be expected that Satan will try to inject into the minds of the consecrated [the anointed, represented by the Watchtower Society] the thought that 1925 should see an end of the [preaching] work. . . . (*WT* 9-1-25, p. 262)

In essence, the Society was saying that Satan had injected his idea into its members' minds, and that he had used the Society's publications in which to print it! In effect, they were saying that despite their being God's sole channel of communication, the Devil had been leading them astray for awhile—that they had actually been the deluded dupes of Satan! If the Watchtower Society had truly been God's organization, surely God was powerful enough to have protected it from Satan's influence. But according to the Society's excuse, it evidently did not agree.

My discovery of these false prophecies triggered something in my memory. I recalled with a queasy feeling an incident I had long ago repressed. It was the day over twenty years previously when I had wandered into the Kingdom Hall library after a meeting, curious as to what kinds of books were kept there. While browsing through the shelves and leafing through several very old publications, a brother approached me. In an accusing tone he asked me what I was doing looking at the Society's older literature. The brother brusquely seized the book, snatching it out of my hands. Without waiting for my response, he curtly remarked, "You don't need to be reading the Society's older writings! Jehovah's Witnesses have an abundance of spiritual food with all the publications that the Society has produced in more recent years." I left the library wondering what that brother was so afraid of me finding and why the Kingdom Hall would even have a library full of books that were so obviously objectionable for the Witnesses to read. It seemed almost as if the older publications that Jehovah had channeled to the Society in years past were now considered to be apostate material! I wondered what the Society had to hide. I restrained my curiosity back then because my security felt so threatened by that brother, and I had a strong emotional need to stay in the perceived safety of the organization.

Amazingly, the Society spoke critically about other groups whose predictions have failed, as though they themselves had never been guilty of doing the same thing:

> The World's End—How Near? Why So Many False Alarms? . . . The flood of false alarms is unfortunate. They are like the wolf-wolf cries of the shepherd boy—people soon dismiss them, and when the true warning comes, it too is ignored. (*AW* 3-22-93, pp. 3–4)

> How will Jehovah show that such clergy prophets are fakes? By not fulfilling what they announce to be "an utterance!" or what they presume to speak in his name. He does not back up their falsehood. (*WT* 9-1-79, p. 30)

In an effort to excuse its many false prophecies, the Society pleads:

> Jehovah's Witnesses, in their eagerness for Jesus' second coming, have suggested dates that turned out to be incorrect. Because of this, some have called them false prophets. Never in these instances, however, did they presume to originate predictions "in the name of Jehovah." Never did they say, "These are the words of Jehovah." (*AW* 3-22-93, p. 4)

The Society's claim of never making predictions in the name of Jehovah is not true, as can be seen by its following statement:

Unlike the clergy class, those of the Jeremiah class [the Watchtower Society][4] have been sent by Jehovah to speak in his name. . . . True, the Jeremiah class back up their message by quoting the words, "This is what Jehovah has said." (*WT* 9-1-79, p. 29)

The Society also has directly attributed its prophecies to God by stating:

- The interpretation of prophecy, therefore, is not from man, but is from Jehovah . . . (*WT* 5-1-38, p. 143)
- *The Watchtower* being the means the Lord is pleased to use to transmit his message of truth to the people. . . . (*Yearbook* [1937], p. 82)
- They are, we believe, God's dates, not ours. (*WT* 7-15-1894, p. 226)
- *The Watchtower* merely brings to the attention of God's people that which he has revealed . . . (*WT* 5-1-34, p. 131)
- As far back as 1880 *The Watchtower* pointed to A.D. 1914 as the date marking the end of the world. . . . All this information came not from or by man, but by the Lord God. . . . (*WT* 2-1-38, p. 35)
- This is not giving any credit to the magazine's publishers, but is due to the great Author of the Bible. . . . He it is that makes possible the material that is published in the columns of this magazine. . . . (*WT* 4-15-43, p. 127)

The Bible advises how we are to view false prophets:

This is what Jehovah of armies has said: "Do not listen to the words of the prophets who are prophesying to you people. . . . The vision of their own heart is what they speak—not from the mouth of Jehovah." (*New World Translation*, Jer. 23:16)

The Society asserts, "*The Watchtower* does not claim to be inspired in its utterances, nor is it dogmatic." (*WT* 3-22-93, p. 4) Its claim of not being dogmatic is false. By definition "dogmatic" refers to asserting one's opinion as if it were fact, acting in an authoritarian manner as though one possesses absolute truth, and being positive in one's manner of utterance. The Watchtower Society demonstrates that it is dogmatic by the following means:

1. By asserting its opinions regarding its interpretations of Bible doctrine are facts, i.e., "the Truth." *The Truth That Leads to Eternal Life* is a publication Witnesses used in their worldwide preaching and teaching work from 1968–1981. Jehovah's Witnesses refer to themselves as being "in the Truth."

2. By acting in an authoritarian manner as though it possesses absolute truth, by requiring its members to accept all of its teachings.

> Approved association with Jehovah's Witnesses requires accepting the entire range of the true teachings of the Bible, including those Scriptural beliefs that are unique to Jehovah's Witnesses. (*WT* 4-1-86, p. 31)

3. By forbidding its members to think independently.

> Avoid Independent Thinking. From the very outset of his rebellion Satan called into question God's way of doing things. He promoted independent thinking. . . . To this day, it has been Satan's subtle design to infect God's people with this type of thinking. (*WT* 1-15-83, p. 22)

4. By disfellowshipping any members who disagree with any of their teachings.

> So important is it never to raise the voice in bitter criticism of the Lord's organization or its appointed representatives. (*WT* 5-15-84, p. 17)

> [I]f a Christian . . . unrepentantly promotes false teachings [disagreements with the Society's teachings], it may be necessary for him to be expelled from the congregation. (*WT* 4-1-86, p. 31)

5. By being positive in its manner of utterance. Although many examples of this have been brought out in the quotes in this chapter, another fine example is demonstrated in the following, as the *Watchtower* speaks of its prophetic dates and chronology:

> [T]his chronology is not of man, but of God. Being of divine origin and divinely corroborated, present-truth chronology stands in a class by itself, absolutely and unqualifiedly correct. (*WT* 7-15-22, p. 217)

The Society reminds its readers of a remarkable declaration it made in *The Watchtower*, January 1883, p. 425: "*The Watchtower*, the official journal of Jehovah's Witnesses, has said: 'We have not the gift of prophecy.' " (*AW* 3-22-93, p. 4) How noteworthy this is when one realizes that the organization had already begun making prophecies in 1877, and continued making prophecies and setting prophetic dates throughout its history.

NOTES

1. David A. Reed, *Behind the Watchtower Curtain* (Southbridge, Mass.: Crowne Publications, 1989)

2. Randall Watters, *Free Minds Journal*, Box 3818, Manhattan Beach, CA 90266; Witness, Inc., P.O. Box 597, Clayton, CA 94517.

3. Asking my husband about this incident several years later only resulted in his denial that it ever happened.

4. That the Watchtower Society refers to itself as "the Jeremiah class" can be seen from the following excerpt:

> Dramatically Jeremiah illustrated Jehovah's prophecy by crashing the earthenware flask at the Valley of Hinnom. By public demonstrations far greater than that, the Jeremiah class has notified Christendom of her impending doom. Take, for example, that convention at Cedar Point, Ohio, in September of 1919. There, before an audience of 10,000, the president of the Watch Tower Bible and Tract Society delivered an address in which he pointed out that the blessing of the clergy upon the then proposed League of Nations would prove fruitless. (*WT* 9-1-79, p. 19)

EIGHTEEN

PLAYING FOLLOW-THE-LEADER

Zigzagging Doctrines That Affect Lives

Next I started avidly researching the Society's history for doctrinal changes. During the years that I was a Witness, I was aware of such changes as they occurred; however, I did not have any idea of the Society's long history of numerous doctrinal modifications and switchbacks. It was only during my research that I learned the extreme degree to which the Society's teachings wavered. Noted here are only the doctrines that seriously hurt people or took their lives.

1. MAY WITNESSES ENGAGE IN ORAL SEX?

NO
(1972)

Nevertheless, if future cases of gross unnatural conduct, such as the practice of oral or anal copulation, are brought to their attention, the elders should act to try to correct the situation. . . . But if persons willfully show disrespect for Jehovah God's marital arrangements, then it becomes necessary to remove them from the congregation as dangerous 'leaven' that could contaminate others. (WT 12-1-72, p. 735)

YES
(1978)

It must be acknowledged that the Bible does not give any specific rules or limitations as regards the manner in which husband and wife engage in sexual relations. (WT 2-15-78, p. 30)

167

In the past some comments have appeared in this magazine in connection with certain unusual sex practices, such as oral sex, within marriage and these were equated with gross sexual immorality . . . in view of the absence of clear Scriptural instruction . . . these marital intimacies do not come within the province of the congregational elders to attempt to control nor to take disfellowshipping action. . . . (WT 2-15-78, pp. 30–31)

NO
(1983)

. . . perverted acts, such as oral or anal sex. . . . However, if it becomes known that a member of the congregation is practicing or openly advocating perverted sex relations within the marriage bond. . . . Such practice and advocacy could even lead to expulsion from the congregation. (WT 3-15-83, p. 31)

This was no insignificant matter. Husbands and wives were "turning each other in" to the elders and subsequently brought before judicial committees for infractions of the Society's view on this issue. Marriages were breaking up, especially marriages where one spouse was not a Witness. Breakups also occurred among Witness couples, as at one point the Society declared that oral sex practiced with one's marriage partner was such a lewd and perverted act that it constituted the basis for a scriptural divorce, with the "innocent" partner having the right to remarry (WT 11-15-74, pp. 703–704).

When the Society reversed its stand, deciding that whether or not a couple practiced oral sex was none of its business, what was done to repair the damage that their erroneous view had caused—the embarrassment, the guilt, the fear, the broken marriages, and the breach of privacy and trust suffered by many during that five years—that resulted from the Society's intruding into an area where they should not have tread? Nothing. No apologies were made to Witnesses who had been disfellowshipped over this issue, nor were they automatically reinstated back into their congregations.

Five years after the Society reversed its stand, it returned to its original position. However, this time practicing oral sex with one's marriage partner was declared no longer a basis for a scriptural divorce, even though it was still a disfellowshipping offense (WT 3-15-83, p. 31).

2. MAY WITNESSES SPEAK WITH DISFELLOWSHIPPED WITNESSES?

YES
(1919)

The brother may merely be treated in the kindly, courteous way in which it would be proper for us to treat any publican or Gentile. . . . (WT 3-1-19, p. 6397 Reprints)

NO
(1952)

Generally speaking, it would be desirable for us to have no contact with disfellowshipped persons, either in business or in social and spiritual ways. (WT 12-1-52, p. 735)

We should not see how close we can get to relatives who are disfellowshipped from Jehovah's organization, but we should "quit mixing in company" with them. (WT 7-15-63, p. 444)

Thus we have established from the Bible itself the basic position of a faithful Christian toward a disfellowshipped one—have no fellowship at all with him, not even speaking with him. (WT 6-1-70, p. 351)

In faithfulness to God, none in the congregation should greet such persons when meeting them in public nor should they welcome these into their homes. (*Organization for Kingdom-Preaching and Disciple-Making* [1972], p. 172)

YES
(1974)

Jesus' counsel about greetings, in connection with his exhortation to imitate God in his undeserved kindness toward "wicked people and good," would seem to rule against such a rigid stand. (WT 8-1-74, p. 465)

So, not "mixing in company" with a person . . . does not prevent us from being decent, courteous, considerate and humane. (WT 8-1-74, p. 468)

As to disfellowshipped family members . . . living outside the home, each family must decide to what extent they will have association with such ones. This is not something that the congregational elders can decide for them. . . . Thus, if a disfellowshipped parent goes to visit a son or daughter or to see grandchildren and is allowed to enter the Christian home, this is not the concern of the elders. Such a one has a natural right to visit his blood relatives and his offspring. (WT 8-1-74, p. 471)

NO
(1952)

Consequently, Christians related to such a disfellowshipped person living outside the home should strive to avoid needless association, even keeping business dealings to a minimum. (WT 9-15-81, p. 29)

Yes, the Bible commands Christians not to keep company or fellowship with a person who has been expelled from the congregation. (WT 9-15-81, p. 22)

I knew a sister who had shunned her disfellowshipped daughter for many years in obedience to the Society. As she told me about the reversal of this doctrine in 1974, she excitedly wrote a letter to her daughter, tears of joy streaming down her face as she did so. She and many others experienced much emotional trauma when this doctrine was again reversed seven years later in 1981, as reunited families once again divided themselves off by shunning the disfellowshipped family members and relatives who had become part of their lives. Witnesses who continued to associate with any disfellowshipped Witness were themselves expelled from the organization. (WT 9-15-81, pp. 25–26)

3. May Witnesses divorce a marriage partner who confesses he/she is gay?

NO
(1948)

When women . . . seek sexual pleasure with other women, committing masturbation among themselves, it is not the fornication for which, or adultery for which, Jesus said a husband could divorce his wife. . . . In parallel fashion, where a man commits sexual filthiness with another male, in other words, sodomy, it does not constitute the Scriptural grounds for his wife to divorce him. (WT 11-1-48, p. 336)

Sodomy . . . Lesbianism . . . are not Scriptural grounds for divorce. . . . Such filthy things by a mate may make life unbearable . . . and are grounds for separation only. . . . Such separation does not free one to remarry and enter thus into adultery. (WT 10-1-56, p. 591)

While both homosexuality and bestiality are disgusting perversions, in the case of neither one is the marriage tie broken. (WT 1-1-72, p. 32)

YES
(1972)

Any married person who goes outside the marriage bond and engages in immoral sexual relations, whether with someone of the opposite sex or someone of the same sex, whether natural or unnatural and perverted, is guilty of committing porneia *or "fornication" in the Bible sense. . . . Therefore, when a mate is guilty of such serious sexual immorality the innocent mate may Scripturally divorce such a one, if he or she so desires. One who obtains a divorce on such Scriptural grounds is also Scripturally free to remarry, not thereby being subject to a charge of adultery. (WT 12-15-72, p. 768)*

For twenty-four years, Witnesses were denied the right to divorce if their husband or wife confessed to being gay, even if that person left the marriage relationship. If a Witness did obtain a divorce on these grounds, remarriage was forbidden—if they did remarry, they were disfellowshipped for adultery, as the Society did not recognize a legal divorce on these grounds as Scripturally allowable. That the Society eventually reversed its position and allowed for divorce and remarriage under this circumstance did not change the lonely years a Witness in this situation may have endured, or the emotional stress they may have suffered as a result of the Society's misinterpretation of Scripture.

4. May Witnesses attend college or prepare for a career?

NO
(1969)

Many schools now have student counselors who encourage one to pursue higher education after high school, to pursue a career with a future in this system of things. Do not be influenced by them. Do not let them "brainwash" you with the Devil's propaganda to get ahead, to make something of yourself in this world. This world has very little time left! (WT 3-15-69, p. 171)

In view of the short time left, a decision to pursue a career in this system of things is not only unwise but extremely dangerous. (Kingdom Ministry 6/69, p. 3)

So by guiding their children away from the so-called higher education of today, these parents spare their children exposure to an increasingly demoral-

izing atmosphere, and at the same time prepare them for life in a new system as well. (AW 6-8-71, p. 8)

College education may present snares. One may become "brainwashed" by human philosophies so that faith in God and the Bible is destroyed. (WT 9-1-75, p. 543)

Going to college will lead you right out of the Truth. (elder addressing the congregation)

YES
(1992)

If Christian parents responsibly decide to provide their children with further education after high school, that is their prerogative. (WT 11-1-92, p. 20)

Suddenly the forbidden thing to do becomes the responsible thing to do! Since my own children had graduated high school before this doctrinal change, they were among the ones who were hurt by the Society's stand against college.

Prior to this change, teenagers who turned down college scholarships found themselves the center of attention at Watchtower assemblies; nearly every one featured the testimony of a young man or woman who chose to serve the organization fulltime as a pioneer, a missionary, or in Bethel service, instead of furthering their education in preparation for a career. Some of them commented that they didn't mind scrubbing toilets to support themselves, since they were confident that soon the entire "system of things" was going down the toilet! Such comments always elicited much laughter and approval from the audience. These testimonies were always met with lots of applause and were followed by remarks of praise and commendation from the speaker, as well as personal comments of encouragement from many Witnesses after the program. In fact, many toilet-scrubbers were found among the ranks of Jehovah's Witnesses, the general attitude being that the more degraded one's profession was, the more one was giving up for the Truth.

During the time I was active in the organization, I knew a young Witness woman who had just graduated from high school. She related that her father had made attending college a condition to her living at home and being financially supported by him; hearing this news, the elders encouraged her to move out of her parents' home and take up the witnessing work fulltime instead. Once her plight was made known to the congregation, an older sister offered to take her in. The young woman immediately availed herself of this "opportunity," moving out of her parents' home, quitting college, becoming a pioneer, and working parttime at a menial job to help defray her expenses.

Two other teenage sisters decided to go to college despite the Society's negative view of getting a higher education. Although they were not disfellowshipped, most of the congregation members considered them to be weak spiritually; consequently, they became the subject of gossip and found themselves socially ostracized from most of the congregation members.

Even back in 1940, the Society equated time spent getting promotions, or earning any money beyond what was absolutely needed, as time lost to Satan. (*Informant* 1-40, p. 2) Believing this type of thinking ruined many people's lives; they gave up the possibility of fulfilling careers for meaningless, low-paying jobs that provided them no retirement pension plans. Several Witnesses I knew who were in their retirement years lived at near-poverty levels, subsisting solely on Social Security checks. Because of the Society's constant emphasis on the imminence of Armageddon, they had felt no need to save money for their later years—doing so was even looked on by many Witnesses as lack of faith in the Society's prophecy of the generation of 1914 as being the marked generation that would live to see Armageddon.

5. MAY A WITNESS ACCEPT ALTERNATIVE SERVICE WORK IN LIEU OF MILITARY SERVICE?

YES
(1898)

We explain our conscientious scruples against war, and seek to be excused; if not excused, that we seek noncombatant positions as nurses, etc. . . . (WT 8-1-1898, p. 231)

AMBIVALENT
(1915)

We have been wondering since if the course we have suggested is the best one. We wonder if such a course would not mean compromise. . . . Would it be any worse to be shot because of loyalty to the Prince of Peace and refusal to disobey his order than to be shot while under the banner of these earthly kings? . . . We are not urging this course. We are merely suggesting it. The responsibility fully belongs with each individual. (WT 9-1-1915, Reprints p. 5755)

YES
(1918)

A Christian might not have been able conscientiously to engage in the military activities of a country offering only combatant service; later, when the opportunity is enlarged so that he may choose some good work such as the hospital or ambulance service, he may with a free conscience take such service. (WT 5-15-1918, p. 168; Reprints p. 6268)

NO
(1974)

It is a matter of strict neutrality. Therefore, any work that is merely a substitute for military service would be unacceptable to Jehovah's witnesses. . . . Civilian servitude as a substitute for military service would be just as objectionable to the Christian. (AW 12-8-74, p. 23)

When global conflict again erupted in 1939, Jehovah provided clear guidance . . . in the form of Bible study material entitled "Neutrality" in the November 1, 1939 issue of the Watchtower. . . . *Whether the issue was shedding blood, noncombatant military work, alternative service . . . faithful Christians took the position that there was no middle ground. In some cases they were executed because of this stand. (WT 9-1-86, p. 20)*

YES
(1996)

Many of these lands make provision for such conscientious individuals not to be forced into military service. In some places a required civilian service, such as useful work in the community, is regarded as nonmilitary national service. Could a dedicated Christian undertake such service? Here again, a dedicated, baptized Christian would have to make his own decision on the basis of his Bible-trained conscience. (WT 5-1-96, p. 19)

As I read the *Watchtower* article that contained this last change, I was horrified that no mention had been made of the Witnesses who were still imprisoned, or others whose lives had been irrevocably altered either from prison terms or from having been victims of brutalities—or who were killed—because of following the Society's mandated refusal of alternative service. I felt incensed that the Society made no apology to these people or their loved ones who were affected by their years of error regarding this matter. As I realized that the *Watchtower* article did not present this changed view in a way that would inform the reader that this was new information and a major change in doctrine, I felt rage well up within me; in fact, no mention was made that their attitude toward alternative service had ever been any different, even though countless lives had been lost or affected by this doctrine for fifty-seven years.

I personally knew several brothers whose records had been tarnished needlessly by prison terms for refusal of alternative service. As medals awarded to soldiers for their bravery in combat, however, so prison sentences were proudly brandished by Witness brothers for their refusal of military alternative service. During the time the Society prohibited acceptance of alternative noncombatant service, a brother was considered to have disassociated himself through his actions if he did accept it, and was viewed as having chosen the death penalty at God's hands in lieu of a prison sentence from the government.

6. IS IT SCRIPTURALLY PROPER FOR WITNESSES TO HAVE CHILDREN?

NO
(1938)

Would it be Scripturally proper for them to now marry and to begin to rear children? No, is the answer, which is supported by the Scriptures. (Face the Facts [1938], p. 46)

It will be far better to be unhampered and without burdens, that they may do the Lord's will now, as the Lord commands, and also be without hindrance during Armageddon. (Face the Facts [1938], p. 47)

YES
(1963)

Let it be noted, however, that at Matt. 24:19, Jesus Christ was not discussing the propriety of Christian married couples having children in these last days. Christians are not under command to have children, but neither are they under a command not to have them. This is a matter to be decided by marriage mates themselves. It is their own business. (WT 10-15-63, p. 640)

AMBIVALENT
(1974)

The circumstance that Jesus foretold proved true: 'Woe to pregnant women and the ones suckling a baby in those days!' (Luke 21:23). . . . One can be sure that flight was more difficult for delaying parents with small children. If you had been living prior to that destruction and knew of its nearness, would you have considered that a time to be having children inside the province of Judea? Today there is a great crowd of people who are confident that a destruction of even greater magnitude is now imminent. The evidence is that Jesus' prophecy will shortly have a major fulfillment, upon this entire system of things. This has been a major factor in influencing many couples to decide not to have children at this time. They have chosen to remain childless so that they would be less encumbered to carry out the instructions of Jesus Christ to preach the good news of God's kingdom Earth wide before the end of this system comes. (AW 11-8-74, p. 11)

Let it be noted, however, Jesus did not say that persons should not have children. At no time did he ever advise against childbearing. . . . So it would be improper for anyone to criticize others for having children. (AW 11-8-74, p. 11)

Interestingly, during all this pre-Flood period, Noah's sons and their wives had no children. . . . This is not to say that the course of action taken by Noah's sons and their wives before the Deluge was meant to set the rule for married couples living today. Nevertheless, since Jesus compared Noah's day to the period in which we are now living, their example can provide food for thought. (WT 3-1-88, p. 22)

It is necessary to have a balanced view of childbearing. While it can bring many joys, it can also bring many heartaches. (WT 3-1-88, p. 22)

WHY DO THEY HAVE NO CHILDREN?

Many Christian couples . . . do not have children. . . . Rather, they have determined to give their full attention to different avenues of the full-time ministry that the rearing of children would not allow. . . . Some couples . . . have decided to remain childless and consider the possibility of bearing children in Jehovah's righteous new world. (WT 8-1-2000, pp. 20–21).

Undoubtedly, the Society's 1938 injunction influenced and changed the lives of many people. In 1941, the Society published a book that told the story of a young couple in love who did not marry, based on the Society's admonition; they reasoned with each other, "We can well defer our marriage until lasting peace comes to the Earth. Now we must add nothing to our burdens, but be free and equipped to serve the Lord." (*Children,* [1941] p. 366) Armageddon did not come as expected; the couple in this story could have been married for over sixty years by now, raised a family, and possibly enjoyed grandchildren and great-grandchildren, had it not been for the Society's interference.

Evidently the Society had no conscience about how their error affected those that they influenced, because during their large conventions in 1970, they exhorted the brothers in like fashion not to marry. At that time, I was divorced from my first husband, with a two-year-old son; I had eagerly looked forward to the convention, hoping it would bring me in contact with some brothers who were seeking a wife. How discouraged, frustrated, and dismayed I felt when one of the talks at that convention urged Witnesses not to marry at this time, so close to Armageddon. I recall a sister telling me that I was living "unscripturally" by working outside the home and having various sisters babysit my young son, as the Society strongly exhorted Witness women to stay home to raise their own children. The organization, however, provided no way to make that possible for its women in my situation. It gave no financial support to destitute Witnesses or to the struggling single mothers in its ranks. And Witnesses are to marry Witnesses only; this prescript radically narrowed the pool from which one may find a marriage partner, and thus also narrowed even the opportunity to marry. And with the Society encouraging the brothers not to marry at this time, even that narrow pool was effectively eliminated!

As noted above, the Society carried on its encouragement for couples to remain childless in 1974. When Armageddon did not occur in 1975 as expected, the Society continued implying in 1988 that couples should not have children, and on into the new millennium with this same implication.

The Society's intimation for over sixty years that Witnesses should not have children has caused much heartache. I have personally heard the regrets of several elderly Witness couples who, following the Society's exhortation, postponed childbearing; they report having suffered much anguish for having given up the opportunity to raise a family. Believing the Society's prophecy about the impending Armageddon, they never planned on growing old. They now suffer considerable anxiety as they face their "golden years" alone, without the help, visitation, or support that one's children normally provide.

And some of the Witness couples I knew who did bring children into the world suffered a great deal of guilt for fulfilling their natural desire to have a family, as such couples were often the subject of much gossip by the couples who acted on the Society's admonition to defer having children. I knew several sisters who, in order to avoid criticism from other Witnesses, felt it

necessary to protest during their entire pregnancies that they had not deliberately planned to have children in this system, insisting that their having
conceived had been an unintentional "accident."

ZIGZAGGING MEDICAL DOCTRINES

The Society's habit of zigzagging their doctrines while declaring them truth
at every turn gave rise to serious life-and-death matters. At least several of
their shifting doctrines involved medical treatments, obedience to which
needlessly cost many Jehovah's Witnesses their lives. I took these changes
very seriously, feeling aghast at the way the Witnesses I knew just accepted
them gratefully as "new light" from God. That these changes were not the
result of new information from God was evident to me. They were instead
the result of the Society playing God. With horror I thought about all of the
people who died under the Society's ban on these medical treatments. With
sorrow I thought about the families that were torn apart by the needless
death of one of their members. Never once did the Society ever publicly
print an apology to these victims or show any remorse for the tragedies their
errors brought to the lives of countless people. The only consolation I ever
heard given to such ones was, "Jehovah will remember their faithfulness
and will reward them by resurrecting them back to life on a paradise Earth
with perfect bodies and perfect health." This was the soothing balm that
was applied to hurting families who lost a loved one due to the Society's
misinterpretation of Scriptures and the incorrect application of them to
medical treatments, which was supposed to excuse the Society's grave
errors—but it does *not* excuse their errors. Even the Society's doctrine of
the earthly resurrection will not reunite families, or replace the childhood
of children that deceased parents missed out on because of obedience to the
Society's medical doctrines. I can't believe that Jehovah would look with
pleasure on the Society, whose ordinances made as God's alleged "mouthpiece," cost the suffering and lives of many.

7. May Witnesses receive vaccinations?

NO
(1921)

*Use your rights as American citizens to forever abolish the devilish practice of
vaccination. (Golden Age 10-12-21, p. 17)*

Thinking people would rather have smallpox than vaccination, because the latter sows the seed of syphilis, cancers, eczema, erysipelas, scrofula, consumption, even leprosy and many other loathsome affections. Hence the practice of vaccination is a crime, an outrage and a delusion. (Golden Age 5-1-29, p. 502)

Vaccination is as effective as the totem pole, and belongs to the same era of intelligence. (Golden Age 9-17-30, p. 814)

Vaccination is a direct violation of the everlasting covenant that God made with Noah after the flood. (Golden Age 2-4-31, p. 293)

Quite likely there is some connection between the violation of human blood and the spread of demonism. (Golden Age 2-4-31, p. 293)

This plainly suggests that much of the looseness of our day along sexual lines may be traceable to the easy and continued violation of the divine commands to keep human and animal blood apart from each other. (Golden Age 2-4-31, p. 293)

Vaccination has never saved a human life. It does not prevent smallpox. (Golden Age 2-4-31, p. 294)

YES
(1952)

After consideration of the matter, it does not appear to us to be in violation of the everlasting covenant made with Noah, as set down in Gen. 9:4 ["Only flesh with its soul—its blood—you must not eat."], nor contrary to God's related commandment at Lev. 17:10–14. Most certainly it cannot reasonable or Scripturally be argued and proved that, by being vaccinated, the inoculated person is either eating or drinking blood and consuming it as food or receiving a blood transfusion. . . . Hence, all objection to vaccination on Scriptural grounds seems to be lacking. (WT 12-15-52, p. 764)

For thirty-one years, the Society spoke out loudly against the practice of vaccination. Viewing it as deliberate blood-poisoning, several of the Society's magazine's even featured cartoons derisive of vaccination; one of these referred to it as a "pus highball," as the Society believed vaccination polluted the bloodstream with pus (*Consolation*, 5-31-39, p. 5).

The Society also objected to vaccination based on the assumption that preparation of the vaccine involved the use of blood and therefore condemned the practice based on Genesis 9:4 and Leviticus 17:10–14, which prohibits the eating of blood. The Society saw no difference between literally eating blood, and receiving a vaccination that it believed was produced using blood.

As the years rolled by, however, the Society became aware of the process through which vaccines were made; learning that vaccines were not produced utilizing blood in the process, it recanted its original position and changed its extremely negative view of vaccination.

The Society had even gone so far as to print a form in one of its magazines that its followers could fill out and use as a legal document to prevent their children from receiving vaccinations (*Golden Age* 1-30-35, p. 269). That the Society's ban on vaccination caused havoc in the lives of some of its members can be seen from the following experience of a Witness who refused to allow his children to be vaccinated, resulting in conflict with secular authorities and a subsequent court trial:

> With the expense I have been put to, including six months in jail . . . I am being forced to refinance my little home. . . . I do not regret what I have been through, as I have saved many little children from being vaccinated. (*Golden Age* 6-22-32, p. 601)

When I learned all of this information, I was in a state of shock. Although I had been in the organization over twenty-three years, I had never known that the Society had ever been opposed to vaccinations; that fact had never been mentioned in any of the Society's literature since I had become associated with it. Having no access to the earlier publications, along with the fact that none of the older Witnesses ever told me about the former doctrine prohibiting vaccinations, combined with the ban against speaking with anyone who had left the organization and reading any books critical of the Watchtower Society, gave me no avenue to even be aware of this damaging teaching that undoubtedly took the lives of many Witnesses.

While doing this research, I visited a support group that served former Jehovah's Witnesses, and Witnesses who were caught in the organization's sticky web and were having difficulty getting out. There I met a woman who showed me a scar on her upper arm that she said was caused by an acid burn. She explained that bribing a doctor to produce a scar on a child's arm that mimicked the scar left from a smallpox vaccination, and then signing a certificate of vaccination to enable the child to go to school, was a common practice among the Witnesses during the years of the Society's ban on vaccinations. One can only imagine how many Witnesses or their children died of smallpox due to this practice of theocratic warfare to avoid vaccinations.

8. MAY WITNESSES ACCEPT A HUMAN ORGAN TRANSPLANT?

NO
(1967)

When there is a diseased or defective organ, the usual way health is restored is by taking in nutrients. The body uses the food eaten to repair or heal the organ, gradually replacing the cells. When men of science conclude that this normal process will no longer work and they suggest removing the organ and replacing it directly with an organ from another human, this is simply a shortcut. Those who submit to such operations are thus living off the flesh of another human. That is cannibalistic. However, in allowing man to eat animal flesh Jehovah God did not grant permission for humans to try to perpetuate their lives by cannibalistically taking into their bodies human flesh, whether chewed or in the form of whole organs or body parts taken from others. (WT 11-15-67, p. 702)

There are those, such as the Christian witnesses of Jehovah, who consider all transplants between humans as cannibalism. . . . (AW 6-8-68, p. 21)

YES
(1980)

Regarding the transplantation of human tissue or bone from one human to another, this is a matter for conscientious decision by each one of Jehovah's Witnesses. . . . While the Bible specifically forbids consuming blood, there is no biblical command pointedly forbidding the taking in of other human tissue. . . . It is a matter for personal decision. (WT 3-15-80, p. 31)

While allowing Witnesses to donate their body organs for use in scientific experimentation or for transplantation purposes in 1961 (*WT* 1961, p. 480), the Society was silent on the matter of allowing Witnesses to accept human organ transplants, although it did allow for Witnesses to make their own decisions about whether or not to accept animal organs for transplantation purposes. In 1967, however, the Society completely banned Jehovah's Witnesses from either donating or accepting human organs for transplantation. Were it simply a matter of pollution of the sacred body vessel, the solution would lie in the donor and recipient both being Witnesses. The Society, however, felt that receiving an organ transplant from anyone—be they Witnesses or not—was literally cannibalism; it deemed sustaining one's life by means of part of the body of another human, i.e., an organ transplant, to be comparable to eating human flesh (WT 11-15-67, pp. 702–703).

When the Society changed its view in 1980 to allow Witnesses to donate and receive human organ transplants, it was with the understanding that the transplantation would have to be accomplished without a blood transfusion. This could be done by infusion into the patient of various non-blood fluids such as salt solution, dextran, lactated Ringer's solution, and Hetastarch (a blood volume expander). Also, administration of a hormone called erythropoietin (EPO) can be used, which stimulates bone marrow to form red blood cells, as well as hyperbaric oxygen chambers. And surgeons can employ blood conservation methods such as electrocautery to minimize bleeding, and blood salvage techniques.

Of interest is that the Society claimed that some recipients of kidney transplants had altered personalities after the transplant and likened this phenomenon to a "personality transplant," i.e., a transplant from an aggressive donor caused a mild-tempered recipient to likewise become aggressive. The Society pointed to the Bible linking the kidneys with human emotions (Prov. 3:16) as the possible correlation (*WT* 9-1-75, p. 519).

Similarly, the Society espoused peculiar ideas about the heart, claiming that the heart is capable of thinking and reasoning; this was cited as the reason heart transplant recipients allegedly have serious mental aberrations (WT 3-1-71, pp. 133–45). A drama at the "Divine Name" district convention, held in a very large baseball stadium during the summer of 1971, made an indelible impression on my mind. The Society erected on the baseball field huge models of a brain and a heart that talked to each other, glowing vividly against the backdrop of the black night sky. The heart pulsated bright red as it argued with the mind all the emotional reasons for wanting to take a certain course. Then the brain, flashing brilliant white light as it spoke back, argued intellectually against the unwise course. The effect was spectacular as the heart and the mind bantered back and forth, carrying the message that the heart is treacherous and is not to be trusted, and that one needs to fortify one's mind with accurate knowledge from the Bible in order for it to prevail over the heart.

The Society's insistence that the Bible does not speak of a symbolic or spiritual heart in contradistinction from the literal heart (*WT* 3-1-71, p. 134) was changed in 1984. It did a complete turnabout by announcing there is indeed a clear distinction between a fleshly heart and a figurative heart; and further, that the functions and capabilities they had previously ascribed to the fleshly heart are actually not so (*WT* 9-1-84, p. 6). I was embarrassed as I remembered the Society's dramatic portrayal of the heart and mind that had previously left me in awe.

For nearly twelve years, the Society forbid potentially lifesaving organ transplants for Jehovah's Witnesses. One sister I knew, who died while a young woman from kidney failure, might have lived if she had undergone a kidney transplant. What of the suffering from Witnesses who went blind because of obedience to the Society in refusing a cornea transplant? What of the many Witnesses who did, whose lives might have been much longer had it not been for the Society forcing its opinion about organ transplants on others? What of the Witness families who suffered from the death of beloved family members due to the Society's mistake? Not one word of apology was given to those adversely affected.

9. MAY WITNESSES RECEIVE A BLOOD TRANSFUSION?

NO
(1948)

According to God's law, humans are not to take into their system the blood of others. (AW 10-22-48, p. 12)

Is it wrong to sustain life by administering a transfusion of blood or plasma or red cells or others of the component parts of the blood? Yes! The law God gave to Noah made it unlawful for anyone to eat blood, that is, to use it for nourishment or to sustain life. Since this is wrong in the case of animal blood, it is even more reprehensible in the case of human blood. The prohibition includes "any blood at all." (Leviticus 3:17) (Blood, Medicine and the Law of God [1961], pp. 13, 14)

According to the law of Moses, which set forth shadows of things to come, the receiver of a blood transfusion must be cut off from God's people by excommunication or disfellowshipping. (WT 1-15-61, p. 64)

There are basically two reasons why Jehovah's Witnesses do not accept blood transfusions:

1. Because the Society contends that God stated that blood represents life, which is a gift from Him; thus blood removed from an animal could only be used in sacrifice, such as on the altar. Otherwise, blood removed from an animal—and, by extension, blood removed from a human—was to be poured onto the ground, in a sense giving it back to God (WT 10-15-92, p. 30).
2. The Society points to the early history of humankind as recorded in

the Old Testament at Genesis 9:3–4, where God ruled that humans should not eat blood: "Only flesh with its soul—its blood—you must not eat." They point also to the New Testament at Acts 15:29 as reaffirming this rule for Christians: ". . . keep abstaining from . . . blood. . . . If you carefully keep yourselves from these things, you will prosper." Jehovah's Witnesses are not prohibited from accepting blood transfusions because they want to keep themselves pure from the blood of non-Witnesses for the final days. They are prohibited from accepting *anyone's* blood because of this scriptural injunction.

The Society feels that accepting a blood transfusion violates God's rule on the prohibition against eating blood; it equates accepting a blood transfusion with eating blood through the following rationale:

Many say receiving a transfusion is not like eating blood. Is this view sound? A patient in the hospital may be fed through the mouth, through the nose, or though the veins. When sugar solutions are given intravenously, it is called intravenous feeding. So the hospital's own terminology recognizes as feeding the process of putting nutrition into one's system via the veins. Hence the attendant administering the transfusion is feeding the patient blood through the veins, and the patient receiving it is eating it through his veins. (*WT* 7-1-51, p. 415)

Some persons may reason that getting a blood transfusion is not actually eating. But is it not true that when a patient is unable to eat through his mouth, doctors often feed him by the same method in which a blood transfusion is administered? Examine the scriptures carefully and notice that they tell us to *keep free* from blood and to *abstain* from blood. (Acts 15:20, 29) What does this mean? If a doctor were to tell you to abstain from alcohol, would that mean simply that you should not take it through your mouth but that you could transfuse it directly into your veins? Of course not! So, too, abstaining from blood means not taking it into our bodies at all. (*WT* 6-1-69, pp. 326–27)

This is the explanation I gave householders during all the years that I participated in the Witness preaching work. It wasn't until 1991, when I became inactive, that I began to reason that a blood transfusion was more like an organ transplant than it was like a meal! And further, the Society's analogy is not legitimate because alcohol and blood are very different fluids. Alcohol is already in a form that can be utilized by the body's cells and absorbed as a food, but blood is entirely different in that after it is transfused, it is not digested or utilized as a food, but remains a fluid tissue. So two separate bodily systems are involved; a blood transfusion involves the circulatory system, whereas food that is eaten involves the digestive system. The Society fails to recognize that blood is the engine oil of the body; the only way blood could be used by the body as a food is if it were actually swallowed, traveling through the digestive tract.

The cover of the May 22, 1994 *Awake!* magazine is filled with the photographs of beautiful children and young adults; the inside cover explains who they are and the significance of their photos:

YOUTHS WHO PUT GOD FIRST

> In former times thousands of youths died for putting God first. They are still doing it, only today the drama is played out in hospitals and courtrooms, with blood transfusions the issue. (*WT* 5-22-94, p. 2)

The next thirteen pages are devoted to the stories of some of these youths, and how they "put God first" by refusing a blood transfusion, which led all of them to an early grave. Sadly, they are but a small fraction of the young people who have died because of the Society's doctrine banning blood transfusions. Ironically, during my many years at the Kingdom Hall, the brothers would often quote from the book of Jeremiah 32:35; they explained that this verse refers to the ancient people of Israel and Judah who offered up their children as burnt sacrifices to false gods, and how God condemned this practice by declaring, ". . . a thing that I did not command them, neither did it come up into my heart to do this detestable thing. . . ." (*New World Translation*) Failing to see the parallel, Jehovah's Witnesses in modern times seemingly offer up their own children as sacrifices to Jehovah by refusing them lifesaving blood transfusions—even to the extent of kidnapping them from their hospital beds to avoid court-ordered transfusions, despite the possibility that this action may make the Witness parent liable to prosecution by the authorities; if punishment from such action results, they view it as "suffering for the sake of righteousness." (*WT* 6-15-91, p. 31) To understand why a Witness parent would do this, one must realize that a Witness's accepting a blood transfusion is much more than just committing a sin; it is literally a life-or-death choice.

> Little do men in general appreciate today that they are under the Creator's law concerning blood and that they will be punished for violating its sacredness. It is no light punishment, but it will call for their very life. (*WT* 11-1-59, p. 645)

> Realistically viewed, resorting to blood transfusions even under the most extreme circumstances is not truly lifesaving. It may result in the immediate and very temporary prolongation of life, but that at the cost of eternal life for a dedicated Christian. Then again, it may bring sudden death, and that forever. (*Blood, Medicine, and The Law of God* [1961], p. 55)

> Jehovah's witnesses do not reject blood for their children due to any lack of parental love. . . . They know that if they violate God's law on blood and the child dies in the process, they have endangered that child's opportunity for everlasting life in God's new world. (*Blood, Medicine, and The Law of God* [1961], p. 54)

Like dangling a carrot before the nose of a rabbit to keep him running, the reward of living on a paradise Earth under God's world government is literally what keeps Witnesses going. They believe that accepting a blood transfusion for themselves or their children would cause them to lose that reward. Thus, they prefer death in the present in order to retain the possibility of receiving that reward in the future, hoping that Jehovah will find them worthy to resurrect back to life in a perfect human body to live forever in paradise on Earth. The extent to which Witness parents have gone to indoctrinate this belief into their children can be seen by the reaction of a Witness girl to the possibility of having a blood transfusion forced on her by the court. She adamantly declared that if an attempt was made to transfuse her with blood, she would scream and struggle and fight it with all the strength she could muster, and further, she would pull the injecting device out of her arm and would attempt to destroy the blood in the bag over her bed (*WT* 6-15-91, p. 17). This account was discussed during a meeting at the Kingdom Hall shortly after it was printed in the *Watchtower*. The brothers praised this girl's determination to avoid a blood transfusion, lauding how strenuously she resisted it, and she was held up to the youth in the congregation as a fine example for them to imitate.

The Society maintains that forcing a blood transfusion on a Witness (as in a court-ordered transfusion) is equivalent to battery, a civil wrong, and a trespass to the person (*AW* 9-8-64, p. 25). They even go so far as to liken it to rape, as the Society teaches, "And since the Bible puts abstaining from blood on the same moral level as avoiding fornication, to force blood on a Christian would be the equivalent of forcible sex—rape." (*How Can Blood Save Your Life?* [1990], p. 20). In an effort to protect Witnesses from this assault, the Society has recommended, "When there is a crisis, elders may consider it advisable to arrange a twenty-four-hour watch at the hospital, preferably by an elder with the patient's parent or another close family member. Blood transfusions often are given when all relatives and friends have gone home for the night." (*Kingdom Ministry* 9-92, p. 4)

Similar to soldiers who die on the battlefield, whom patriotic citizens view as having honorably given up their lives for their country, Jehovah's Witnesses who die due to refusal of blood transfusions are considered to have died honorable deaths, having given up their lives for God. Some Witnesses I knew looked upon such deceased ones with envy, as they had proven their faith unto death—which, Witnesses generally believe, guarantees them a ticket to paradise, with the bonus of avoiding the ordeal of having to go through Armageddon.

The Watchtower Society declares, " . . . our Maker forbids the use of blood to sustain life" (*WT* 1-15-95, p. 6). In making this statement, however, the Society is overlooking the fact that the function of blood *is* to sustain life! Another example of the Society's illogical reasoning about blood transfusions is that although they have allowed Witnesses to have organ transplants since 1980, and although they have referred to a blood transfusion as an organ transplant (*Jehovah's Witnesses and The Question of Blood* [1977], p. 41), still they staunchly deny Witnesses blood transfusions. They have even allowed bone marrow transplants (*WT* 5-15-84, p. 31), from which red blood cells originate, yet they do not allow Witnesses to accept a transfusion of red blood cells (*Journal of the American Medical Association* 11-27-81, Vol. 246, No.21, pp. 2471–72). Further, the Society realizes that the marrow that is withdrawn from live donors used in bone marrow transplants may have some whole blood with it—and they allow this, even though the blood obviously contains red blood cells—yet they deny Witnesses to accept transfusions of red blood cells.

While a Witness, I always carried in my wallet a card supplied by the Watchtower Society, which functioned as a legal document to ensure that no blood would be given me should I be found unconscious as a result of an accident. The Society provided new cards for Jehovah's Witnesses annually, and time was taken at the Kingdom Hall meeting for all to fill them out and have one of the elders sign them. In addition, the brothers in my congregation strongly encouraged Witness parents to obtain identification bracelets for their minor children, engraved with the directive, "No blood to be given in any form."

Instruction from the brothers in my Kingdom Hall for teaching potential converts included the admonition, "Save the blood doctrine for last; your Bible students will be more receptive to it after they have developed an appreciation for the Truth." Introducing the Society's mandate forbidding blood transfusions too early to a person who was newly studying with the Witnesses was considered a cause for "stumbling that person out of the Truth," i.e., they might become alarmed and drop their study with the Witnesses. Now, however, I can easily see that the real reason the blood issue was not presented to newly interested ones right away was because they needed time to associate with the Witnesses long enough to come under the mind control of the Society before they could accept a doctrine that might cost them their own lives or the lives of their children. Of interest is a statement in the Society's *Awake!* magazine: "Nor is the blood issue an organizational dictum but rather a heartfelt personal belief" (*AW* 3-22-95, p. 19). That statement is not true. The blood issue *has* been an organizational dictum since 1961. This can be seen by the following decree set forth in the *Watchtower* magazine:

> According to the law of Moses, which set forth shadows of things to come, the receiver of a blood transfusion must be cut off from God's people by excommunication or disfellowshipping. (*WT* 1-15-61, p. 64)

Because the action of accepting a blood transfusion carried with it the severe punishment of being ousted from the organization, it has indeed been an organizational dictum ever since it was declared to be a disfellowshipping offense on January 15, 1961, in the *Watchtower* magazine. On June 14, 2000, however, the Society's Public Affairs Office released an official statement to the media in an effort to make it appear to no longer be an organizational dictum. By announcing that the Watchtower Society will no longer disfellowship Witnesses who accept blood, the appearance is given that there is no Watchtower policy banning its members from receiving blood transfusions, which is a gross misrepresentation.

> If a baptized member of the faith willfully and without regret accepts blood transfusions, he indicates by his own actions that he no longer wishes to be one of Jehovah's Witnesses. The individual revokes his own membership by his own actions, rather than the congregation initiating this step. This represents a procedural change instituted in April 2000 in which the congregation no longer initiates the action to revoke membership in such cases. However, the end result is the same: the individual is no longer viewed as one of Jehovah's Witnesses because he no longer accepts and follows a core tenet of the faith. (Jehovah's Witnesses Public Affairs Office *Statement to the Media* 6-14-2000)

So while the Society allows the public to think that taking blood is not a disfellowshipping offense, the fact remains that Witnesses are not free to accept blood without dire repercussions—they will still be shunned. There is no difference in the way the Society and fellow Witnesses treat a disfellowshipped person or one who has disassociated himself.

Although the Society claims it no longer initiates the action to remove from the organization a Witness who accepts a blood transfusion—in reality it still does—through its interpretation of what it means for a Witness to accept a blood transfusion. A Witness may disagree with the Society's prohibition of accepting blood; however, he may still want to be a Witness, and may have no intention of disassociating himself from the organization even though he may have a blood transfusion. So the action is still coming from the Society through its choice to label him "disassociated."

The Watchtower Society's Website on October 23, 2000, contained information from the Public Affairs Office of Jehovah's Witnesses discussing medical care and the beliefs of Jehovah's Witnesses, which proclaimed, "The type of medical treatment selected is a matter of personal choice." This is a deceptive declaration, since the statement to the media quoted above shows that if a Witness's personal choice is to accept a blood transfusion, the Society will no longer view that person as one of Jehovah's Witnesses. A true "personal choice" would carry with it no such punitive measure. This statement also deceives in that it leads one to think that Witnesses have always had the freedom to choose the type of medical treatment they want; that this is not true is clearly demonstrated in this chapter.

10. MAY A DOCTOR WHO IS ONE OF JEHOVAH'S WITNESSES GIVE A BLOOD TRANSFUSION TO A PATIENT WHO IS NOT ONE OF JEHOVAH'S WITNESSES?

YES
(1964)

In harmony with Deuteronomy 14:21, the administering of blood upon request to worldly persons is left to the Christian doctor's own conscience. (WT 11-15-64, p. 683)

NO
(1975)

Also, if one were a doctor responsible for the decision, one could not order a blood transfusion for a patient. . . . (WT 4-1-75, p. 215)

11. MAY WITNESSES ACCEPT SERUM INJECTIONS SUCH AS ARE USED TO FIGHT AGAINST TETANUS, DIPHTHERIA, HEPATITIS, RABIES, BOTULISM FOOD POISONING, SNAKEBITES, AND SPIDER BITES?

NO
(1931)

The blood of man is sacred. It may not be polluted by . . . the insidious method of serums. (Golden Age 2-4-31, p. 291)

YES
(1958)

The injection of antibodies into the blood in a vehicle of blood serum . . . is not the same as taking blood, either by mouth or by transfusion. . . . It would therefore be a matter of individual judgment whether one accepted such types of medication or not. (WT 9-15-58, p. 575)

AMBIVALENT
(1961)

The entire modern medical practice involving the use of blood is objectionable from the Christian standpoint. . . . As to the use of vaccines and other substances that may in some way involve the use of blood in their preparation, it should not be concluded that the Watch Tower Society endorses these and says that the practice is right and proper. . . . It would therefore be a matter of individual judgment whether one accepted such types of medication or not. (WT 11-1-61, p. 670)

NO
(1963)

As to blood transfusions . . . this is an unscriptural practice . . . it is not just whole blood but anything that is derived from blood and used to sustain life or strengthen one that comes under this principle. (WT 2-15-63, p. 124)

AMBIVALENT
(1964)

The Society does not endorse any of the modern medical uses of blood, such as the uses of blood in connection with inoculations. Inoculation is, however, a virtually unavoidable circumstance in some segments of society, and so we leave it up to the conscience of the individual to determine whether to submit to inoculation with a serum. . . . (WT 11-15-64, p. 682)

The fact that serums are made from blood makes them undesirable to Christians because of the Biblical law against the use of blood. However . . . their use is a matter that must be decided by each person according to his conscience. (AW 8-22-65, p. 18)

YES
(1978)

What, however, about accepting serum injections to fight against disease . . . ? This seems to fall into a "gray area." . . . Hence, we have taken the position that this question must be resolved by each individual on a personal basis. (WT 6-15-78, pp. 30-31)

While finally leaving the decision as to whether one will or will not accept serum injections up to the individual, the Society nevertheless exerted a lot of pressure on the Witnesses to refuse them by repeatedly stating their opinion against them for many years, as noted above. When one considers that Witnesses believe the Society's view that they must respond to the Society's directions as they would to the voice of God Himself, one can understand how difficult it is for Witnesses to make a truly independent decision based solely on their own conscience. Because of believing the elevated claims the Society makes for themselves, Witnesses have extraordinary difficulty making a decision different from the opinion of the Society, even though at times they ostensibly have the freedom to do so.

This point is illustrated by an incident that happened to me in 1974. I had been cleaning our bathroom and found I couldn't reach the dusty window ledge above the bathtub, so I stood on the edge of the tub to give myself a boost. My rubber-soled shoes slid on the wet edge of the tub; I suffered a broken nose and a nasty gash near my eye from falling against the faucet. Dazed, I called my husband. Unable to get away from work to help me, he called a sister from the congregation who lived nearby to take me to the hospital.

As the emergency room doctor stitched my wound, he gave me a tetanus shot. Afterward, when the sister asked me what treatments I had received, I told her about the tetanus shot; she was appalled that I didn't refuse the injection, repeatedly insisting how wrong it was for me to have accepted it. This sister, who was older than I and in the organization for a much longer time, was evidently still under the influence of the Society's many years of expressing its negative opinion about the use of serum injections. Still, her insistence that Jehovah did not approve of my taking the injection caused me emotional upset and worry, especially because Armageddon was believed to be only a year away—I feared accepting the tetanus shot might cost me Jehovah's protection at Armageddon.

12. May Witness hemophiliacs receive injections containing a blood-clotting factor such as factor VIII, to control against fatal bleeding?

NO
(1961)

The receiver of a blood transfusion must be cut off from God's people by excommunication or disfellowshipping. (WT 1-15-61, p. 64)

(NOTE: The blood-clotting factor came under this prohibition since it is contained in blood, and the taking in of blood in any form was forbidden.)

Certain clotting "factors" derived from blood are now in wide use for the treatment of hemophilia, a disorder causing uncontrollable bleeding. . . . Of course, true Christians do not use this potentially dangerous treatment, heeding the Bible's command to "abstain from blood"—Acts 15:20, 28, 29. (AW 2-22-75, p. 30)

YES
(1978)

What, however, about accepting serum injections to fight against disease, such as are employed for . . . hemophilia . . . ? This seems to fall into a "gray area." . . . Hence, we have taken the position that this question must be resolved by each individual on a personal basis. (WT 6-15-78, pp. 30-31)

The Governing Body, a prestigious group numbering between approximately eleven and seventeen "anointed" brothers (most of whom are quite elderly), residing at Watchtower headquarters in New York City, is responsible for all changes to doctrine. Ostensibly these men pray together, and Jehovah directs them what to do, i.e., in His due time, God causes the Governing Body to realize if a doctrine needs to be changed, and what changes should be made. These changes are then attributed to "new light" from God. Past doctrines that are discarded are commonly depicted as "God's will for that time" instead of as mistakes. As these men die off, the remaining members of the group decide what exemplary elder they will invite to be part of the

Governing Body. Some of the changes in doctrine are triggered by the letters of the Witnesses themselves written to the Society. If many letters are received asking the same question about a particular doctrine, the Governing Body will discuss the matter and decide if a change should be made; any changes are made known through the *Watchtower* magazine.

The Society did not take responsibility for the suffering caused to families who had lost a beloved father, brother, son, or husband due to bleeding to death because of its previous view on this issue. When this change finally did appear in the *Watchtower*, a point was not even made of it—in fact, no mention was made that this was a change from the previous policy! Instead, this important change was obscured in a "Questions from Readers" column about serum injections used to fight against disease—inappropriate, since hemophilia is not a disease, but a hereditary defect.

Witnesses believe that the Bible's injunction to "abstain from blood" includes not eating blood; thus, a Witness wrote to the Society expressing concern about eating meat, as it may naturally contain blood fractions. The Society's response was:

> There may remain in the meat some very small amounts of blood even after proper bleeding has been done. . . . The important thing is that respect has been shown for the sanctity of blood, regard has been shown for the principle of the sacredness of life. (*WT* 11-1-61, p. 669)

I was enraged that the Society's concern about showing regard for the principle of the sacredness of life in connection with meat being properly bled before eating it, was so inconsistent with their disregard for the principle of the sacredness of life in connection with the lives of hemophiliac victims to whom they denied a blood fraction to prevent them from bleeding to death, and others who needed blood derivatives to survive surgery or other medical treatments.

This issue becomes even more unconscionable when one considers that by the time the Society printed its statement in the *Awake!* magazine (*AW* 2-22-75, p. 30) denying injections of the blood clotting factor for hemophiliacs—which is a blood fraction—the Society had already ten years previously printed an article in the *Awake!* magazine explaining its decision to permit Witnesses to make their own choice whether or not to accept serum injections containing blood fractions! (*AW* 8-22-65, p. 18) Yet because hemophiliacs required ongoing injections of the blood fractions to control against fatal bleeding, the Society treated them differently. Ray Franz, former member of the Watchtower Society's Governing Body, reports:

For many years inquiries sent by hemophiliacs to the headquarters organization (or its Branch Offices) received the reply that to accept such blood fraction *one time* could be viewed as not objectionable, as, in effect, "medication." But to do so *more than once* would constitute a "feeding" on such blood fraction and therefore be considered a violation of the Scriptural injunction against eating blood.[1]

Mr. Franz relates that although this change in policy was made official at the June 11, 1975, session of the Governing Body, it was not until June 15, 1978, that the change was put into print[2]; one can only imagine how many lives were lost in the interim.

During the years when the lifesaving blood-clotting factor was being denied to hemophiliacs, the Society came up with an alternative solution in a small blurb in their *Awake!* magazine. Fear not, brothers—peanuts could be the answer!

American scientist H. Bruce Boudreaux, a victim of hemophilia, in which disease the blood does not clot, suddenly noticed that his condition had greatly improved; seeking the cause, he found that it was due to his having eaten many peanuts. Experiments with other hemophiliacs corroborated his findings. (AW 11-22-65, p. 19)

13. MAY WITNESSES ACCEPT TREATMENTS INVOLVING BLOOD FRACTIONS?

NO
(1956)
While this physician argues for the use of certain blood fractions, particularly albumin, such also come under the Scriptural ban. (AW 9-8-56, p. 20)

YES
(1958)
[T]he use of blood fractions to create . . . antibodies is not the same as taking blood either by mouth or by transfusion. . . . While God did not intend for man to contaminate his blood stream by . . . blood fractions, doing so does not seem to be included in God's expressed will forbidding blood as food. It would therefore be a matter of individual judgment whether one accepted such types of medication or not. (WT 9-15-58, p. 575)

NO
(1961)

Is God's law violated by such medical use of blood? Is it wrong to sustain life by infusions of . . . the various blood fractions? Yes! (WT 9-15-61, p. 558)

Jehovah's witnesses will not . . . in medical use consent to . . . an infusion of any blood fraction. . . . (Blood, Medicine, and the Law of God, [1961] p. 39)

AMBIVALENT
(1961)

The infusing of some blood fraction to sustain one's life is wrong. . . . As to the use of . . . substances that may in some way involve the use of blood in their preparation. . . . It would therefore be a matter of individual judgment whether one accepted such types of medication or not. . . . However, the mature Christian is not going to try to find in this a justification for as many other medical uses of blood substances as possible. To the contrary, recognizing the objectionableness of the entire practice, he is going to stay as far away from it as he can. . . . (WT 11-1-61, p. 670)

NO
(1963)

As to blood transfusions, he knows from his study of the Bible and the publications of the Watch Tower Society that this is an unscriptural practice. . . . He need only ask the doctor . . . "Where did you get this substance?" If the answer is "Blood," he knows what course to take, for it is not just whole blood but anything that is derived from blood and used to sustain life or strengthen one that comes under this principle. (WT 2-15-63, p. 124)

AMBIVALENT
(1964)

The Society does not endorse any of the modern medical uses of blood, such as the uses of blood in connection with inoculations. . . . we leave it up to the conscience of the individual to determine whether to submit to inoculation with a serum containing blood fractions. . . . (WT 11-15-64, p. 682)

NO
(1965)

As for prevention of the Rh threat to childbirth . . . there are reports of prevention having been realized by means of the use of Rh-positive haptens. These haptens are a blood fraction. . . . Those using this method have reported perfect results. However, this involves the use of blood fractions, which is objectionable on Scriptural grounds. (AW 4-8-65, p. 18)

AMBIVALENT
(1974)

As initially stated, out of full respect for what the Bible says about blood, we refrain from endorsing any use of it outside the body of the animal or human to whom it naturally belongs. We believe that the use of . . . a blood component . . . is obviously in conflict with the Scriptural command to "abstain . . . from blood." . . . What, then, of the use of a serum containing only a minute fraction of blood . . . ? We believe that here the conscience of each Christian must decide. (WT 6-1-74, p. 352)

NO
(1975)

Certain clotting "factors" [fractions] derived from blood are now in wide use for the treatment of hemophilia, a disorder causing uncontrollable bleeding. . . . Of course, true Christians do not use this potentially dangerous treatment, heeding the Bible's command to "abstain from blood." (AW 2-22-75, p. 30)

YES
(1975)

What, however, about accepting serum injections . . . ? This seems to fall into a "gray area." . . . accepting a small amount of a blood derivative [fraction] for such a purpose . . . we have taken the position that this question must be resolved by each individual on a personal basis. (WT 6-15-78, pp. 30–31)

AMBIVALENT
(1982)
BLOOD PLASMA IS NOT ALLOWED

While these verses [Gen. 9:3-4; Lev. 17:13-14;Acts 15:19-21] are not stated in medical terms, Witnesses view them as ruling out transfusion of whole blood, packed RBCs [red blood cells], and plasma as well as WBC [white blood cells] and platelet administration. (AW 6-22-82, p. 25)

COMPONENTS OF BLOOD PLASMA ARE ALLOWED

However, Witnesses' religious understanding does not absolutely prohibit the use of components such as albumin, immune globulins, and hemophiliac preparations [fibrinogens]; each Witness much decide individually if he can accept these. (AW 6-22-82, p. 25)

YES
(1990)
(Fractions of plasma only)

Q. *Do Jehovah's Witnesses accept injections of a blood fraction such as immune globulin or albumin?*

A. *A common issue involves the plasma proteins . . . globulins, albumin, and fibrinogen. . . . A pregnant woman has an active mechanism by which some immune globulin moves from the mother's blood to the fetus. . . . That some protein fractions from the plasma do move naturally into the blood system of another individual (the fetus) may be another consideration when a Christian is deciding whether he will accept immune globulin, albumin, or similar injections of plasma fractions. . . . Each must resolve the matter personally before God. (WT 6-1-90, pp. 30, 31)*

YES
(2000)
(Fractions of any component of blood)

Just as blood plasma can be a source of various fractions, the other primary components (red cells, white cells, platelets*) can be processed to isolate smaller parts. For example, white blood cells may be a source of interferons†️ and interleukins†️, used to treat some viral infections and cancers. Platelets can be processed to extract a wound healing factor. And other medicines are coming along that involve (at least initially) extracts from blood components. Such therapies are not transfusions of those primary components; they usually involve parts or fractions thereof. Should Christians accept these fractions in medical treatment? We cannot say. The Bible does not give details, so a Christian must make his own conscientious decision before God. (WT 6-15-2000, p. 30)

I noticed an astonishing contradiction in two of the quoted statements; in essence, the Society was allowing the use of blood fractions *to prevent a disease*, to create antibodies (*WT* 9-15-58, p. 575)—but was not allowing the use of blood fractions *to prevent a death*, as they do not allow their use to sustain a life (*WT* 11-1-61, p. 670).

Amazingly, the Society spoke out of both sides of its mouth at the same

---

*A component of blood that is small, colorless, and disk-shaped, that plays an important role in the blood-clotting process. Platelets constitute a tiny percentage of blood volume (about .17 percent).

†️Fractions of white blood cells, used for treatment of some viral infections and cancer.

time, as in the same paragraph of an article they wrote about blood therapy, they both *disallow* transfusions of blood plasma *while allowing* transfusions of the separate components of blood plasma! (*AW* 6-22-82, p. 25)

While the Society still holds that transfusing whole blood or any of the four primary components of blood—red cells, white cells, platelets, or plasma—violates God's law and are thus unacceptable for Jehovah's Witnesses, they did announce a significant change to their blood policy in the June 15, 2000 *Watchtower* magazine by permitting Witnesses to accept medical treatments utilizing fractions extracted from *any* of the primary components of blood, i.e., not only from plasma, but now also fractions of white blood cells, red blood cells, and platelets. This new policy will likely be a boon to Jehovah's Witnesses, as new products from the medical field make use of hemoglobin, the oxygen-carrying fraction of red blood cells; Witnesses will be able to take advantage of these treatments, and likely many lives now lost annually because of the Society's blood transfusion prohibition will then be saved. One such development is Hemopure®, a highly purified oxygen-carrying hemoglobin solution made from fractionated bovine (cow) blood manufactured by Biopure Corporation. The Society's new policy, however, does not absolve the Society for the thousands of deaths that have occurred due to their prohibition of blood transfusions and their zigzagging views about blood fractions.

Even though Jehovah's Witnesses may avail themselves of the blood stored in blood banks by receiving the various fractions of blood into which whole blood had been separated, they may not help replace that blood so that others may likewise be helped. One of the reasons the Society prohibits Witnesses from donating blood is explained in a booklet produced by the Society, which states, "We cannot drain from our body part of that blood, which represents our life, and still love God with our whole soul, because we have taken away part of 'our soul—our blood—'and given it to someone else." (*Blood, Medicine, and The Law of God* [1961], p. 8) The other reason is that the Society maintains, "The Bible shows that blood is not to be taken out of a body, stored, and then later reused." (*AW* 4-8-72, p. 30) They insist that once blood has left a person's body, it is to be poured out onto the ground. This, however, is clearly inconsistent with their allowing Witnesses to accept blood fractions which have been stored.

14. MAY WITNESSES ACCEPT AN AUTOLOGOUS BLOOD TRANSFUSION? (I.E., MAY A WITNESS HAVE SOME OF HIS BLOOD WITHDRAWN AND STORED, FOR THE PURPOSE OF TRANSFUSION BACK INTO HIMSELF DURING A FUTURE SURGERY?)

NO
(1961)

Mature Christians . . . are not going to feel that if they have some of their own blood stored for transfusion, it is going to be more acceptable than the blood of another person. They know that God required that shed blood be poured out on the ground. Nor are they going to feel that a slight infraction, such as momentary storage of blood in a syringe when it is drawn from one part of the body for injection into another part, is somehow less objectionable than storing it for a longer period of time. (Blood, Medicine and the Law of God [1961], pp. 14–15)

How was blood to be dealt with under the Law if it was not used in sacrifice? We read that when a hunter killed an animal for food, "he must in that case pour its blood out and cover it with dust." (Leviticus 17:13, 14; Deuteronomy 12:22–24) So the blood was not to be used for nutrition or otherwise. If taken from a creature and not used in sacrifice, it was to be disposed of on the Earth, God's footstool.—Isaiah 66:1; compare Ezekiel 24:7, 8

This clearly rules out one common use of autologous blood– preoperative collection, storage, and later infusion of a patient's own blood. (WT 3-1-89, p. 30)

Witnesses believe that blood removed from the body should be disposed of, so they do not accept autotransfusion of predeposited blood. (Journal of the American Medical Association, 11-27-81, Vol. 246, No. 21, pp. 2471, 2472)

AMBIVALENT
(2000)
"Questions From Readers"

Q. *In the light of Bible commands about the proper use of blood, how do Jehovah's Witnesses view medical procedures using one's own blood? (WT 10-15-2000, p. 30)*

A. *. . . [I]t is a matter between him and Jehovah. . . . Occasionally, a doctor will urge a patient to deposit his own blood weeks before surgery (pre-operative autologous blood donation, or PAD) so that if the need arises, he could* *transfuse the patient with his own stored blood. However, such collecting, storing, and transfusing of blood directly contradicts what is said in Leviticus and Deuteronomy. Blood is not to be stored; it is to be poured out—returned to God, as it were. Granted, the Mosaic Law is not in force now. Nevertheless, Jehovah's Witnesses respect the principles God included in it, and they are determined to 'abstain from blood.' Hence, we do not donate blood, nor do we store for transfusion our blood that should be "poured out." That practice conflicts with God's law. . . . The details may vary, and new procedures, treatments, and tests will certainly be developed. It is not our place to analyze each variation and render a decision. A Christian must decide for himself how his own blood will be handled in the course of a surgical procedure, medical test, or current therapy. Ahead of time, he should obtain from the doctor or technician the facts about what might be done with his blood during the procedure. Then he must decide according to what his conscience permits. (WT 10-15-2000, pp. 30-31)*

For the past forty years, Jehovah's Witnesses have not been allowed to have their own blood drawn and stored in preparation for operations they may undergo, for the purpose of subsequent transfusion back into themselves during surgery. This prohibition of autologous blood transfusion—which is based on the premise that the Bible forbids the storage of blood—is clearly inconsistent with the fact that since 1982, Witnesses could accept transfusions of components of blood plasma which had been stored. The June 15, 2000, *Watchtower* points out that the other primary components of blood (red cells, white cells, and platelets) can be processed to isolate smaller parts—and since that date have allowed Witnesses to decide for themselves whether to accept medical therapies that make use of these blood fractions—even though such processing of blood requires the storage of the blood as well as of the resultant blood fractions. Further, the Society has permitted Witness hemophiliacs since 1978 to accept injections of Factor VIII, a blood-clotting factor to control against fatal bleeding; the Society itself points out that each batch of Factor VIII is made from plasma that is pooled from as many as 2,500 blood donors (*WT* 6-15-85, p. 30)—obviously requiring a great deal of stored blood—as well as storage of the isolated Factor VIII. One can easily see the Society is contradicting itself in a grave way by telling Jehovah's Witnesses they cannot store their own blood temporarily for use during their own surgery. One can well imagine the numbers of lives lost to this illogical doctrine. Further, the Society's argument against storage of one's blood for later use during one's surgery derives from a requirement in the Law of Moses that blood from an animal that had been hunted and killed be poured out (Deut. 12:22–27). Obedience demonstrated that a person understood that the animal's life had come from God. One might wonder how this rule could apply to autologous blood transfusions, since no one has died. The blood is put back into the person from whom it was taken.

The quotation from the *Watchtower* (10-15-2000, pp. 30–31) cited above is itself a paradox. The Society begins its answer to the question of how Jehovah's Witnesses view medical procedures using one's own blood by stating that this is a matter between the individual Witness and Jehovah. Subsequently, however, it delves into detail about various medical procedures, and singles out autologous blood transfusion as a practice that conflicts with God's law—that Jehovah's Witnesses do not store for later transfusion back into themselves their withdrawn blood that should be "poured out." At the end of the article, however, it puts the decision for how one's own blood is to be used regarding surgical procedure, medical testing, or any current therapy, back into the lap of each Witness to decide for himself. From the way this article is written, whether or not this includes autologous transfusions is anyone's guess. This article is an excellent example of Watchtower "double-talk," where it is difficult to know just what the Society means.

In the above quotation, the Society boasts that Jehovah's Witnesses are "determined to abstain from blood"; however, it doesn't seem to realize that this statement makes it look foolish, as it is incongruent with the fact that it allows Witnesses to accept all the components of blood plasma and all of the fractions of the rest of the components of blood from blood donors.

To illustrate just how deeply indoctrinated Witnesses are about the prohibition of storing blood, I recall my experience at a doctor's office in 1973, when I was receiving weekly intravenous hormone and vitamin injections to treat my hypoglycemia. The doctor asked me to lie down, and as usual inserted the syringe into a vein in my arm and began the slow injection. This time, however, something went wrong, as instead of the medication being injected into my vein, the syringe—which was only partially filled with the medication—began to fill up with blood. I watched with alarm as the expensive medication mixed with my blood, nervously wondering what the doctor would do about this mishap. In the midst of this procedure, the doctor was unexpectedly called away to attend to an urgent telephone call. He laid the syringe down on a sterile cloth and left the room for about five minutes; when he returned, much to my horror, he picked up the syringe to attempt the injection again. "No!" I shrieked, and quickly pulled my arm away from him. The doctor, obviously wondering what was going on, asked me what my panic was about. I explained the Society's blood policy proscribed injecting the now contaminated medication, as storing blood for later use was prohibited, even if that storage time was only five minutes long. The doctor grew agitated, exclaiming how costly the medication was, and if I demanded that he throw the syringe away, then he would have to charge me a second time for the new injection. Feeling disrespected and even suspecting the doctor an agent of Satan trying to test my loyalty to Jehovah, I indignantly left his office and never went back again.

Just how far Witnesses will go in their application of the Society's doctrine prohibiting storage of blood is shown in the following incident in 1974, when I tried to produce my own compost for my garden. I had purchased a bag of blood meal, a type of fertilizer that was said to speed up the decomposition time of a compost pile. I reasoned that this must surely be an appropriate use of blood, since Jehovah demands that blood be poured out onto the ground. An elder, however, spotted the bag in my yard during a visit to my home; he counseled that using any product in which blood was a component was offensive to Jehovah, repugnant, and unacceptable, as it defamed the sacredness of blood. He insisted I throw the rest of the fertilizer away.

15. MAY WITNESSES ACCEPT HEMODILUTION IN LIEU OF A BLOOD TRANSFUSION?

The Society has further demonstrated inconsistency in its position forbidding autologous transfusion through its wavering policy about a procedure known as "sever hemodilution," which is a type of autologous transfusion. In this procedure, at the beginning of an operation, some of the patient's blood is drawn and stored in a plastic bag which remains connected to the patient by a tube. The drawn blood is replaced by a plasma volume expander, which dilutes the blood in the patient's body. Some of this diluted blood is lost during the operation; then at the end of the operation, the blood in the plastic bag is elevated, and reinfused into the patient.

NO
(1972)

These techniques [hemodilution and autologous transfusion] are noteworthy to Christians, since they run counter to God's Word. The Bible shows that blood is not to be taken out of a body, stored and then later reused. (AW 4-8-72, p. 30)

YES
(1990)

It is with this in mind [the risks of blood transfusions], and not just to honor the requests of Jehovah's Witnesses, that Denton Cooley has performed open-heart operations . . . limiting transfusions whenever possible by substituting hemodilution. . . . (AW 3-22-83, p. 16)

NO
(1990)

Techniques for . . . hemodilution that involve blood storage are objectionable to them. (How Can Blood Save Your Life? [1990], p. 27)

YES
(2000)

When it comes to hemodilution . . . a Christian must decide for himself how his own blood will be handled in the course of a surgical procedure. . . . (Jehovah's Witnesses Public Affairs Office News Release 9-19-2000)

In an effort to save their own lives in spite of the Society's blood policies, some Witnesses have become very resourceful, finding innovative ways to skirt around the obstacle of the prohibition against storing blood. One example was found in a newspaper article I read many years ago, in which a doctor created a novel way to extend a little Witness girl's circulatory system by inserting a long tube into one of her veins, and inserting the other end of the tube into another part of her vein. The blood would flow out of her body, into the tube, and then back into her body. Because her blood was kept constantly flowing, it was not technically being stored. Her body was thus fooled into thinking that the tube was part of her vein, and would produce extra blood in order to keep up the proper volume of blood for her body. Gradually the doctor lengthened the tube to extend her circulatory system and thus increase the amount of blood her body would make. The newspaper printed a photo of the little girl in her hospital room, surrounded by this special apparatus—by that time the tube was so long that it was draped about the room. As blood was lost during the little girl's surgery, the blood in the tube would flow into her body, making a blood transfusion unnecessary.

Recent developments in the medical field, in conjunction with the

Society's latest changes in its blood doctrine, may make such extreme measures unnecessary for Witnesses in the future.[3] An interesting development has been the formation of an underground group known as the Associated Jehovah's Witnesses for Reform on Blood, a diverse group of Witnesses from many countries. Some of its members are presently serving as elders and [Witness] Hospital Liaison Committee members or have previously served in that capacity, while other members are from the medical field or have friends or relatives who are Witnesses. All have volunteered their time and energies in an effort to educate other Witnesses and the medical community, and to encourage change in the Watchtower's blood policy. They work in the hope that Jehovah's Witnesses will someday be allowed to freely choose whether or not they will accept various forms of blood therapy or products without fear of being disfellowshipped. It is their hope that the Watchtower Society will acknowledge that some Witnesses, after carefully studying the scriptures and medical science, have concluded that it is not a violation of God's law to accept blood or blood products since these do not serve as food in the body. They can be contacted through their Website at www.ajwrb.org.

WATCHTOWER MEDICAL ADVICE

Further research into the Watchtower's history astounded me, as it revealed that the Watchtower has a long history of giving questionable medical advice and recommendations to its followers, even advertising and selling suspect medical contraptions in their magazine, *The Golden Age*. One can only guess how many people were hurt or died by following the advice, advertisements, and sanctions of the Society, who claims to be "God's mouthpiece."

- *"Aspirin—The Menace of Heart Disease"*

   By the excessive and continuous use of aspirin, the heart muscles become soft and flabby, the heart valves relax and lose the power to properly perform their normal function, and by degrees the blood begins to regurgitate or flow back through the weakened heart-valves with each heart pulsation, thus gradually and unawares producing a valvular heart-lesion, which, when once established, is never cured, but continues to grow worse and worse until death results. Acetylsalicylic acid, aspirin, is potentially a dangerous drug, and its unqualified use as a home remedy is a menace to good health, and should be discouraged. (*Golden Age* 9-23-36, p. 822)

- *The medical profession is demonized.*

> We do well to bear in mind that among the drugs, serums, vaccines, surgical operations, etc., of the medical profession, there is nothing of value save an occasional surgical procedure. Their whole so-called science grew out of Egyptian black magic and has not lost its demonologic character. . . . Readers of *The Golden Age* . . . should also know the truth about the medical profession, which sprang from the same demon-worshiping shamans (doctor-priests) as the 'doctors of divinity'." (*Golden Age* 8-5-31, p. 727)

> Medicine originated in demonology and spent its time until the last century and a half trying to exorcise demons. During the past half century it has tried to exorcise germs. Its methods are the same in both efforts at exorcism, and instead of injuring the demon or the germ, the injury is often to the patient. (*Golden Age* 8-5-31, p. 728)

- *A simple cure for appendicitis.*

> **"Some simple Remedies."** The following recipes are entirely harmless and have proved effective when all other means have failed. They may be given to feeble and aged individuals without fear of harm resulting, and should be persisted with until the desired effects are produced. . . . Appendicitis: One ounce each of elderblossom, peppermint and yarrow; best crushed ginger, half an ounce. Simmer in three pints of water for twenty minutes. Sweeten with old-fashioned black treacle (not golden syrup) and take a wineglassful every fifteen minutes until relieved. The medicine must be taken hot every time, and you must keep it up, sometimes for twenty-four hours. A cure is usually certain in the most severe cases. Do not be afraid of the perspiration caused. You may vomit at first, but that will pass off and you will be all the better for having an empty stomach. (*Golden Age* 7-6-32, p. 627)

- *Osteopathy cures insanity.**

> The object of this article is to emphasize the fact that there is a cure for most types of insanity. The seventeen-year record of one of our osteopathic institutions for the treatment of mental disorders has shown that osteopathy, when given a fair trial, cures more than fifty percent of the insane. (*Golden Age* 10-26-32, p. 53)

---

*Osteopathy is a system of medical practice based on the theory that disease is due chiefly to mechanical derangement in tissues, placing emphasis on structural integrity by manipulation of the parts. Similar to chiropractic, except that the osteopath is a medical doctor.

- *Avoid medicines and surgery.*

  Avoid the use of stimulants, intoxicants, drugs, and patent medicines. Avoid the loss of organs of the body by surgical operations. (*Golden Age* 11-13-29, p. 107)

- *Chewing gum is unhealthy because it uses up your saliva.*

  Stop chewing gum, as you need the saliva for your food. (*Golden Age* 11-13-29, p. 107)

- *Avoid medical injections and vaccinations.*

  Avoid serum inoculations and vaccinations, as they pollute the blood stream with their filthy pus. (*Golden Age* 11-13-29, p. 107)

- *A blood transfusion is a personality transplant.*

  The poisons that produce the impulse to commit suicide, murder, or steal are in the blood. (*WT* 9-1-61, p. 564)

  Transfusing blood, then, may amount to transfusing tainted personality traits. (*WT* 5-15-62, p. 302)

- *Eating starchy foods with foods containing sugar is not advised, since it produces pus in the body.*

  Starches taken into the body are changed into a form of sugar, and, when fortified by other sugars, such as syrups, jellies, jams, pies, cake and pastries, it requires the expenditure of a great amount of vital energy to get this excess chemically changed into some form of pus so that it may be expelled from the system. Do you wonder that you have that "tired feeling" . . . ? (*Golden Age* 11-13-29, p. 107)

- *Drinking scalded milk can be deadly.*

  Scalded milk, for either adults or children, is very constipating. This in turn causes more deaths and resulting ailments than do all other causes combined. . . . (*Golden Age* 7-24-1929, p. 682)

- *Grapes cure cancer.*

  "The Grape Cure." Don't use ANY other food while on the "Grape Cure" diet; you will only cause yourself (and perhaps others) trouble by so doing. DON'T do it. . . .

  In case of internal cancer or cancer that has not become active, it has been found very effective . . . to begin taking a small amount of grapes every two hours or so throughout the day, not using over two pounds a day for the first day or two, gradually increasing the quantity for a week up to not over four pounds a day. Continue the diet as long as the case requires, or until the patient grows too weak. Many continue without breaking away from the diet for six weeks or longer. . . .

  When the cancer is active and suppurating, the pulp of the grape may be made into a poultice and renewed as frequently as indicated. This poultice will eat its way down into the foreign mass, not injuring normal cells and tissues, however. . . . We suggest changing from one variety of grapes to another, when convenient, although the dark-skinned varieties seem to be the best. But even the little green hot-house grape is better than none to arrest the progress of the cancer till another grape season comes in. (*Golden Age* 5-29-29, p. 563)

- *You won't die if you don't eat for one or two days—or even fifty-six days!*

  Don't let anyone frighten you by telling you that you will die if you stop eating for a day or two; Moses (the Israelite) fasted for forty days. So did our Lord Jesus. Others have fasted for as long as fifty-six days with dandy results. (*Golden Age* 5-29-29, p. 563)

- *Dreams are caused by demons.*

  No one should pay any attention to dreams or visions now. They are certainly not to be considered as from the Lord. Quite often . . . they may be, and no doubt are, caused by the demons' toying with our thinking faculties while we are resting. (*Golden Age* 7-13-27, p. 646)

- *A level-headed doctor does not study disease germs.*

  Secure the services of a level-headed physician (one who has been devoted to the study of *health* and not to the study of *disease germs*). . . . (*Golden Age* 5-29-29, p. 563)

- *Germs do not cause disease.*

    It has never been proven that a single disease is due to germs. (*Golden Age* 1-16-24, p. 250)

- *Disease is caused by wrong vibrations.*

    Any disease is simply an "out of tune" condition of some part of the organism. In other words, the affected part of the body "vibrates" higher or lower than normal. It has a different vibratory rate than the rest of the body. (*Golden Age* 4-22-25, p. 453)

- *Cure whatever ails you with Dr. R. A. Gamble's Electronic Radio-Biola!*

    The Biola works on the same principle as the Radio and gets its power from the Electro-Magnetic Earth Currents. The Biola is a Disease Wave-Trap Reservoir for catching and storing up the Disease Vibrations. These Disease-Vibrations can be then used to assist nature in destroying the very disease that produced them. Send for a Biola today. Price $35.00. (*Golden Age* 4-22-25, p. 479)

    The Biola automatically diagnoses and treats diseases by the use of the electronic vibrations. The diagnosis is 100 percent correct, rendering better service in this respect than the most experienced diagnostician, and without any attending cost. (*Golden Age* 4-22-25, p. 454)

- *Tonsillectomy is worse than suicide.*

    If any overzealous doctor condemns your tonsils, go and commit suicide with a case-knife. It's cheaper and less painful. (*Golden Age* 4-7-26, p. 438)

- *Basking in the sun is good for you, as the UV rays are healing.*

    The earlier in the forenoon you take the sun bath, the greater will be the beneficial effect, because you get more of the ultra-violet rays, which are healing. (*Golden Age* 9-13-33, p. 777)

- *Ovaries are more than what they seem to be.*

    Cutting into the ovaries is like cutting into the brain. (*Golden Age* 6-8-32, p. 865)

• *An anti-typhoid injection turns one into stone.*

Do you want to turn to stone? You might try receiving anti-typhoid injections. (*Consolation* 12-1-37, p. 14)

• *Radium, a radioactive element, cures what ails you.*

It is now known that the curative agent in certain baths in Europe which have been famous throughout the world is the Radium which the waters of their springs contain. (*Golden Age* 2-2-21, p. 260)

Radio-activity . . . This wonderful energy finds its principal use and application in dealing with our physical bodies in the relief of human suffering. (*Golden Age* 6-23-20, p. 607)

Radio-Active Pad Restores Health—or Money Back. *No matter what your ailment may be, we can help you.* (*Golden Age* 5-11-21, p. 480)

• *The only thing our Radio-Active Pad will do is improve your circulation.*

This is what our Radio-Active Pad will do for you or me. It gives forth energy rays that penetrate your body, causing a vibration that exercises the tissues, the blood cells, veins, arteries, etc. This causes the circulation to attain its normal flow. That's all our Pad does. It restores your circulation to normal. (*Golden Age* 5-11-21, p. 480)

• *Radium energy is akin to the life force.*

Moreover, it has given us a new branch of human wisdom and that branch is the science of radio-activity. . . . Its force is strikingly akin to the actual, vital forces of the cells of the body by which all the life functions of our bodies are sustained. (*Golden Age* 6-23-20, p. 607)

• *The demons say radium is close to being the secret of life; they could be right, because even liars tell the truth sometimes.*

The demons that infest the atmosphere of our Earth now, just as they did in the days of our Lord, are said to have made the statement, either through the Ouija boards which they operate, or through the so-called spiritualist mediums whom they control, that in the discovery of Radium humanity has come very close to the secret of life. Of course these "lying spirits," as the Scriptures call them, cannot be trusted; and yet even a liar will sometimes tell the truth, so that he may have the greater influence when he does lie. (*Golden Age* 2-2-21, p. 260)

- *OOPS!*

> Not a cure for cancer or anything else has ever been caused by radium, so far as known, but terrible sufferings have been caused by it. (*Golden Age* 8-1-34, p. 692)

> We now have a new disease known as radium poisoning. . . . Now a new case has occurred at the Ottawa, Ill., factory. Eight of these have died, and the others are condemned to a living death of paralysis known as radium poisoning. (*Consolation*, 9-21-38, p. 10)

- *The E.R.A. machine will cure what ails you!**

> The many marvelous cures made by Dr. Abrams, and those who practice the Electronic Reactions of Abrams, or ERA, as it is called, have forced the attention of the whole world upon it. (*Golden Age* 4-22-25, p. 452)

- *Or does it?*

> In this article proof is set forth that the "Diagnostic Machine of Dr. Albert Abrams" is nothing more and nothing less than a complex ouija-board; that this said diagnostic machine cannot possibly be used to diagnose disease unless the operator thereof is a spirit medium; and, furthermore, that the whole theory known as the Electronic Reactions of Abrams, or the "E.R.A.," is an absolute farce, unproved, and unprovable . . . (*Golden Age* 3-5-30, p. 355)

- *Yes, it does!*

> While the E.R.A. system is true and genuine, there are fakirs and frauds endeavoring to associate themselves with it and to take advantage of its good name and reputation. (*Golden Age* 4-30-30, p. 483)

As if oblivious to its own history of medical doctrine, the Watchtower Society had the audacity to make this claim:

---

*The abbreviaion "E.R.A." stands for the "Electronic Reactions of Abrams," which was a theory of disease and how to cure it by canceling out the disease vibrations with a current of the same wavelength. Dr. Albert Abrams was the apparent originator of this electronic theory to medicine. Dr. Abrams (and his students after he died) developed several machines which were recommended in the *Golden Age*, machines which purportedly diagnosed and cured various diseases. The ERA machine was also known as an Oscilloclast.

The Watch Tower Society does not make recommendations or decisions for individuals on medical and diagnostic practices. If certain practices have aspects that are questionable in the light of Bible principles, however, attention may be called to these. Then each person can weigh what is involved and decide what to do. (*WT* 12-15-94, p. 19)

The Society's statement is dishonest; as shown through the foregoing, the Society has indeed made many recommendations through the pages of its magazines on medical and diagnostic practices. It is also dishonest in making the situation appear that Witnesses have had free choice about personal medical decisions. As has been documented in this chapter, the Society *has* made numerous decisions regarding the unacceptability of many medical practices throughout its existence—even forbidding some medical treatments on pain of disfellowshipping if a Witness chooses them. In an effort to influence the congregation members to obey the Society even when no other Witnesses are observing them—as in obedience to their medical doctrines, for example—I recall an elder warning the congregation: "Jehovah can disfellowship, even if the elders can't."

The Society silences in advance any who disagree with its doctrines by instructing all Witnesses in the following way, and in doing so, it lays responsibility for the tragic results of its errors onto God:

If we have become thoroughly convinced that this is Jehovah's organization, that he is guiding and directing his people, then we shall not be unsettled by anything that happens. If something comes up that we do not understand we will wait patiently until it is made thoroughly clear to us. . . . We will not 'forsake our mother's teaching' by immediately beginning to criticize and find fault. We will realize that Jehovah knows what is going on in his organization, and if he is willing to permit it, who are we to insist it should be different? If we really have faith, we will know that if it is wrong he will straighten it out eventually, and we are far safer inside his organization even with these minor difficulties than we would be on the outside where only chaos and destruction await us. (*WT* 5-1-57, p. 284)

The Society here warns that "only chaos and destruction" lie outside of the organization—but it says nothing about the chaos and destruction that lie *within* the organization, the destruction of so many lives within its ostensibly safe confines. The Society's confused medical teachings along with their resultant fatal consequences cannot be classified as "minor difficulties."

My experience throughout my long association with the organization had been that the Watchtower Society frequently pointed its finger at other religions as being responsible for loss of lives in wars because of their blessings and prayers for their soldiers going off to battle, while contrasting itself as being free of bloodguilt because of its refusal to participate in war—but it, too, is responsible for the deaths of many.

The Society itself tells how to view organizations that are bloodguilty before God:

> The Scriptures show that if we are part of any organization that is bloodguilty before God, we must sever our ties with it if we do not want to share in its sins. (*United in Worship of the Only True God* [1983], p. 155)

The Society has attempted to absolve itself of responsibility for its zigzagging doctrines in many and varied ways, as demonstrated in chapters 6 and 7. As if in final summation, regarding itself the Society has pleaded: "In their human fallibility, they misinterpreted matters." (*AW* 3-22-93, p. 4) One must keep in mind, however, that the Society has exalted itself far above an imperfect organization of mere fallible men (see chapter 4) by laying claim to being God's channel of communication, God's mouthpiece, possessing Divine authority, and being God's organization—the only organization directed by God's Holy Spirit; therefore, in view of all of the Society's zigzagging doctrines, one is lead to the conclusion that the God of the Watchtower Society is a hurtful, sadistic God, and a very confused God, or the Society is just not being truthful when it makes those lofty claims about itself.

When I told my therapist about the extreme anger I felt about the harmful effects following these erroneous doctrines produced, he asked: "Do you think a religion that is so hurtful could be *right*?" His question touched a place inside of me that knew that for God to require obedience to such hurtful, zigzagging teachings was indeed unthinkable; the Watchtower Society's claim to being the only true religion could not possibly be right.

My research revealed twenty-five nonmedical doctrinal flip-flops as well, which likely constitute only the tip of the iceberg. I exclaimed to my therapist how outraged I felt that the Society went so far as to equate acceptance of its "tacking in the wind" explanation for its ever-changing doctrines—which amounted to forced acceptance of falsehoods—with loyalty to God! "Of course, such development of understanding, involving 'tacking' as it were, has often served as a test of loyalty. . . ." (*WT* 12-1-81, p. 31)

My therapist reflected, "It's so twisted that they can end up using something that doesn't make sense to justify their faith! People get hurt. People *die* from this!" Though the Society touts each turn of its sailboat as "new light" from God—that its sailboat had instead gone astray, adrift in waves of chaos and lightlessness, was clearly evident to me.

The Society frequently condemned religious wars for blood spilled "in the name of God," but the Society has also caused much blood to be spilled "in the name of God," through its insistence that its interpretations of the Bible from which it formulates its medical edicts are channeled to it from God. Untold lives have been and continue to be lost, for which it takes no responsibility; that it appeared to be without moral sense about these deaths infuriated me. I could see no reason why God would allow such falsehoods to be palmed off as truth, especially when precious lives were being lost waiting for God to correct the Society's mistakes of medical doctrine.

Comparing itself to other religions, the Society boasts:

> Many of such denominations allow widely divergent views among the clergy and the laity because they feel they cannot be certain as to just what is Bible truth. They are like the scribes and Pharisees of Jesus' day who were unable to speak as persons having authority. (*WT* 4-1-86, p. 30)

Ah, yes, the Society is better than the churches and the Pharisees, for it speaks with authority, regardless of the fact that what it says is wrong much of the time!

When I considered the long time that often transpired before a "truth" was found to be in error and then corrected, I came to the realization that the Society had been teaching falsehoods as truth much of the time. The Bible book of 1 Corinthians 14:33 says: "For God is not the author of confusion" (*King James Version*), and in Hebrews 6:18, ". . . it is impossible for God to lie" (*New International Version*); thus, I could not see how the God of truth could possibly have channeled these flip-flopping teachings to the Society.

I was mortified as I thought about the countless Witnesses who died during the many years that ensued before the Society changed its medical views, which it formerly had printed as unqualified truth. The Society says, "It does not mean that the writings in this magazine *The Watchtower* are inspired and infallible and without mistakes." (*AW* 3-22-93, p. 4) Honesty would therefore dictate that the Society not present its writings as absolute truth, forcing all Witnesses to accept them under pain of being expelled from the congregation and ostracized by God; however, as has been seen, that has not been the case. Just how the Watchtower Society requires Jehovah's Witnesses to view all of its teachings can be seen from the following:

... the "faithful and discreet slave" ... found to be the anointed witnesses of Jehovah operating today in all parts of the Earth through ... the Watch Tower Bible and Tract Society of Pennsylvania. (*WT* 7-15-60, p. 438)

God interprets and teaches, through Christ the Chief Servant, who in turn uses the discreet slave [the Watchtower Society] as the visible channel, the visible theocratic organization. (*WT* 2-1-52, p. 79)

We should meekly go along with the Lord's theocratic organization and wait for further clarification, rather than balk at the first mention of a thought unpalatable to us and proceed to quibble and mouth our criticisms and opinions as though they were worth more than the slave's [the Watchtower Society's] provision of spiritual food. Theocratic ones will appreciate the Lord's visible organization and not be so foolish as to pit against Jehovah's channel their own human reasoning and sentiment and personal feelings. (*WT* 2-1-52, p. 80)

And if the heavenly Father would not give a stone or serpent or scorpion to a child who asked for bread or fish or an egg from him, are we to take the spiritual food he provides through the slave [the Watchtower Society] into our hands as if we were going to be bruised by a stone or bitten by a serpent or stung by a scorpion? Are we to be doubtful and suspicious about each new provision? (*WT* 2-1-52, p. 80)

If we have once established what instrument God is using as his 'slave' [the Society] to dispense spiritual food to his people, surely Jehovah is not pleased if we received that food as though it might contain something harmful. We should have confidence in the channel God is using. (*WT* 2-15-81, p. 19)

The spiritual food from the Society, however, has contained many harmful things! How can anyone have confidence in a parent who is abusive? The Watchtower Society, "the Mother," has abused it members by forcing them to submit to medical doctrines that have claimed the lives of countless Witnesses, which ended up being reversed many years later; this gives no basis for confidence in the organization, or in its present ban of blood transfusions. In view of its history, I am utterly amazed that the Society could even question anyone who is doubtful and suspicious about its teachings; blindly accepting everything the Society has declared as truth has had far more disastrous consequences than being bruised by a mere stone—it *has* often had the consequence of being bitten by a poisonous serpent or scorpion! Jehovah's Witnesses have good reason to be hesitant to hold out their hands to accept more of the Society's "spiritual food." The organization is like a skeleton with osteoporosis! Its doctrines are like bones that appear solid, but are actually full of holes. In unwitting condemnation of its own zigzagging doctrines, the Society printed in the *Watchtower*, the vehicle through which it claims God channels truth:

> Seeing the strenuous efforts needed to succeed in the race for life, Paul went on to say: "Therefore, the way I am running is not uncertainly. . . ." (1Cor. 9:26) Hence, to run "not uncertainly" means that to every observer it should be very evident where the runner is heading. *The Anchor Bible* renders it "not on a zigzag course." If you saw a set of footprints that meanders up and down the beach, circles around now and then, and even goes backward at times, you would hardly think the person was running at all, let alone that he had any idea where he was heading. But if you saw a set of footprints that form a long, straight line, each footprint ahead of the previous one and all evenly spaced, you would conclude that the footprints belong to one who knows exactly where he is going. (*WT* 8-1-92, p. 17)

I chuckled as I read this paragraph, as the Society—using the metaphor of footprints in the sand that wander up and down a beach, circling around now and then, and even going backward at times—was inadvertently describing its own history of what was supposed to be divine revelation of truth. Amazingly, in spite of its long history of zigzagging changes of many of its doctrines, the Society still claimed:

The Watchtower—an outstanding Bible study aid

> Since 1879 it has been published regularly for the benefit of sincere students of the Bible. Over that extended period of time *The Watchtower* has consistently proved itself dependable. (*New World Translation of the Christian Greek Scriptures* [1950], p. 793)

> With the exception of the Bible, do you know of any other literature that supplies as much divine wisdom as does a year's subscription to *The Watchtower*? (*Kingdom Ministry* 4-83, p. 3).

> What a priceless treasure we have in *The Watchtower* and *Awake!* (*WT* 1-1-94, p. 25)

These statements would be comical were it not so utterly tragic that Jehovah's Witnesses believe them, many of whom have been led to a needless death because of putting faith in the "wisdom" of the *Watchtower*.

Notes

1. Raymond Franz, *Crisis of Conscience* (Atlanta, Ga.: Commentary Press, 1983, 1992), pp. 106–107.

2. Ibid., p. 107.

3. For a more detailed discussion of Jehovah's Witnesses and the issue of blood, see David Reed, *Blood on the Altar: Confessions of a Jehovah's Witness Minister* (Amherst, N.Y.: Prometheus Books, 1996); and Jerry Bergman, *Blood Transfusions: A History and Evaluation of the Religious, Biblical, and Medical Objections* (Clayton, Calif.: Witness Inc., 1994).

NINETEEN
THE GUISE OF SPIRITUAL AUTHORITY

Researching the Society's history had not been an easy task for me emotionally. Often the material my investigation uncovered caused enormous rage within me about the indignities the organization had perpetrated on its faithful followers. At other times, however, I suddenly felt like I was falling through thin ice, being submerged in terrifying uncertainty that maybe the Society *is* God's organization—albeit a very imperfect one—and that I was leaving the only true religion. My confidence in myself and in my research would spiral downward, my mind becoming a minefield, tripping over words that triggered explosive and petrifying doubts. Frequently I experienced "mental paralysis," a very frightening feeling that suspended my continued examination of the organization for a while. This feeling of immobility and numbness, which would arrest my scrutiny of the organization for weeks at a time, would hit me in waves. Sometimes I felt like I was going under, drowning in the undulations; however, when the surging waves of doubts and fear would recede, I would take up my analysis of the organization with renewed fervor; I truly felt like I was fighting for my very life. At times I felt so driven that I would carry on my research despite crushing migraine headaches.

Trying to break free of the Society's control in order to leave the organization was the toughest thing I had ever tried to do; I wondered if I would ever stop feeling so afraid. As a means to that end, I decided to analyze just how the Society has the authority to affect people's lives so dramatically.

I found that its claim of divine authority stems from its assertion that Jesus inspected all the churches during 1919, and that He found that the

Watchtower Society was the only religious group having spiritual wisdom (*WT* 12-15-77, p. 751), and serving quality spiritual food (*WT* 12-1-84, p. 17); on this basis, the Society contends that Jesus chose it as the sole channel through which God would communicate truth to humankind.

> Their faithfulness and spiritual wisdom in the Master's service determines their worthiness to be put in charge of all the earthly belongings of their Master. (*WT* 12-15-77, p. 751)

> When the enthroned Lord Jesus inspected his household in 1919, he found the group of Christians associated with the *Watchtower* magazine loyally striving to "keep on the watch" with the help of spiritual "food at the proper time." (*WT* 12-1-84, p. 17)

I resolved to research the organization's history in order to check on the quality of the "spiritual food" the Society had served in 1919, in order to ascertain if there was any possibility that Jesus could have selected them and given them divine authority. I discovered that the Society had published a book entitled *The Finished Mystery* in 1917; this book would have been the "spiritual food" that Jesus would have found the Society serving to His people during His alleged inspection. I wanted to read it to see for myself what kind of "spiritual wisdom" they had, and the quality of the "spiritual food" they were serving.

Obtaining a copy of *The Finished Mystery* presented quite a challenge, though, since it was so old and thus very rare. The logical place to possibly find it was the Kingdom Hall library; however, I knew that the elders had long ago passed a rule prohibiting any of the library materials to be checked out. I was anxious to read it, since during my long association with the organization, many times speakers and the Society's literature had referred to it in a boastful manner and with great pride:

> It has been sweet to the spiritual taste of the remnant to feed upon the prophetic book of the Revelation. During World War I they did, by means of the book *The Finished Mystery,* feed on a commentary on the whole book of Revelation.... (*Then Is Finished The Mystery of God,* [1969], p. 258)

Eventually, I learned through an ex-Witness newsletter[1] that a copy of *The Finished Mystery* was for sale as a collector's item. Excitedly, I contacted the editor of the newsletter; finding that the book was still available, I quickly purchased it. I was dumbfounded at the quality of the "spiritual food" that it contained; the following list is a sampling of what I found.

"Spiritual Food" from *The Finished Mystery* [1917]

- Demons will invade the minds of churchgoers in 1918, leading to their destruction. (p. 128)
- Nahum 2:3-6 describes a railway train. (p. 93)
- The "valiant men" of Nahum 2:3 are an engineer and a fireman. (p. 93)
- "The chariots rage in the streets, they jostle one another" of Nahum 2:4 are the clanking and the bumping of railway cars. (p. 93)
- "Leviathan" of Job 41:2-19 is a locomotive. (p. 85)
- "Also, in the year 1918, when God destroys the churches wholesale and the church members by millions. . . ." (p. 485)
- "Behemoth" of Job 40:15-24 is a stationary steam engine. (p. 84)
- "Even the republics will disappear in the fall of 1920. . . . Every kingdom of Earth will pass away, be swallowed up in anarchy." (p. 258)
- The "voice from heaven" of Revelation 18:4 is the voice of The Watch Tower Society. (p. 276)
- The glory of the angel of Revelation 18:1 refers to modern discoveries such as correspondence schools, celluloid, *Divine Plan of the Ages* [a Watchtower publication], talking machines, vacuum cleaners, induction motors, pasteurization, Panama Canal, shoe sewing machines, subways, skyscrapers, Roentgen rays. (p. 273)
- Michael the Archangel is the pope of Rome. (p. 188)
- The Lord's Second Advent had taken place in 1874. (p. 54)
- The Watchtower Society's elite "anointed" group of its members would all be taken from Earth up to heaven in the spring of 1918. (p. 64)
- Revelation 14:20 predicted the precise distance from the place where the Society's book, *"The Finished Mystery"* [1917], was produced in Scranton, Penn., to its shipping destination in Bethel (the Society's head-quarters) in New York City (p. 230).
- The Lord assumes responsibility for *The Finished Mystery.* (p. 295)
- One function of hair is to lead off vapors which could otherwise choke and make the brain smoky, which "leads to the conclusion that all modern church organizations were founded by bald-headed men, and the smoke being unable to find its way out through their scalps naturally had to come out of their mouths!" (pp. 165–66)

I shared this list with my therapist; regarding the last quote, he observed, "That's a good example of how logic can be used abusively. Just because things are logical doesn't mean they're true. Their statement starts with a wrong assumption." All of the ridiculous nonsense presented as truth in *The Finished Mystery* was clear evidence to me that the Watchtower Society showed a lack of spiritual wisdom and a lack of quality in the spiritual food it was serving during the time that Jesus supposedly examined all the churches; on that basis, I believe Jesus would never have chosen the Society to serve as God's channel. If Jesus had actually chosen the Watchtower Society as God's channel, undoubtedly He would have corrected their false doctrines immediately after choosing them—which He did not do, as exemplified by the fact that the Society continued printing absurdities in 1921, most notably in their book, *The Harp of God*. It contains a list of discoveries and inventions, which the Society points to as evidence of Jesus' second presence since the year 1874.

> It was in the year 1874, the date of our Lord's second presence, that the first labor organization was created in the world. From that time forward there has been a marvelous increase of light and the inventions and discoveries . . . mention is made of some of those that have come to light since 1874, as further evidence of the Lord's presence since that date, as follows:

gas engines	South Pole	submarines
disk ploughs	illuminating gas	electric welding
railways	fireless cookers	match machines
smokeless powder	railway signals	radium
linotypes	aluminum	barbed wire
adding machines	artificial dyes	automatic couplers
antiseptic surgery	aeroplanes	automobiles
bicycles	carborundum	cash registers
motion pictures	Darkest Africa	dynamite
cream separators	electric welding	escalators

(Partial list from *The Harp of God* [1921] pp. 234, 235)

Continuing in my research, I learned that the organization had been very involved with pyramidology (now considered to be an occult practice) at the time of Jesus' alleged inspection.

- The Testimony of God's Stone Witness and Prophet, The Great Pyramid in Egypt. (*Thy Kingdom Come* [1903], p. 313)

- The Great Pyramid . . . seems in a remarkable manner to teach, in harmony with all the prophets, an outline of the plan of God, past, present, and future. . . . The Great Pyramid, however, proves to be a storehouse of important truth—scientific, historic, and prophetic—and its testimony is found to be in perfect accord with the Bible. . . . (*Thy Kingdom Come* [1903], p. 314)

- The Great Pyramid . . . Soon it became apparent that the object of its construction was to provide in it a record of the divine plan of salvation. . . . (*Thy Kingdom Come* [1903], p. 320)

- The Society was so convinced about the meaning of the Great Pyramid, that a large pyramid serves as the headstone for the grave of its first president, Charles Taze Russell!

The Watch Tower Society burial lots in Rosemont United Cemeteries, five miles due north of Pittsburgh City . . . In the exact center of the Bethel lot will be erected diagonally the Pyramid Shape Monument as . . . *accepted by Brother Russell* as the most fitting emblem for an enduring monument on the Society's burial space. The size of this structure is 9 feet across the base and its apex stone is exactly seven feet above the ground surface level. (*Souvenir Report of the Bible Students Convention* 1/2-5/19, pp. 6–7)

Ironically, by 1928 the Society's beliefs about the pyramid took a complete turnabout to the opposite view:

- It is more reasonable to conclude that the great pyramid of Gizeh, as well as the other pyramids thereabout, also the sphinx, were built by the rulers of Egypt and under the direction of Satan the Devil. (*WT* 11-15-28, p. 344)

- Then Satan put his knowledge in dead stone, which may be called Satan's Bible, and not God's stone witness. (*WT* 11-15-28, p. 344)

- Those who have devoted themselves to the pyramid have failed to see some of the most important things that God has revealed for the benefit of his church. The mind of such was turned away from Jehovah and his Word. (*WT* 11-15-28, p. 344)

The Society failed to acknowledge *who* it was that turned the people's minds away from God and His word by promoting the pyramid as God's truth for over twenty-five years: *the Watchtower Society itself!*

My research also revealed some additional peculiar teachings that I believe could not have come from God:

- *God lives on a star called Alcyone.*

  Alcyone, the central one of the renowned Pleiadic stars. . . . Alcyone . . . from which the Almighty governs his universe. (*Thy Kingdom Come* [1903] edition, p. 327)

- *The desire to worship God is dependent on the shape of one's brain.*

  Some have a strong desire to worship God, others have a weak desire, and others have no desire at all. This difference is due to the shape of the brain. (*WT* 3-15-13, p. 84)

- *Early modern-day Witnesses were Gods.*

  ### YE ARE GODS

  Our high calling is so great, so much above the comprehension of *men*, that they feel that we are guilty of blasphemy when we speak of being "new creatures"—not any longer human, but "partakers of the *divine nature*." When we claim on the scriptural warrant, that we are begotten of a divine nature and that Jehovah is thus our father, it is claiming that we are divine beings—hence all such are Gods. (*WT* 12-1881, p. 301)

- *God's plan can be known through astrology.*

  It is quite probable that the divine plan is shown in the stars. . . . (*WT* 11-15-1928, p. 340)

- *Blacks will become white under Jesus' millennial rule.*

  Can Restitution Change The Ethiopian's Skin? The following from the *New York World*, is the third we have seen reported. These suggest and illustrate the process of restitution soon due. . . . "From Black to White He Slowly Turned." Though once as black as charcoal, the Rev. Mr. Draper is now white. His people say that his color was changed in answer to prayer. (*WT* 10-1-1900, p. 296)

- *The healthiest sleeping position is with your head pointed north.*

  Sleep on the right side or flat on the back, with the head toward the north so as to get the benefit of Earth's magnetic currents. (*GA*, 11-13-29, p. 107)

- *Blacks are the cursed race.*

  Certain it is that when Noah said, "Cursed be Canaan, a servant of servants shall he be unto his brethren," he pictured the future of the Colored race. They have been and are a race of servants. . . . (*GA*, 7-24-29, p. 702)

- *Pure hatred is OK for Christians, as it does not belong to the Devil.*

  Haters of God and his people are to be hated, but this does not mean that we will take any opportunity of bringing physical hurt to them in a spirit of malice or spite, for both malice and spite belong to the Devil, whereas pure hatred does not. (*WT* 10-1-52, p. 599)

- *We should accept truth, even if it comes from the Devil.*

  We should learn to love and value truth for its own sake; to respect and honor it by owning and acknowledging it wherever we find it and by whomsoever presented. A truth presented by Satan himself is just as *true* as a *truth* stated by God. (*WT* 7-1879, p. 8)

During my investigation, I discovered several books[2] that exposed many of the Watchtower Society's:

- contradictions
- deceptions
- twisted logic
- misrepresentations of quotes
- unbiblical teachings
- illogical thinking

Quoting the Society's own book, Insight on the Scriptures *[1988]:*

Being "the spirit of the truth," God's holy spirit could never be the source of error but would protect Christ's followers from doctrinal falsehoods. (p. 1132)

Comparing that statement with the history of the organization, one finds that Jehovah's Witnesses have not been protected from doctrinal falsehoods; indeed, they have suffered from the Society's doctrinal errors for over 120 years! Thus, according to the Society's own statement, their doctrines could have not been the result of God's direction.

Not only did the Society lack spiritual wisdom at the time that Jesus allegedly chose it to be God's channel, but all the zigzagging doctrines my research had uncovered were evidence that the Society has lacked spiritual wisdom throughout its existence, and the quality of its spiritual food has been found to be wanting as well. Amazingly, the Society still maintains that it has been serving spiritual food "at the proper time."

> Who really is the faithful steward, the discreet one, whom his master will appoint over his body of attendants to keep giving them their measure of food supplies at the proper time? (Luke 12:42, *New World Translation*) For over 120 years now, spiritual "food supplies at the proper time" have been provided in *The Watchtower*, as well as in other Bible-based books and publications. Note the expression "at the proper time." At the right moment, our "Grand Instructor," Jehovah, by means of his Son and the slave class [the Watchtower Society], has guided his people in matters of doctrine and conduct. (WT 10-1-2000, p. 21)

The Society's history disproves its claim of having provided spiritual food "at the proper time," i.e., "at the right moment"—as has been shown, untold numbers of Witnesses have either suffered or died during the interims between the changes in their doctrines.

All the evidence I had uncovered points to the conclusion that God is not using the Watchtower Society, and that He had not channeled any information to the Society at all. I found it impossible to believe that Jesus chose this organization, so riddled with falsehood, on which to establish the only true religion. The Watchtower Society has no support for its claim of divine spiritual authority. The authority of the Watchtower Society is a false authority, and it has set up a false need for others to believe in it.

NOTES

1. Randall Watters, *Free Minds Journal*, Box 3818, Manhattan Beach, CA 90266.
2. The following publications:

Raymond Franz, *Crisis of Conscience* (Atlanta, Ga.: Commentary Press, 1983).

Raymond Franz, *In Search of Christian Freedom* (Atlanta, Ga.: Commentary Press, 1991).

Randall Watters, *Thus Saith The Governing Body of Jehovah's Witnesses* (Manhattan Beach, Calif.: Bethel Ministries, 1982).

Duane Magnani, *The Watchtower Files* (Minneapolis, Minn.: Bethany House Publishers, 1983).

M. James Penton, *Apocalypse Delayed* (Toronto: University of Toronto Press, 1985).

TWENTY

CODEPENDENCY HELD ME HOSTAGE

As a Witness, I had to give up what I really felt and my freedom to doubt openly, which resulted in my feeling trapped intellectually. I now saw the organization as a completely repressive system built on shame, guilt, and the threat of rejection. I felt disgusted for having allowed myself to be controlled by the Watchtower Society for half of my life. My therapist helped me to develop compassion and forgiveness for myself for becoming a Witness and staying in the organization for so many years. I was abused as a child; as an adult, I became involved with an abusive religion. Through therapy, I came to understand that this was not just a coincidence. I learned that part of the reason I was involved with the organization for so long and was unable to leave it was because of what was psychologically leftover from my childhood experience of abuse. The struggle I experienced with the organization was essentially the same struggle I had when I was a child; it was just being played-out differently: "Could I stand up to my abusive parent without getting killed?" As a four-year-old child, the answer obviously would have been no; my abusive experiences as a child blinded me to seeing that the answer to that question as an adult would be much different. I was carrying those helpless, vulnerable feelings into the present in my relationship with the Watchtower Society.

My therapist explained to me that as the child of an abusive mother, I learned how to be a victim; and that as an adult, I had carried this propensity into my involvement with the organization. After abusing me, my mother would tell me that she loved me; thus, I grew up with a very warped view of love—that control and abuse was part of the deal when someone loved me. This way of thinking was in part responsible for my being trapped in this abusive religion, as on some level I had come to see their abuse as love, which fit precisely with the adage heard so often in the congregation, "Those whom Jehovah loves, He disciplines." The congregation members thus viewed harsh discipline from the elders as evidence of God's love.

I came to see that my involvement with the organization was also partly a product of the insecurity I felt when I left home as a teenager; my mother made it clear that once I left home, I would never be allowed to come back—not even to visit—unless she invited me. Life was frightening when my marriage fell apart, and I found myself without friends or any way of supporting myself adequately. One of the reasons I found the Witnesses appealing was because they presented themselves as concerned people who I could count on for friendship and help. The organization offered enticing idealistic promises about the future, and a unique culture that drew me by providing the illusion of safety within its structured environment.

In addition to therapy, I read books about adults who were abused as children, and books about codependency; all of these helped me to understand that the feeling of powerlessness I felt due to childhood abuse led to my developing a codependency relationship with the organization and resulted in my being held hostage in it.

Children who grow up in dysfunctional families are not allowed to grow up emotionally,[1] and therefore they make a perfect fit for an organization that does not want their members to mature. The Watchtower Society wants its members to stay as children in relation to its authority, referring to the organization as "Mother"; thus, Jehovah's Witnesses spend most of their time in the "child" mode, looking to the organization as their "parent." When a Witness voices any disagreement with this "parent," the organization disrespectfully views that disagreement as tantamount to a child throwing a tantrum.

Abused children can see everyone as a potential attacker,[2] but with the visible organization as "Mother," and Jehovah as "Father," and the congregation members as "brothers and sisters," I finally felt safe in this "family" and was thus drawn to the organization. Because my emotional needs as a child were not fully met, I carried the desire to have those needs met into adulthood. I looked to the organization to meet those emotional needs, as it offered the appearance of a nurturing and caring environment, which in turn caused my emotions to short-circuit all my critical thinking about the organization. Children who have been abused tend to make very rigid divisions in the way they think and in the way they view people and issues; they tend to see things as either all good or all bad.[3] Because I had developed this type of thinking pattern, the organization's rigid black-and-white way of viewing matters seemed completely normal to me.

My immersion in an abusive religion was partly the result of my unconscious mind looking for a place that was familiar and that validated how I had been brought up to view life. The organization's strict consequences about leaving it fit my feelings about how the world worked; this prevented me from acknowledging how I really felt inside for a long time, and contributed to my feeling stuck in the organization.

Adults abused as children seek to regain power in various ways, sometimes by appearing to know all the answers.[4] The Watchtower Society is an organization that claims to have all the answers, even to life's most perplexing problems. This claim of having exclusive knowledge that no other group has imparts the feeling of power to its members, thus the organization tends to draw to it adults who were mistreated as children. In talking confidentially with many Witnesses over my long involvement in the organization, I was surprised how many Witnesses confessed that they had been abused during their childhood.

The Watchtower Society tells the Witnesses what to do and think and feel about nearly everything; consequently, they experience a strong sense of containment and security, as they believe that God is behind them. Jehovah's Witnesses are required to accept all of the Society's interpretations and the full range of its doctrines. While that requirement may appear confining, it also creates a sense of freedom—freedom from the responsibility of having to figure out what one believes. This "freedom," however, carries with it a heavy price which I believe few Witnesses consciously think about: relinquishment of one's free will and one's ability to think for oneself. This "freedom," though, very powerfully holds people in the organization; leaving it means giving up that "freedom" and having to shoulder the responsibility oneself for figuring out what the truth really is, which is a terrifying prospect because of the life-or-death qualification the Society puts on possessing accurate knowledge of the Bible.

It was as if Jehovah God had set before humankind the ultimate riddle: to find the one accurate set of beliefs about God and the Bible. Only those accurately solving the riddle will receive eternal life, while those not solving it will receive eternal death. Finding this absolute answer on one's own is just too overwhelming a task for a Witness, and too great a risk because of the high stakes that are involved; thus, having doubts often causes the doubter to flee back into the "safety" of the organization, the vehicle through which they believe God channels the answer to the riddle.

The Society teaches that the only way Jehovah will excuse a person following a path of error is if the Society has directed them onto that path through its error; thus, most Jehovah's Witnesses feel safer staying with the organization, even if they feel the organization is in some ways wrong. They are confident that Jehovah will cause the Society to change its errors according to His "timetable." Jehovah's Witnesses believe that obeying the Society, whether it is right or wrong, is God's requirement.

As an abused child, I was frequently preoccupied with fantasies and make-believe. I became a "master of pretend" in order to deal with frightening aspects of my life over which I had no control; I utilized that same "skill" as an adult as a way to deal with my frightening doubts so I could still stay in the organization. My sense of security was so tied up with being a Witness that, subconsciously, I was willing to overlook or excuse the negative aspects of the organization just to maintain the illusion of security. My therapist said, "You wanted to pretend everything was okay; and because of the way you grew up, you were able to put on a mask." I had been so used to pretending in order to escape the frightening and painful aspects of my childhood, that to do so while in the organization was second nature for me. I desperately wanted to believe the Society's resplendent precept of living forever on an Earth restored to paradise, free of problems. This desire was a great motivator for me to overlook or suppress any negative feelings or doubts I had about the organization, and enabled me to put on a "mask" and pretend that I agreed with it about everything. With the Society was an all-or-nothing deal—either demonstrate belief and agreement with it about everything, or be thrown out and excluded from God and the paradise that was so soon to become a reality.

As a child, I felt protected in school, as I knew no one would abuse me there. The school day followed a program governed by strict rules; because of this schedule, school was predictable and made me feel safe. Small wonder that I initially felt safe in the Kingdom Hall, as its appearance was that of a lecture hall, and its meetings followed a set schedule and were conducted much like classes in school; thus the setting felt familiar and, in the beginning, I felt safe in its disciplined structure.

Jehovah's Witnesses believe they will be the only people who will survive God's War of Armageddon. Because of the organization's wartime mentality of "Us vs. Them," i.e., "Jehovah's Witnesses vs. the World," it tended to attract people who had been through their own "wars"—their own trau-

Because I had this codependent characteristic:[5, 6]	I tolerated this organizational attitude:
• Focus on pleasing others	• Directs nearly every aspect of members' lives
• Giving up personal needs and interests when they conflict with the needs or interests of others	• Directs nearly every aspect of members' lives
• Basing one's responses to others on fear of their rejection or anger	• Requires total acceptance of and obedience to all of its teachings; disagreement or disobedience results in punishment or disfellowshipping
• Not defending one's own values when they are challenged by others	• Does not allow its members to disagree with any of it teachings
• Basing one's self-image on what other people say or think about oneself	• Requires total acceptance of and obedience to all of its teachings; disagreement or disobedience results in punishment or disfellowship
• Not defending one's own values when they are challenged by others	• Does not allow its members to disagree with any of its teachings
• Basing one's self-image on what other people say or think about oneself	• Gives acceptance and love based on degree of one's loyalty and obedience to the organization
• Fearing reality, fantasizing how things will be different when "something" happens	• Offers enticing vision of Paradise, "the new system of things on Earth"
• Being out-of-touch with one's own feelings	• Condemns certain feelings, resulting in members denying, suppressing, or ignoring their feelings
• Difficulty developing or maintaining intimate relationships	• Discourages trust of other Witnesses by warning members to always "keep their guard up," and by requiring members to "turn each other in" to the elders for any infraction of the Society's rules.
• Having low self-esteem	• Reminds members that they are worthless; shames and humiliates its members
• Difficulty making decisions	• No independent thinking
• Pushing your own thoughts or feelings out of awareness because of guilt, fear, or lack of trust of oneself	• "Put your questions 'on the shelf!' Don't let your lack of ability to understand our doctrines cost you your life!"
• Not believing one can take care of oneself	• "You can't get along without Jehovah's organization!"
• Pretending problems are not there	• Refusal to take responsibility for its errors and false prophecies
• Having expectations of oneself that are unrealistic	• Demands increasingly more amount of members' time and energy
• Feeling unimportant	• "You are but a speck of dust."
• Feeling different than the rest of the world	• "We are different than the rest of the world! We have the Truth!"

matic difficulties in life—which was yet another reason why I was attracted to the organization.

The codependent characteristics I developed as a result of childhood abuse are the same characteristics that kept me in the organization, because the Watchtower Society is an organization in which those codependent characteristics define their attitudes.

Many people who were abused early in life possess many of these codependent characteristics, and are drawn to and held in the organization because of them. Many people who were not abused early in life do not possess many of these codependent characteristics, but instead are drawn into the organization by various emotional needs. It is my opinion, however, that such individuals will develop many of these codependent characteristics as a result of their involvement with the organization, in order to keep themselves in the organization. If they do not develop these codependent characteristics, they will eventually experience an intolerable level of internal dissonance, and will leave the organization.

NOTES

1. Brian DesRoches, *Reclaiming Your Self* (New York: Bantam Doubleday Dell, 1990), p. 52.

2. Eliana Gil, *Outgrowing the Pain* (New York: Bantam Doubleday Dell, 1983), p. 37.

3. Gil, *Outgrowing the Pain,* p. 37

4. Ibid., p. 73

5. DesRoches, *Reclaiming Your Self*, p. 11

6. Melody Beattie, *Codependent No More* (New York: Harper & Row, 1987), pp. 37–43.

TWENTY-ONE

THE ILLUSION OF CHOICE

Mind Control

T he Society pulls out every psychological ploy it can to make Witnesses who have disagreements with it feel bad about their opinions, in order to punish them and make them feel like they are betraying God, so as to keep them in submission. The reality is, though, that they are *not* betraying God; they are rejecting the organization's thinking on matters and its control over their lives. Often the reason behind Witnesses' rejection of the organization is to become free to serve and worship God according to their personal sense of what is right, since the Society demands obedience to its teachings—even if those teachings go against the conscience of any of its members.

For twenty-three years, I had not felt loved, consoled, and cared for by the organization; instead, I had felt controlled and manipulated by it. I began to read some books about the general techniques of mind control; these books described various manipulative methods that cultlike groups in general use to control their members. Although the books never specifically mentioned the Watchtower Society or Jehovah's Witnesses, I felt as if they *were* written about them, for a majority of the methods and attitudes of groups using mind control matched the methods and attitudes of the Watchtower Society. I felt greatly relieved to learn that all the years that I had been angry with the Society, I had not been rebelling against God, as the elders led me to believe; I had instead been rebelling against the mind control techniques and manipulative methodology of the Society.

During most of the years that I was an active Witness, if anyone would have asked me if I was in the organization by my own free will, I would have answered in the affirmative—even though I was often angry with the "imperfections" of the organization. I eventually came to see that those "imperfections" amounted to abuse of its members, however, and that the suffering the organization causes them is unconscionable. The fact that I wanted to leave the organization but found myself *unable* to leave, suggests that something else was at play. The mental and emotional agony that accompanied my struggle to free myself from entanglement with the organization attests that something much greater was involved; the pieces of the puzzle began to fall together when I started learning about mind control.

Entire volumes have been written by others on this subject; the following does not attempt to cover the totality of this topic, but is aimed only at familiarizing the reader with some of the basic tenets of mind control and how they apply to Jehovah's Witnesses and the Watchtower Society.

I learned that mind control has four basic components: behavior control, emotional control, information control, and thought control.[1]

Behavior Control

The Society controlled behavior by controlling certain aspects of the Witnesses' environment; i.e., its strict rules regarding grooming, clothing styles, rigid and demanding schedule requirements, and its enforcement of discipline, which can be extremely severe. During the years I was active in the organization, punishment took various forms: personal chastisement given privately, a public announcement of reproof, humiliation in the form of restriction of one's privileges or responsibilities in the congregation, individual members "marking" specific Witnesses and avoiding socializing with them, or expulsion from the organization.

An example of punishment via humiliation through having one's privileges taken away was an occasion when I met with a group of Witnesses at the Kingdom Hall one weekday morning before going out into the witnessing work. These brief meetings were for the purpose of organizing the group, giving encouragement, and praying for guidance. Brothers preside over all Witness meetings; however, if there is no brother present, then a sister may conduct the meeting. This particular day, there was one brother in attendance among the group of sisters; naturally, all expected this brother, who had been serving as a pioneer and was looked-up to by the congregation as exemplary, to lead the group. Unbeknownst to any of us, this brother had been privately reproved by the elders for some infraction of the Society's rules, and was stripped of his privilege of offering prayer before leading the group out into the territory. The brother, his face crimson with embarrassment, asked one of the sisters to say the prayer. Witness women, viewed as subservient to the men, are not allowed to pray in the presence of a male Witness unless her head is covered. As this situation is so rare, Witness women do not usually carry any sort of head covering with them; consequently, one sister pulled a facial tissue of out her purse, plopped it on top of her head, and said the prayer. The brother was obviously humiliated at being replaced by a woman with a tissue perched on top of her head.

Another means through which the organization controls the behavior of its members is utilizing peer pressure to get wayward Witnesses to conform. Witnesses know that "Big Brother" is always watching, as all Witnesses are directed to keep an eye on each other; charged with the responsibility to "keep the congregation clean," they must report to the elders any brothers or sisters who seem to be straying away from the straight and narrow path that the Society has defined. Witnesses are instructed to "mark," i.e., avoid socially, any who manifest a disgruntled attitude, or who demonstrate lack of respect for the Society or any of its rules. Dissenters are quickly expelled from the congregation and shunned to evade their contaminating influence.

A further aspect of behavior control can be seen by what occurs when a newly interested person comes to the Kingdom Hall. A mature brother or sister is quickly assigned to particularly "befriend" him or her, introducing the new person to various congregation members, sitting with that person, and endeavoring to start a personal, one-on-one home Bible study. The only road to becoming a Witness is through the individual home Bible study program; the brother or sister conducting the study is responsible for the gradual molding of that person to conform to Society standards.

Even the odd, clonelike similarities of mannerisms and facial expressions that I had long observed among the Witnesses were a form of behavior control, as the brothers modeled off the leaders of the organization.

The most effective way the Society controls the behavior of its members is by setting itself up as the authority from God, thus giving itself the right to be the sole interpreter of the Bible, to lay down all the rules for Jehovah's Witnesses, and to demand unquestioned obedience from them. "The leaders cannot command someone's inner thoughts, but they know if they command *behavior*, hearts and minds will follow."[2]

Thought Control

The Society's habit of assigning its own meanings to normal words is a key contributor to its control of the thoughts of Witnesses; the words with special meanings convey specific thoughts, and are used repetitiously to indoctrinate Jehovah's Witnesses in Watchtower thinking patterns. Witnesses are taught that the Society channels information from God to them, thus independent thinking is neither needed nor tolerated; anyone speaking to others independent thoughts that run counter in any way to the opinions or teachings of the Society is disfellowshipped. Speaking to any former Witnesses is forbidden, as is reading or possessing of any literature critical of the Watchtower Society; this effectively limits the Witnesses' thoughts about the organization to only the positive thoughts which the Society implants in the minds of its members through continual repetition of such in its abundant literature which Witnesses are required to read, and during its many meetings. If any negative thoughts about the organization or its doctrines do creep into their minds, Witnesses are taught to stop them by immediately dismissing them, dwelling instead on the new system or some other positive aspect of Witness theology.

In my congregation, thought control was exercised to some extent through fear that the demons could read one's mind. If they could, it was reasoned, then the need to be ever vigilant of one's thoughts was even more imperative, lest the demons know one's weaknesses and bring temptation across one's path.

Witnesses will insist that they are in the organization by choice; they do not realize, however, that they have been deceived and manipulated into making that choice. "Those who do make the commitment to join are rarely aware of the subtle techniques of persuasion and control shaping their behavior, thoughts, and feelings."[3] If asked, Jehovah's Witnesses will vehemently deny being under mind control. "It is absurd, however, to expect an objective answer from someone under mind control."[4] "In any event, when thought is controlled, feelings and behaviors are controlled as well."[5]

Emotional Control

Guilt, humiliation, shame, and blame are effective tools that the Society uses to control the Witnesses and keep them in submission. The Society uses fear to instill phobias of the outside world into the minds of the Witnesses, which deters them from leaving the organization. Fear of punishment from the elders and fear of embarrassment in front of fellow Witnesses is used to prevent dissention and preserve unity. Fear of Armageddon and of Jehovah's wrath is used to keep all in obedience. Fear of doubts, of other religions, and of people on the outside is used to keep all in the confines of the organization. Feelings are also redefined so that a person will feel happiness even though she may be suffering. "The result of this process, when carried to its consummation, is a pseudo-personality, a state of dissociation in which members are 'split' but not 'multiple,' in which they proclaim great happiness yet hide great suffering."[6]

Negative emotions, such as are betrayed by criticism or complaints, are condemned and are not tolerated. Positive emotions, such as loyalty to Jehovah as demonstrated by complete obedience to the organization, are given great praise. Many people are drawn to the organization because of emotional needs that they have; if they find those emotional needs satisfied by being in the organization, their thoughts and behavior will often adjust to the stipulations and limits of the Watchtower Society.

Information Control

Through its teaching that every religion outside of its own is of the Devil, the Society instills the fear that reading or possessing outside religious literature is an invitation to demon attack. By contrast, it presents its own literature as truth, knowledge of which is a protection in avoiding demon attack; some Witnesses believe that the actual literature itself has the power to ward off demons, hence they leave it scattered about the house for protection. "Critical words have been explained away in advance as 'the lies about us that Satan puts in peoples' minds'. . . . Paradoxically, criticism of the group confirms that the cult's view of the world is correct. The information presented does not register properly."[7]

I remember an elder speaking to the congregation disparagingly about people who learn about the organization by reading books written by former Witnesses. He exclaimed with indignity, "If people want to know about Jehovah's Witnesses—*let them ask Jehovah's Witnesses!*" I remember agreeing, thinking that the most accurate information could be obtained only by "going to the source" instead of getting an outsider's distorted view. I later learned, however, that former Witnesses—those who Jehovah's Witnesses had to most especially avoid—could provide the most accurate information about the organization, especially its history. Reading any information critical of the organization is forbidden, and Witnesses are kept so busy with the large amount of required reading of the repetitious Watchtower publications that there is little time left for reading any outside information. "People are trapped in destructive cults because they are not only denied access to critical information but also lack the properly functioning internal mechanisms to process it."[8]

Another way Witnesses experienced information control was through the Society's dramatic warnings against attending college and watching television, conveyed through its literature and also skits at the Kingdom Hall and assemblies. Television was often referred to as the "Devil's Eyeball." Witnesses who had disposed of their television sets were literally applauded at the congregation meetings, and they would usually boast about how much more time they now had to study the Society's literature.

Information control reached new heights the time that an elder gave me strict instructions that should the deaf disfellowshipped brother show up for a meeting, I was not to translate the meeting into sign language for him; the elder claimed that doing so would amount to spiritual fellowshipping with a disfellowshipped person, which was forbidden. I argued the point, explaining that disfellowshipped hearing persons who want to come back to the organization can gain spiritual strength by coming and listening to the meetings; my interpreting the meetings for the deaf man would only be giving him the same opportunity. My argument, however, fell on deaf ears.

As computers are increasingly becoming commonplace in many homes, the Society has issued stern warnings against using the Internet; they are obviously aware of the easy and private access it provides to an abundance of information about the organization that the Watchtower would prefer be kept hidden. Issuing such warnings ostensibly to protect the Witnesses from "apostate influence," the Society may be looking to conceal its checkered history and the tragedy it has brought to the lives of many.

        ❧   ❧   ❧

In part, I think the Society's methods of control are a defense against it seeing things in ways that it doesn't want to see them, and are an outgrowth of its investment in seeing things in its own particular ways. The Society has such a huge investment in believing everything it says is reality and is the truth, that for it to have even a thought of disagreement is so internally forbidden; to let itself think even for a second that it could be wrong would be so frightening, that I feel it sets up a psychological mechanism of denial that gets put in motion all the way down the line from the Governing Body to the rank-and-file Witness, so that all negative thinking about the Society is banned for everyone. I feel the Society develops various methods of control to ensure no one thinks critically of it because it is so scared of being wrong. Since its pride and its sense of security comes from maintaining its superior position as "God's channel," psychologically it will do a lot to support that belief, as is evidenced by its finding all manner of excuses when its prophecies fail or its doctrines are found to be in error.

NOTES

1. Steve Hassan, *Combatting Cult Mind Control* (Rochester, Vt.: Park Street Press, 1988, 1990), pp. 59–66.
2. Ibid., p. 61.
3. Michael Langone, *Recovery from Cults* (New York: W. W. Norton & Company, 1993), p. 7.
4. Hassan, *Combatting Cult Mind Control*, p. 110.
5. Ibid., p. 63.
6. Langone, *RecoveryFrom Cults*, p. 9.
7. Hassan, *Combatting Cult Mind Control*, p. 62.
8. Ibid., p. 65.

TWENTY-TWO

THE FINAL HURDLES

Although intellectually I understood that the organization exhibited cultlike characteristics, that the Society was guilty of false prophesy many times over, that its numerous vacillating doctrines betrayed the fact that it didn't really know what the truth was, that it utilized mind-control techniques, and that it had no basis for its claim of possessing divine authority—on an emotional level, I was still unable to free myself from the entrapment of the organization. My therapist noted, "You're clinging to this empty thing." The organization was an empty thing that left me feeling empty because it had failed to nourish me. Using the metaphor of a well symbolizing the organization, my therapist pointed out that I kept throwing the bucket in with the hopes of getting refreshing water; he reminded me, however, that there was no water for me in the well, and that the bucket will continue to hit the bottom and come up dry. He recognized my anger about the organization's failure to provide the nurturance that it had promised, but suggested that there is also sadness beneath that anger—and that I would likely have to grieve the deep disappointment of finding that the organization was not the loving mother that it claimed to be.

I felt that leaving the organization would be so much easier if I knew there was something on the outside to fill the void it would leave in my life. A smorgasbord of churches existed, but the sheer number of them only made me feel confused; I just didn't know how to choose the right one to visit. My therapist gently probed by asking, "What touches you spiritually?" His question gave me a joyful feeling of liberation—the idea that there could be a choice based on what personally touched me, instead of my being coerced into obeying a set of rules and ignoring my feelings, gave me an excited feeling of hopefulness. No one had ever asked me that question before; the organization didn't care about what I felt; it only cared about my saying what it wanted me to say and looking like I agreed with it. It didn't listen to me, try to understand me, or do much to help me understand it—it only wanted me to follow Society rules and keep quiet about my feelings. I came to see that the Society was just not capable of doing more than that. As to what touched me spiritually—I knew at once the answer to that question: jubilant singing and triumphant music!

The dreary music at the Kingdom Hall had not fed me spiritually. The Society no longer even allowed any live instruments to accompany the congregational singing, such as the piano that we customarily had, or the occasional treat of an elderly brother playing his violin. Only a tape recording of music prepared by the Society was permitted. The songs were written by the Society also, many of which sounded like funeral dirges and were depressing; others that had lyrics about going from house-to-house in the preaching work were sung to a zippier cadence, but still left me feeling unsatisfied.

I remembered long ago when a visitor, after sitting through two hours of lecture and classroom-like instruction at the Sunday morning Kingdom Hall meetings, asked me, "When is your worship service?" I, too, had wondered the same thing. The Kingdom Hall meetings lacked the spirit of worship and reverence that I had experienced as a child in church; obviously that was evident to outsiders, as well. I responded by rote, with the preprogrammed Witness answer that Jehovah's Witnesses do not have worship services, since they worship Jehovah through participating in the house-to-house preaching activity and through living their lives in strict obedience to the Watchtower Society. During all my years as a Witness, churches in general were regularly ridiculed during the meetings. An elder frequently singled out one particular nondenominational church in a nearby town as being the most evil of all the churches in the area, allegedly because a group of former Witnesses—now considered to be part of the "evil slave" class—attended there. The elder's berating of this church piqued my curiosity about it.

Coincidentally, I learned that this church was putting on a concert, so I secretly decided to go. My excitement, however, was dampened by the fear that the elders would somehow discover that I went and would then disfellowship me for apostasy. I also felt frightened because the Society had indoctrinated me with the belief that demons live inside of churches. As I cautiously approached the church, I was drawn by the lively music wafting in the breeze, beckoning me to come in. I sat in the back row next to the door just to be sure I could beat a hasty exit if any demons came after me. The triumphant music of the orchestra and the choir's jubilant singing of joyous songs, however, were uplifting to me; as I began to relax and enjoy the music and feel comforted by it, my thoughts drifted back to the many times that the elders at the Kingdom Hall mocked, "Being in a church only feels good because Satan has 'got you' when you're there!" Their premise was that Satan disguises himself as an "angel of light," and thereby keeps people out of the Truth—i.e., out of the organization—by causing them to feel good in churches. I never felt the presence of demons in the church, though; instead, I felt like I was being spiritually nurtured, as the "empty space" inside of me began to be filled. Interestingly, I learned—contrary to what the elder had declared—that there was no group of ex-Witnesses attending this church; instead, their only former Witness member was one elderly woman.

I noticed the emphasis the church songs put on Jesus; although the Society recognized Jesus, its emphasis was on Jehovah. Any Witness speaking too much about Jesus received a reprimand from the elders, because they viewed such talk as a step toward apostasy and leaving the Truth. As a Witness, I often thought it strange that there was always a sense of competition between Jehovah and Jesus, and the Society was determined to make sure Jehovah won! One of the ways this "competition" was evident was with the Society's production of a new songbook in 1984. I remember the elders emphasizing at the meetings one of the significant changes in the new songbook—that the number of songs about Jesus was reduced to only seven, whereas the songs about Jehovah had increased to forty-four. In discussing this with my therapist, he observed, "God gave His Son to redeem humankind, but Jehovah's Witnesses are afraid of displeasing the Father by being loyal to the Son!" Hearing him mirror the essence of the organization's teaching reminded me how little sense most of its doctrines made in my life.

When I told my therapist how lost I felt because I didn't have any beliefs with which to replace those that I had discarded, he counseled, "No one can tell you the right way to believe. The basic issue is respect for the person and their autonomy and their right to have their point-of-view about things and not to intrude on you with that or force or coerce you to believe a certain way." In a word, he was speaking of freedom—the freedom for people to decide for themselves what they believe to be truth, and to respect everyone else's right to make that same decision for themselves. That freedom was one of the basic concepts upon which our country was founded, yet the Society continues to deny it to Jehovah's Witnesses. My therapist commented, however, that many churches do respect that freedom. "Some churches have Bible studies; they want you to discuss. *They respect your disagreement.*" I thought how refreshing finding a church with that kind of attitude would be! How strikingly different than the Bible studies I participated in as one of Jehovah's Witnesses, where everyone had to parrot—and that with enthusiasm—only the Society's opinions of matters. Personal viewpoints that differed in any way from the Society's expressed viewpoints were prohibited. I remember one brother who had an inquisitive nature; he delighted in preparing for the congregational *Watchtower* study by doing additional research on whatever topic the *Watchtower* was featuring, finding interesting details that complemented the Society's views. Often the comments he offered during the study, based on this research, were fascinating and added a great deal of interest to the otherwise boring meeting. Instead of this brother being commended for his extra effort, though, the elders eventually reprimanded him for "drawing attention to himself."

The Society used yearly conventions to reinforce their old doctrines, and also to introduce new doctrines—or revisions of old ones—as "new light" from Jehovah. In June of 1992, my husband came home from one such convention, excitedly exclaiming, "The Society says there has been a great influx into the organization! That proves we are God's organization because it shows we have His blessing!" I pointed out that many people were also *leaving* the organization every year; he replied, "That *also* proves it is God's organization! The Bible foretold that just before Armageddon, 'the love of the greater number will cool off.' "

This was a typical example of Watchtower reasoning: whether people join or leave the organization, both are proof that the Watchtower Society is God's organization! I remember hearing this sort of "double-talk" often during my years in the organization; the Society would always rationalize matters so that whatever the outcome was, it still proved the same thing— namely, that the Watchtower Society is God's organization. One example that comes to mind that caused much disturbance and talk among the congregations was an incident in Australia a number of years ago. A bomb exploded inside a Kingdom Hall, killing several Witnesses and injuring many others. Although there was a lot of speculation among the Witnesses as to why Jehovah did not protect His "name people," the Society remained undaunted, for it had a knack of manipulating the outcome of any situation to prove the organization is God's people. I heard a talk given by a brother dealing with this very incident; he rationalized that had Jehovah's hand not been with that congregation, many more would have perished, proving that Jehovah's Witnesses were God's people. Had all escaped injury, however, undoubtedly he would have pointed to that as divine protection and evidence that the Jehovah's Witnesses were God's people.[1]

Another example of this "double-talk" can be seen in how Witnesses use the Society's errors to prove that the Watchtower Society is God's organization. A typical Witness comment would be, "The world thinks that our belief of _____ (one of any number of beliefs the Society has changed over the years) is silly, but what do *they* know? *We* have the Truth!" Then, when the Society changes this "truth," Witnesses commonly laugh, exclaiming, "Look how far we've come! See how much Jehovah has corrected us!" as proof that Jehovah's Witnesses are God's sole people.

My therapist helped me to understand that for the Witnesses, the fact that many leave the organization is a powerful reason for them to remain in it, by explaining, "It's a psychology that people can get into that becomes a vicious cycle and once it starts, it can be incredibly hard to get out of—that every step you take out, to the others justifies their position. It's set up that way. It's part of the system. And the more you protest, the more they look at you and say: 'You're influenced by the Devil!' "

My husband returned home from the last day of the four-day Watchtower convention, catching me off-guard by suddenly thundering, "This is the 'great testing time'!" The final test, I murmured to myself, and here I am failing it! I felt like I had been pinned to the wall with someone holding a gun to my head while demanding, "Either accept that the Watchtower Society is the truth—or *die!*"

I was stunned by my extreme reaction to my husband's declaration, and how quickly I could be pulled back into the Witness mindset. My therapist put this experience into perspective for me by explaining that fear had gripped me so intensely because for that moment, I had slipped back into believing in "the power of the gun" to kill me. "Jehovah's Witnesses perfectly match your fears. Your anxiety about your belief in yourself gets acted out in this worry that what they say has any bearing at all on your fate," he said. As I pondered all the things I had learned about the Watchtower Society, remembering that the authority of the Society was merely a self-assumed authority, I realized that the security I saw in the organization was a false security, an illusion of security, and an abusive security. The real security lay in trusting in my own ability to decide what I believed the truth really was. My experience in the organization was a replay of my childhood experience—that even though I had been abused, it was still "home" and therefore hard to leave. As long as I was afraid of the Society, my therapist counseled, it would still have power over me and affect my life. He sensitively suggested, "The only way the fear will go away is if you let yourself *feel* it. It's an illusion that you're stuck in the organization. *Feel the fear* and find another way to deal with it." My being "stuck" in the organization felt real to me; I wondered how it was that it was only an illusion.

Lying in bed one night, puzzling over my dilemma of feeling too paralyzed to leave the organization, I fell asleep and had a dream—a dream in which I was huddled on the floor, a large and extremely heavy blanket thrown over my head, which draped down over my whole body. I felt fearful and paralyzed—unable to move, unable to scream, unable to even breathe, and no one would take the blanket off of me. Frustrated and angry, with tremendous effort I finally mustered-up enough strength to hurl the blanket off of myself. My therapist interpreted this dream as symbolizing my feelings of being suffocated by the organization, and my wish for a rescuer from this oppressive situation. Through this dream, my subconscious mind provided the solution to my dilemma, for it was telling me that I was the only one who could rescue me. I would have to feel the fear and find a way to deal with it other than staying paralyzed—I would have to muster-up the strength to leave the organization myself. I finally understood that feeling stuck in the organization *was* just an illusion, and I realized that I had the capacity and the strength within me to rescue myself.

Trying to help me see the separation between God and the Watchtower Society, my therapist offered some thought-provoking words: "If the way the Society deals with people is the way God deals with people—punishing them, forcing them to lie to themselves and pretend—*what kind of God is that?* Do you want a God who coerces you into loving Him? Give yourself a chance to know a different kind of God." The kind of God he was describing was the God I had feared for half of my life, the God of the Watchtower Society. I thought about my vision, and how intensely I had felt love and kindness emanating from Jesus' hands; what a striking comparison to how frightened I was of Jehovah. Having been proven wrong about so many things, the Society could likely be wrong about the kind of God Jehovah is, too. I felt excited about the prospect of finding out. I was hindered in doing so, though, because I had not yet left the organization.

My husband's reactions to my pulling away from the organization made my leaving the Jehovah's Witnesses especially painful. Being an elder, he was deeply involved in the Witness lifestyle and belief system; naturally he was very upset when I confronted him with my doubts about this religion really being "the truth." Our entire marriage was not centered around our relationship—it had been centered around the organization, involvement in its activities, and obedience to its rules. My becoming inactive had been a public embarrassment to him, as Witness husbands are to have their wives in subjection; my absence at the Kingdom Hall meetings was a sign of rebelliousness, a far cry from the subjection Witness wives are to show. My husband did not share many of his feelings with me, except that he was plenty angry about the fact that I had led him into the Watchtower, and now I was the one walking away from it. And I am sure he worried that he might be stripped of his position as elder for failure to keep me "on the straight and narrow," as husbands are the head of their households and responsible for the spiritual health of each member of their family.

A former elder who lived nearby, who was himself on his way out of the Watchtower, was close friends with an elder of a neighboring congregation; this elder told him that the elders of our congregation had had a secret meeting during which my husband had been discussed. The elders had decided at this meeting to put my husband under surveillance, to see if he was straying off the straight and narrow, too. He relayed this information to me, which I passed on to my husband. My husband felt quite betrayed upon finding out that his fellow elders had had a meeting from which he had been specifically excluded in order to talk about him behind his back. All of this caused a lot of stress and tension between my husband and me, and made me fear that my marriage might fall apart if I left the organization.

My daughter was of course relieved and happy that I was finally "seeing the light," and that the organization would no longer be able to drive a wedge between us.

Leaving was additionally difficult because my entire social system was tied up with the organization. Since it requires Jehovah's Witnesses to limit their friends to only other Witnesses, disassociating from it would leave me completely isolated socially. This prospect was very frightening to me, and it contributed greatly to my delay in leaving the organization. I knew that disassociating myself would result in being shunned by all of Jehovah's Witnesses forever. The Society teaches that Witnesses who voluntarily leave the organization are the very personification of evil. Because the Society believes its religion is the only true religion, anyone leaving it is said to have left Christianity entirely— even if they remain morally upright, and attend a church that they feel more accurately reflects the teachings of Christ.

It is interesting to note that while an announcement to the congregation that someone had been disfellowshipped was usually met with sadness by the Witness audience, an announcement that someone had disassociated himself was met with gasps of horror. Disassociation was so rare in my congregation, that during the twenty-three years that I was active there, I can recall only two persons who had left the congregation in that manner. To disassociate oneself was considered the worst thing that a Witness could do, because it is a public announcement of a deliberate decision to reject the organization. A person who is disfellowshipped is not viewed as permanently lost, as the hope remains that they will repent of their wrongdoing and return to the congregation and request reinstatement; whereas there is little hope that the person who disassociates himself will ever return, disassociation being a premeditated, conscious decision. Those who are disfellowshipped are seen as having temporarily been overtaken by Satan's temptations, while those who disassociate themselves are viewed as having willfully taken up the Devil's side.

The Society depicts those who leave the organization as:

- Having an attitude of ingratitude and presumption
- Having a lack of faith
- Being detestable to God
- Being rebellious against the Society
- Having spiritual weakness and a breakdown of spirit
- Having yielded to enmities, strife, jealousy, fits of anger, contentions, divisions, sects, drunken bouts, loose conduct, and fornication
- Having abandoned "the straight path" (*WT* 8-1-80, pp. 19–20)

- Having renounced being a Christian
- Being "self-condemned"
- Having sinned
- Having God's judgment against him (*WT* 9-15-81, p. 23)

- Having become part of the "antichrist"
- Having become wicked, practicing wicked works
- Having become a sow that has returned to the mire (*WT* 7-15-85, p. 31)

- Having come into the organization with a bad motive
- Having selfish reasoning, ambitions, and desires
- Having allowed his associates to mold his thinking
- Having allowed the Devil to affect his heart (*WT* 3-15-86, p. 16)

Witnesses who disassociate themselves are shunned and are treated as are those who have been disfellowshipped for wrongdoing. Further, since the Society associates any who leave the organization with having become part of the "antichrist," they consider these to be haters of God—and so they instruct the Witnesses to hate them: "Haters of God and his people are to be hated. . . . We must hate in the truest sense, which is to regard with extreme and active aversion, to consider as loathsome, odious, filthy, to detest." (*WT* 10-1-52, p. 599)

The Society labels those who leave the organization "apostates"; all Witnesses are indoctrinated to immediately associate that label with the foregoing negative characteristics, and on that basis to immediately dismiss *everything* that person says, never considering if that person has any valid points. The word "apostate" makes any Witness cringe with abhorrence; not wanting to be connected with that label and the associated negative characteristics, few Witnesses openly express their disagreements with the Society by formally disassociating themselves.

Those who do disassociate themselves are not able to give any explanation to their Witness friends as to why they are doing so, because Witnesses are trained to stop a brother or sister in their tracks if the conversation drifts into doubts or complaints about the organization or its doctrines. An immediate report to an elder must be made, which often results in a citation to the complaining Witness to a speedy judicial committee hearing. Thus when a Witness does leave, it often comes as quite a shock to the congregation members. A cliché Jehovah's Witnesses commonly use to comfort one another whenever any leave the organization is, "They were in the Truth, but the Truth was not in them." No matter how many years of loyal service the person had given to the organization, no matter how devout a Witness the person had been, this trite saying always provided the bottom-line reason why a brother or sister would forsake the "spiritual paradise" for the outside world.

A much more common way for Witnesses to leave the organization is by quietly "drifting away"; they accomplish this by becoming inactive—minimally participating in the witnessing work, and attending the meetings at the Kingdom Hall sporadically—until their attendance eventually dwindles away more or less unnoticed. The longer they stay away, the less the Witnesses and the elders have to do with them, until they are ultimately forgotten. At this point, these inactive Witnesses are fairly free to live as they wish without interference or punishment by the elders, as long as they do not declare themselves to still be Witnesses. Most of the time such ones will move out of the area and not inform the elders that they are moving away, eliminating the possibility of being disfellowshipped—thus, the traumatic ordeal is avoided. "Drifting away" avoids the negative labels and severe punishment meted out to those who boldly stand up for what they believe and publicly denounce the religion. Witnesses who drift away will not be shunned if by chance they encounter a Witness in the course of everyday life, as they would if they had taken a definite stand instead by disassociating themselves.

Witnesses who have severe disagreements with the organization, but who cannot leave the organization because of wanting to keep Witness family ties intact, or who cannot move away because of their job, etc., have little choice but to suffer in silence. Some of these remain active Witnesses and endure a tremendous amount of pressure and turmoil within themselves because of their outward pretext of being a Witness. For some, "drifting away" is not always possible, especially if one had been active for many years and served in positions of responsibility in the organization. And for others, drifting away is not always the desired choice, as some Witness families exclude from their social gatherings those who have become inactive. Often, too, Witnesses work for other Witnesses; if these Witness employees allow their doubts or disagreements with the Society to surface, they will almost certainly lose their jobs.

I believe the Society has great fear of anyone questioning their doctrines because questions infer doubts and mistrust, both of which could cause dissentions and divisions among the Witnesses, which would cause the Society to lose its tight control over its members. My therapist helped me deal with the indignant feelings I had about the maligning expressions the Society uses against those who leave. He noted a technique it employs to discredit everything anyone could possibly say that was critical of the organization: "They label a person 'apostate,' and then they take everything that person says as coming from that down position." I was incensed that the mind of every Witness had been poisoned to believe that those negative descriptions are true of every person who leaves the organization, and that the mind of every Witness I knew was thus primed to believe these slanderous statements would be true about me. Putting the matter into perspective, my therapist said, "These are people who believe things that you feel are absurd; so, why do their beliefs about you carry so much weight?" His question "woke me up" and enabled me to see that if the Witnesses believe all the defamatory expressions associated with the label "apostate" apply to me, then that is just another of a long line of absurd beliefs that they hold. He helped me to see that although I couldn't control what the Witnesses would think about me, I could control how what they think about me affects me. A feeling of relief flooded over me as I realized that their attitude about me was one less hurdle I had to cross before I could leave.

My therapist assisted me in understanding that the Witnesses would not really be reacting to *me* with their shunning, but would in reality be reacting to me as a symbol of evil set up by the Society. He suggested also another motive behind the Witnesses' shunning those who leave the organization: "This is how they're going to react to defend themselves, because your leaving is a threat to them." My leaving the organization would be a threat to the security of Witnesses who knew and respected me because it could cause them to begin to question the organization and its teachings; shunning me would be their way of protecting themselves against the terrifying threat of doubt. Additionally, my therapist said, "Jehovah's Witnesses need to have others believe what they believe, because it strengthens their own faith. They are working out of an insecurity, and not a real faith." His statement called to mind the vivid memory of the elders repeatedly asking the congregation, "When we go out in the preaching work, who are we benefiting the most?" The answer was always a resounding, "Ourselves!" As Witnesses, we needed the constant reinforcement of our faith provided by meeting attendance and the preaching work; it was well known that Witnesses who slacked off doing either of these activities often fell into "spiritual sickness" and disbelief. The belief system of Jehovah's Witnesses is not established upon a foundation of truth that is firm enough to allow them to tolerate discussing challenges to those beliefs by anyone who had left the organization.

Now I wanted a true faith that wasn't so brittle that it needed the protection of shunning those who honestly question it, a faith that didn't require such constant reinforcement in order for me to convince myself that I believed it—and a faith where I wouldn't feel so afraid all the time.

Although I knew the descriptions the Society associated with their "apostate" label were not true about me, still I felt the need for some social support while I gathered the courage to leave the organization. I wrote to a former Witness, the editor of a newsletter which promoted awareness of the

Watchtower[2]; through him I learned of the location of a local support group which met monthly for ex-Witnesses, people who had lost friends and family to the Watchtower, Witnesses who were unhappy in the organization, and for Witnesses having difficulty leaving it. I was excited to learn about the support group, but I felt apprehensive about attending its meetings. If the organization knew of the existence of this group, the real possibility existed of their sending a spy to the group meetings—under the pretext of being a Witness who was struggling to get out of the organization—in order to find any Witnesses having doubts, so they could take action against them before their dangerous "leaven" spread in the congregation. I knew this was a genuine risk because although a basic belief of Jehovah's Witnesses is that liars will receive eternal death with no hope of a resurrection, exception is made when it comes to lying or pretending to be someone one is not if the purpose is for the good of the organization.

An example of this sort of deception that I had personally experienced was the time a Witness friend invited me and several other Witnesses to her house when a Witness missionary from Israel was visiting her, as he was to give a slide presentation about his work in Israel. The Society had sent him there to oversee the secret construction of a printing facility for their literature, which would house several Witness workers as well. The Jews in that area were known to effect violence against the Witnesses, and they were very suspicious when they saw this large building being constructed, especially since every room had a sink in it. To protect the facility and the other Witnesses who were to live there, the Society instructed this missionary to pose as an eccentric millionaire who has a fetish about being clean, and to inform any inquirers that this was his own house that was being built. This story was fabricated to cover up the real purpose of the building—that of being a Watchtower factory having bedrooms with sinks in them to house the factory workers. This incident was another example of theocratic war strategy. Knowing this, for a Witness to come to a support group and pose as a Witness struggling to escape the organization was definitely in the realm of possibility—I knew special caution would be necessary if I decided to go.

My need for social support was so great that I decided to take the risk and go to the support group meeting. To protect myself from being "turned in" to the elders before I felt ready to leave the organization on my own, I remained anonymous to the group; I didn't tell them my name, where I lived, or to what congregation I had belonged. I attended this group monthly for several months; my confidences were never betrayed, and I found it to be a safe place where I could vent my frustrations and anger with the organization and receive empathy, support, encouragement, and friendship.

I heard some interesting experiences while attending the support group. One Witness woman there bewailed the lack of love among the elders in her congregation; she exclaimed that they had reprimanded her sternly for using some of her time to visit and read to a sister who was blind, telling her she should be using that time in the house-to-house preaching work instead. A young woman who had been raised in the organization told how her father, who served as an elder, habitually befriended frail, elderly persons with ailing health. His kindness and helpfulness were not extended out of Christian love, however, for she knew he had an ulterior motive: coercion to change their wills to leave their money to the Watchtower Society instead of their families, under the guise that this will facilitate their achieving everlasting life in the paradise soon to come in the new system. Another Witness woman who was in the throes of trying to leave the organization told the group that she and her Witness husband wanted to see what going to a church was like before they decided to leave the organization. It was a sticky situation, though, because their next door neighbor was a Witness elder; despite knowing they would be disfellowshipped for apostasy if they were caught, they decided to take the gamble. She related that as they were driving to the church, she sensed that they were being followed. Turning around to see who was behind them, she observed that it was none other than the elder next door. Sure enough, every time they turned a corner, he turned a corner; when they pulled into the parking lot of the church, he was right there—flashing his car headlights, shaking his fist angrily at them while shouting, "I see you! I *see* you!" to let them know they had been caught.

I enjoyed the association with the former Witnesses at the support group so much that when I received an invitation to have lunch with Ray Franz, former member of the Governing Body, I eagerly jumped at the chance. This came about after I had lamented to an ex-Witness friend that I felt like I needed a boost, a final push, to be able to leave the organization. Learning that Ray Franz was planning to visit some mutual friends in a nearby town, she arranged for me to be invited to join them for lunch. Having heard the elders in my congregation speak out against Mr. Franz, calling him "sour grapes," I was anxious to meet him in person to judge his attitude for myself. I had already read his book, *Crisis of Conscience*, and noted that he had not given off a disgruntled, faultfinding attitude at all. To the contrary, his book simply reflected factual events as a member of the

Society's elite Governing Body that he himself had witnessed, events which eventually caused him to experience a crisis of conscience, leading to his voluntary departure from the Governing Body.

I spent several hours in the company of Mr. Franz and a small group of his personal friends, and had the opportunity to speak at length with him personally. I found him to be the exact opposite of what the elders had said about him; he was one of the kindest, most gentle men I had ever met. There was not even a trace of "sour grapes" to be found in anything he said. I remember thinking, Jesus must have been like him! How different he was in comparison to the rude, coldhearted Governing Body member I had spoken to about the tubal ligation issue years ago. Seeing how Mr. Franz emulated the spirit of Christ, I believed the experiences he described in his book were accurate. Learning about the inside workings of the Governing Body—which were in fact very different than the Governing Body leads the Witnesses to believe—gave me renewed strength.

A turning point in my struggle to escape from the organization came when I unexpectedly encountered a man one day who I recognized as having attended the Kingdom Hall regularly several years ago. He asked me how things were at the Kingdom Hall, and was astonished when I announced, "I'm leaving the organization!" Expecting him to shun me, I was excited when he asked why I was going to disassociate myself. I mentioned one of my reasons was that the Society hurts people, briefly citing some of the medical issues they had zigzagged about and the suffering that had caused many Witnesses. He retorted, "Maybe the Society's errors were just a test!" I grew hot with rage, remembering that argument was one of the Society's justifications for their errors. I told him that was impossible, reminding him of what the Bible said at James 1:13: ". . . with evil things God cannot be tried, nor does He Himself try anyone." (*New World Translation*) If God used the Society's doctrinal errors as a test of loyalty to Him, that means He would be testing with falsehood posing as truth— deception—certainly an "evil thing," since the Bible says, "A man of . . . deception Jehovah detests." (Prov. 5: 6, *New World Translation*) The man responded, "Surely you have a teeny part of you that believes the organization is the Truth!" to which I adamantly declared, *"No, I don't!"*

The next time I saw my therapist, I expressed frustration about this man's reticence to believe my position regarding the organization. He responded, "You're frustrated that he didn't take your position seriously, but you don't take it seriously either, *because you don't act on it.*" I was shocked, stunned, and convicted by stinging words that spoke the truth. I had come to a crossroads in my life; I couldn't continue just blindly following the Society wherever it went. Things that didn't make sense to me when I was baptized twenty-three years ago still didn't make sense to me now. In the past, I was willing to defer the issues I didn't understand, because of my emotional need to be in the organization—but now, I was no longer willing to do so. My therapist challenged: "You need to think about what you really believe, and start to feel more comfortable acting on it."

NOTES

1. See Appendix B, "Closed Belief Structure."
2. Randall Watters, *Free Minds Journal*, Box 3818, Manhattan Beach, CA 90266.

TWENTY-THREE

THE LAST STRAW

Rape

he Watchtower Society's assigning the meaning of "fornication" to the word "rape" if the woman does not scream during the attack had angered me ever since I had become associated with the organization. The Society's literature will now be considered in the order in which each was published, noting in particular the effects that the Society's zigzagging doctrine would have on Witness women who had been raped but were either unable to scream, or who—for whatever reason—chose not to.

> Thus if a Christian woman does not cry out and does not put forth every effort
> to flee, she would be viewed as consenting to the violation. . . . [I]f she should
> submit to the man's passionate wishes, she would not only be consenting to
> fornication . . . but be plagued by the shame. (*WT* 1-15-64, p. 63)

Rape is not an act of passion, it is an act of violence! Apparently the God of the Watchtower Society is so limited that He cannot read the heart of the victim so as to know that she is being raped, and not engaging in lustful fornication. The Society went even a step farther, inferring that just screaming might not be enough to prove that a woman is resisting the rapist and is innocently defending her virtue: "A Christian woman is entitled to fight for her virginity or marital fidelity to the death." (*WT* 1-15-64, p. 64) Nowhere does the Bible demand that a woman fight a rapist until she dies! The Watchtower Society does not make any allowance for a woman to feel her life is more sacred in God's eyes than is protecting her chastity! I wondered how many Jehovah's Witness women had died needlessly by obeying the Society's admonition.

> Would it be different if the man had a weapon and threatened to kill you if you did not submit? No, the Scriptures plainly state that Christians are under obligation to "flee from fornication." (1 Cor. 6:18) It is true that you face the possibility of death in this case. (*WT* 6-1-68, p. 348)

The Society confirmed its view that dying is preferable to saving one's life through submission to the attacker. With this article, the Society took a firmer stance; not only is the woman "entitled to fight for her virginity or marital fidelity," as it formerly stated, but it became more adamant that a woman resist rape to the point of death.

A year later, the Society inferred that it had changed its view equating "rape" with "fornication" through publishing opposing definitions for those two words in its publication *Aid to Bible Understanding*, as follows:

> **RAPE:** Rape is defined as unlawful sexual intercourse without the woman's consent, effected by force, duress, intimidation. . . . (*Aid to Bible Understanding* [1969], p. 1374)

> **FORNICATION:** Sex relations by mutual agreement between two persons not married to each other. (*Aid to Bible Understanding* [1969], p. 601)

Five years later, however, the Society reverted to its former view that if a woman were raped and did not scream, she had committed fornication and would be disfellowshipped:

> [I]f she did not scream she would be as good as dead anyhow. . . . Also, that if she did not scream she would ruin her relationship with Jehovah God and the Christian congregation; that then she would be disfellowshipped or excommunicated from it and that this would be worse than being killed as far as she was concerned. (*AW* 3-8-74, p. 14)

The Society teaches that disfellowshipping is a complete cutting-off from the congregation and from God; hence, the Society punished rape victims who were unable to scream during the assault by forbidding other Witnesses to associate with them. Instead of the victim being assured of God's love, the Society added to their pain by psychologically isolating them from God, for it teaches that God will have nothing to do with anyone who is disfellowshipped from the organization. Since the Society teaches that God will kill all who are in a disfellowshipped state when Armageddon occurs, the rape victim who did not scream was not only denied comfort, but was deemed deserving of death.

Sometimes it may be better to fight the rapist, but other times it may not be; it is a judgment call that should be based on the woman's instinct at the moment of the attack. It is this judgment call that the Watchtower Society has denied its women. By its punishing attitude, the Society made victims of the victims all over again. The woman is first the victim of the rapist, then becomes the victim of the Watchtower Society. Just who is the villain here? Most people would think it is the rapist. The Society evidently thinks it is the victim.

Six years later, the Society reversed its viewpoint again. In an article entitled, "The Growing Terror of Rape," the Society made the following comments:

- "Profound terror in the face of physical threats simply renders most women helpless."
- "Rape is the fastest growing crime in America."
- "I never physically fought him off in any way . . . I was overwhelmingly confused and defenseless against the whole suddenness."

(*AW* 7-8-80, pp. 5, 6)

The Society showed a softening of its previous attitude by portraying rape as causing terror, in contrast to its former depiction of rape as being a demonstration of passionate or lustful desires. In this article, acknowledgment is made that a woman's fear may render her helpless, inferring that she may be unable to scream—yet she still is not labeled a "fornicator." The article reflects a feeling of compassion for rape victims, recognizing the confusion they feel and the inability of some women to fight back due to their being overwhelmed by fright. The Society finally seemed to be recognizing rape as the crime that it really is. Witness women who had been raped could now feel some relief that God really does understand a woman's emotions after all, and their relationships with God could now begin to mend.

Astoundingly, just three months later the Society reaffirmed its former position about rape: that if a rape victim did not scream during the attack, she was again considered to have committed fornication and would be disfellowshipped.

She told him that if he touched her she would scream as he had never heard anyone scream before. She explained that if she did not she would ruin her relationship with Jehovah God and the Christian congregation. . . .

> A Christian woman is under obligation to resist, for the issue of obedience
> to God's law to 'flee from fornication' is involved. (*WT* 10-15-80, p. 7)

One may wonder why being rendered speechless from fright while being
raped would ruin a woman's relationship with God! Does God not understand her fright and her disorientation? Does He not know of her inno-
cence? Is He not loving and just? Does the Society's view honor God?
Whatever relief rape victims may have felt due to the previous compassionate view was short-lived; evidently Jehovah did not understand a
woman's emotions after all. I wondered how many rape victims who didn't
scream felt condemned all over again, and gave up hope for a relationship
with God because of the Society's reversal of this doctrine. The broken relationships with God that had been mended were now broken again.

Two and a half years later, however, the Society unequivocally stated
that a rape victim would *not* be guilty of fornication:

> What do we understand here by "fornication"? The Greek word in this
> text is *porneia*. . . . A male or a female who is forcibly raped would not be
> guilty of porneia. (*WT* 3-15-83, p. 30)

Rape victims who couldn't scream could breathe a sigh of relief; they had
been acquitted! The organization maintains that every change in its doctrine is a result of God's illumination of truth.

> What is one thing that distinguishes the righteous from the wicked, the true
> servants of Jehovah God from those in bondage to God's adversary, Satan
> the Devil? Doubtless more than anything else it is the fact that the right-
> eous, the true servants of Jehovah God, enjoy light. For them, indeed, "light
> itself has flashed up." . . . Note that the shining of light on the path of the
> righteous is progressive. It keeps shining ever brighter. (*WT* 12-1-81, p. 16)

That this "light" progressively shined ever brighter just was not true; I
could see by this rape issue alone that the light flashed off as much as it
was on, as the Society zigzagged its teaching back to the former views that
it supposedly had left behind in the darkness! Jehovah was either a very
confused God—or a very fickle one—to keep changing the truth this way
and that at His seeming whim. The explanation that I felt would best
explain all these back-and-forth changes was that the Society was not God's
channel, and that these changes were merely results of the efforts of a confused group of men who pridefully enjoyed the prestigious position of control over others.

Amazingly, only eleven months later, the Society's light beam swung back the other way to reilluminate the falsehood it had been enlightened to leave behind! I was shocked that the acquitted rape victims who didn't scream were now again guilty of fornication! "But the rapist is asking a person to break God's law by committing fornication." (*AW* 2-22-84, p. 24)

Unbelievably, the Society went even a step further, instructing women to treat the man raping her with respect!

Treat Him Respectfully

The intended victim should remember that the rapist is a human. No doubt there are circumstances in his life that have precipitated his behavior. So although a woman should not cower in fear and permit a rapist to intimidate her, at the same time she should treat him understandingly as a fellow human. (*AW* 2-22-84, p. 24)

I was aghast! Rubbing salt in the wound, the Society not only informed rape victims that their fear is unacceptable, but that they should treat rapists with respect and understanding! This directive flies in the face of a woman's natural reaction to defend herself, and it is in direct contradiction with the instructions the Society had given three and a half years earlier: "May she properly inflict damage on her assailant? Indeed she may . . . she may use any means at her disposal to resist intercourse." (*AW* 7-8-80, p. 12) I wondered how respectful one of the members of the Governing Body would be if he were attacked and raped! How could the men who wrote these articles and made this decision about how women should react during a rape attack possibly understand what a woman would experience while being raped and threatened with injury, when many of them have spent most of their lives cloistered in the protection of the Watchtower Society's buildings in New York City?

Incredulously, the Society did not even stop there; in the same magazine article in which they counseled women to respect their rapist, they went on to warn about the dire consequence that would befall a woman if she did not fight the rapist! The article quoted a Witness who had been raped: "But if I gave in and he raped me, I would eventually die and have no hope of a resurrection." (*AW* 2-22-84, p. 25) Now the crime of being raped without having screamed or actively resisted was so offensive to God that the victim deserved to die eternally—without hope of a resurrection. In essence, the Society was saying that being raped under such circumstance is "the unforgivable sin!" One might wonder when even the sin of *intentional fornication* became "the unforgivable sin!" The Society itself has acknowledged that sins, including fornication, can be forgiven if the sinner is repentant (*Organized to Accomplish Our Ministry* [1983], p. 146); consequently, for rape to be classified as a sin worse than that of deliberately committing fornication makes no sense. It is a violation of humanity to tell someone they're wrong for being victimized.

Four months later, the Society printed a couple of letters that they had received from readers who were upset and indignant that the Society could ever consider a victim of rape to be guilty of fornication. One such letter protested:

> You say to show a rapist respect. These men show no respect for their victim. They don't care that they are shattering a woman, leaving in her memory horror for the rest of her life. (*AW* 6-8-84, p. 28)

The Society responded by again doing a 180° turnabout: "For the victim to be considered guilty of fornication, there would need to be proof of willing consent." (*AW* 6-8-84, p. 28) Rape victims who didn't scream were again exonerated! One would think that the Society would have felt embarrassed by this chastisement from its readers, at least enough to cause it to really think before printing anything further about the rape doctrine—but not so. Two years later, it printed an article lauding the valiant efforts one woman made in fighting her attacker, commenting:

> Why you should resist an attacker from the first moment: . . . Your conscience will be clear. (Even if you are raped, you will not sacrifice your self-respect or cleanness before God.) (*AW* 5-22-86, p. 23)

Rape victims who didn't scream were again guilty of fornication. Just four months later, the Society printed a letter received from the Metropolitan Organization to Counter Sexual Assault which criticized the Society's position; they advised that if a woman is paralyzed by fear, or her instincts tell her not to resist, they recognize that as appropriate. They explained that they would rather have the victim live through the experience than to be killed or mutilated. The Society responded:

> True, the woman has to respond according to her assessment of the danger to her life, and we believe that is covered in the advice given . . . on page 23 (May 22, 1986). (*AW* 9-22-86, p. 28)

Instead of the Society admitting it was now accepting this constructive criticism and changing its view back again, it tried to wheedle out of its uncomfortable position by saying it had already covered that point in its article; of course it had not, which was the reason that the Metropolitan Organization to Counter Sexual Assault had written! Through its statement, the Society was now allowing a rape victim to make her own choice of whether to resist or not; no mention was made that they would consider her choice to be fornication if she decided not to resist. Through their statement, the Society was rescinding its requirement for a woman to fight a rapist to the death, and relieving rape victims of guilt and condemnation if they chose not to resist a rapist; nevertheless, the Society also expressed ambivalence at the same time by asserting that the Bible does support the thought that a woman attacked by a rapist should scream and resist. (*AW* 9-22-86, p. 28)

Unbelievably, the Society three years later re-established its original position of equating rape with fornication if the woman does not scream, through the following statement:

> It was then that I remembered the scripture in Deuteronomy 22. It says that if a woman does not cry out when attacked, it indicates she is submitting to the man and is committing a sin against Jehovah. (*AW* 8-22-89, p. 24)

By this time, the Society's zigzagging doctrinal changes about rape caused Jehovah's Witness women to feel like ping-pong balls being played between the yes-and-no paddles of the Watchtower Society.

RAPE

Perhaps too few people know about the emotional suffering that the Watchtower Society has caused women through its damaging views of rape. I personally experienced the terror of being raped. Through poetry I express the pain and turmoil that I felt as a result of the Watchtower Society's fluctuating teachings about rape.

The Raping of a Witness

A Man.
Hands of steel.   Flashing eyes.   A grip of iron.
I can't believe this is happening to me.
Feelings of unreality.
This is just a dream.

"Don't touch me!"
Words
screaming to be spoken
yet
I cannot speak.
Captive.
The pawn of a man's twisted desires.
Terror.
Will he kill me?
I can't move.
Petrified
as if made of stone.

Clothing
lying in a heap.
Whose are they?
Frightened.   Vulnerable.   Exposed.
Revulsion.

Thrown onto a table
my body
like
some rag doll.
My dignity shattered.

Everything
is
far away   removed
cloudy   hazy
vague   fuzzy
blurry
unreal.
I'm not really here.

Numb.

A body
powerful, heavy
like lead
pressing down on me.

I can't breathe!
Helpless.   Terrified.   Powerless.
I can't scream!
When will this be over?

Silence.
Survival.
Staggering.
Scared.   Stunned.
Shock.
Shame.
Secret.

This isn't really happening.
It's just an illusion.

Deceived.
Defeated.
Disoriented.
Dazed.   Dizzy.
Distant
Denial.
Damned.

Violated.
Used.   Abused.
Tossed aside
like
so much chaff.

Alive!
Feeling dead
for
Jehovah
has left me.

Feeling dirty.
I bathe.
But
I'll never be clean,
for
I couldn't scream.

Guilt.
I couldn't stop him.
Depressed.   Distressed.
No one will understand.
Despondent.
Alone.

Despair.   Dread.

Defenseless
Powerless.   Paralyzed.

God doesn't understand a woman's fear?
How could He be so unjust!

Confused.   Despondent.
Shattered faith.

Anger
at
The God of The Watchtower
for
considering
threats and force
from a rapist
as
requests to commit fornication.

Anger
at
The God of The Watchtower
for
leaving me forever
because
I was sexually attacked
and
I did not scream.

Anger
at
The God of The Watchtower
for
judging me guilty of illicit passion

when
I was the victim
of crime.

Anger
at
The God of The Watchtower
for
asserting
the absence of a scream
changes
terror
into lust.

Anger
at
The God of The Watchtower
for
His Uncompassionate Heart
that
condemns me
to
eternal death.
Had I committed "the unforgivable sin"?

I was raped.

THE LAST STRAW

Jehovah's Witnesses are compelled to accept whatever doctrinal view the Society has at any given moment as absolute truth from God. My believing the Society was God's channel, coupled with its fluctuating and hurtful views about rape, severely affected my relationship with God; for many years, I hated Him for being so unjust and without compassion about this issue of rape.

The last straw for me was the Society's article about rape in which it presented as "myth," views it had previously insisted were "truth"; and as "fact," views it had previously insisted were "false." (*AW* 3-8-93, p. 5)

- "*Fact:*   When a woman is forced to submit to arapist out of terror or disorientation, it does not mean that she consents to the act. Consent is based on choice without threat and is active, not passive."
- "*Myth:*   A rape victim bears part of the blame unless she actively resists."
- "*Fact:*   A rape victim is not guilty of fornication."
- "*Myth:*   Rape is an act of passion."
- "*Fact:*   Rapists bear sole responsibility for the rape."
- "*Myth:*   A woman can "ask" to be raped by wearing provocative clothing."

In reference to the foregoing, the Society commented:

Rape Myths and Realities
The following are some of the long-held misconceptions about rape that serve to blame the victim and to perpetuate attitudes that encourage the perpetrators. (*AW* 3-8-93, p. 4)

What the Society left out was the reason for those misconceptions. Those misconceptions had been the Watchtower Society's misconceptions which it forced upon all of Jehovah's Witnesses as truth from God! The Society never took any responsibility for nor offered any apology for the guilt and emotional distress it had inflicted upon countless rape victims through its zigzagging "truths" about rape. I wondered how many of these rape victims experienced such despair that they gave up on God completely, or how many committed suicide, or how many turned to a debauched way of life due to depression that came out of feeling so rejected by God.

I felt the Society had finally gotten it right in its issue of March 8, 1993 *Awake!* regarding its position on rape. Why did the Society's changed teachings about rape push such a sensitive button in me that I viewed them as being "the last straw"? Because for the past twenty-five years, I had experienced the raping of my spirit by the Watchtower Society.

SPIRITUAL RAPE

I had endured twenty-five years of spiritual rape, as the Watchtower Society assaulted me with their doctrines, forcing me under threat of "death"—disfellowshipping—which results in spiritual death immediately and literal death at Armageddon, to teach and profess belief in doctrines that did not make sense to me and that I did not believe.

I became incensed when I read the checklist in the *Awake!* magazine (3-8-93, p. 7) entitled "Profile of a Potential Rapist"; I felt the list could be applied to the Watchtower Society and aptly be entitled "Profile of a Spiritual Rapist," as a majority of the listed characteristics of a potential rapist fit the attitudes the Watchtower Society has toward its members:

- Emotionally abuses you by insulting you, ignoring your views, or getting angry or annoyed when you make a suggestion.
- Tries to control elements of your life, such as how you dress and who your friends are. Wants to make all the decisions. . . .
- Gets jealous for no reason.
- Talks down about women in general.
- Can't handle frustration without getting angry.
- Doesn't view you as an equal.
- Intimidates you. . . .

The Society says: "Rape flourishes in societies that tolerate violence and sexual manipulation." (*AW* 3-8-93, p. 4) What a striking parallel to "spiritual rape," which flourishes in a society that tolerates spiritual abuse and mind manipulation!

The Spiritual Raping of a Witness

An organization.
Promises:
Problems are things of the past!
Peace!   Perpetual youth!   Plenty!
Paradise!

I can't believe this is happening to me!
Feelings of unreality.
This is just a dream!

The Watchtower Society
Channeling truth from God.

I feel
Confidence.   Contentment.

Commitment.
Focused
on
"The Road That Leads to Eternal Life."

The Watchtower Society
creating black-and-white doctrines
from
the Bible's shades of gray,
forcing obedience to their interpretations
of matters the Bible presents as vague.

The Watchtower Society
demanding conformity to
"Truth"
which is not truth at all
except
to the Organization that created it.

Zigzagging doctrines.
Conflicts.   Chaos.   Confusion.
Forbidden to complain!   Forbidden to question!
Blind acceptance
or
Death.

The heavy weight of the rapist
pressing down on me
like
the heavy weight of the Organization
oppressing me.
Both holding me captive.

Forced
To be a hypocrite.   To be untrue to myself.
To violate my conscience.
To believe and do what is wrong
in order to
be right with God.

Forced
to embrace

twisted thinking　　　and　　　doctrines that kill.
Forced
to cover up the truth
to mask The Lie.

As a Rapist
demands submission under threat of death
The Watchtower Society
demands submission under threat of death.
Spiritual Death by disfellowshipping.
Literal Death at Armageddon.

The Raping of my Spirit
like
The Raping of my Body.
Used. Abused.
Tossed aside like so much chaff.
Forced to be silent.

The Governing Body of the Watchtower Society
making rules that dictate lives.
The Governing Body of the Watchtower Society
Paper Tigers
posing
as
God's Channel.

Anger
at
The God of The Watchtower
Who says
with
my independent thoughts,
I commit fornication
with
evil.

Anger
at
The God of the Watchtower
Who wants me to play Follow-The-Leader
without question or doubt

with
a Leader who commits fornication
with
truth.

TWENTY-FOUR

ESCAPE

I felt indignant and incredibly angry with the Society, about which my therapist said, "Your anger comes out of the power they claim, because they lord it over other people, and they hurt people with it." How elders lord their power over congregation members is illustrated by a comment an elder once made to me: "Nobody better ever tell me that I can't disfellowship them, because *I'll disfellowship them!*"

As has been shown throughout this work, the Watchtower Society makes many decisions about how Jehovah's Witnesses must live. It asserts its authority is from God, thus coercing the Witnesses into living their lives according to those decisions; but those decisions hurt people, and at times cost them their lives. Instead of humbly acknowledging its errors and asking forgiveness for the pain it has caused others, the Society presumptuously continues in its insistence that its authority is from God, shifting its doctrines to and fro without conscience as to how these doctrines are affecting those over whom it lords its power. Ironically, my research of the organization's early history turned up some statements in the Society's own literature denouncing what the organization had become—an organization based on the vacillating, contradicting teachings of a singular collective group of mere men.

> If we were following a man . . . undoubtedly one human idea would contradict another and that which was light one or two or six years ago would be regarded as darkness now. But with God there is no variableness, nei-

ther shadow of turning, and so it is with truth. . . . A new view of truth never can contradict a former truth. "New light" never extinguishes older "light," but adds to it. (*WT* 2-1881, p. 188)

These statements are those of Charles Taze Russell, founder of the Watch-tower Society; I remembered similar thoughts being conveyed in the Bible verse of Ephesians 4:14:

That we henceforth be no more children, tossed to and fro, and carried about with every wind of doctrine, by the sleight of men, and cunning craftiness, whereby they lie in wait to deceive. (*King James Version*)

Then we will no longer be like children, forever changing our minds about what we believe because someone has told us something different, or has cleverly lied to us and made the lie sound like the truth. (*The Living Bible*)

Amazingly, the Society speaks out in criticism of vacillating teachings as though it had never been guilty itself:

It is a serious matter to represent God and Christ in one way, then find that our understanding of the major teachings and fundamental doctrines of the Scriptures was in error, and then after that, to go back to the very doctrines that, by years of study, we had thoroughly determined to be in error. Christians cannot be vacillating—"wishy-washy"—about such fundamental teachings. What confidence can one put in the sincerity or judgment of such persons? (*WT* 5-15-76, p. 298)

In making these comments, the Society precisely mirrored my thoughts about itself.

I had come across an article that the Society had written in the *Awake!* magazine, recommending that the reader place confidence in the Bible—and hence in itself as the only avenue for understanding the Bible—instead of in science; a paragraph, written in reference to science and scientists, more aptly describes the Society instead:

But what is also clearly shown in the history of science is that scientists are only imperfect humans. They make mistakes just like everybody else. And often, because of the desire for fame, or because of pride and stubbornness, they will cling to ideas that are not the truth and that can even result in harm to people. (*AW* 12-8-76, p. 9)

What is clearly shown in the history of the Watchtower Society is that the Governing Body is made up of only imperfect humans who make mistakes just like everybody else, who have clung to ideas that were not the truth, which resulted in harm to many people. The Society unwittingly admitted that its zigzagging, erroneous doctrines are products of mere men when it stated, ". . . Jehovah, the God who gives himself absolutely no 'scope for getting it wrong.' " (*WT* 12-15-92, p. 32) The Society's gravest error lies in its claim of being more than imperfect humans; it lies in its blasphemous claim of being the channel of communication between Almighty God and all of humankind. The Society's statement of long ago is particularly apropos: "Jehovah never makes any mistakes. Where the student relies upon man, he is certain to be led into difficulties." (*Prophecy* [1929], pp. 67–68) This work has drawn attention to the many serious difficulties into which following man can lead, especially when one is deceived into thinking he is actually following God. During my research, I found a *Watchtower* article that discussed what it means to worship God with truth:

> What should elevate true worship far above all other worship? Is it not TRUTH? It should be founded on *reality*, be in conformity with the *actual state of things*, rather than being based on the guesswork or imagination of the worshipers. Would not any other form of worship be just a counterfeit, belittling to One known as the "God of truth"? (*WT* 4-1-76, p. 208)

The Society's statements unintentionally condemned itself; by its own definition, counterfeit worship is the kind of worship the Society practices, as manifested by its many false prophecies and flip-flopping teachings which are obviously based on guesswork and imagination of men and not Divine direction from God. Its ever-changing teachings are not founded on reality, but are wrong about as much as they are right—if indeed they are ever right at all.

In an article dealing with counterfeit Christianity, the Society issued a warning against apostates—a warning that, from my experience, better fits itself instead: "If we keep listening to subtle arguments and specious reasoning, 'twisted things' can sound as though they were straight." (*WT* 3-15-86, p. 14) This is exactly what happens to the Witnesses—they become so overwhelmed with the skillful, cunning arguments and deceptive reasoning of the Society that after a while its twisted doctrines seem straight—the Society even succeeds in getting its members to believe that all of the twists and turns of its zigzagging "sailboat" are really a straight route to truth. Interestingly, the advice the Society intended for others applies particularly to itself as well:

It follows, then, that all doctrines or teachings of men, which are contrary to the Word of God, are false teachings; and if such doctrines or teachings tend to do injury to others, then such doctrines or teachings are lies. (*Riches* [1936], p. 178)

Although the Society cites scriptural support every time it changes its doctrines to a new point of view, and then later switches them back to the former view, and so on—common sense testifies to the fact that not all of those viewpoints represent the truth—hence, some of the time they represent false teachings. That some of those teachings have done injury to others is written in the journals of history. The Society's own counsel under such circumstances is fitting:

If you find that a doctrine or teaching is a lie, you should quickly forsake it, regardless of who teaches it or how long you have believed that teaching to be true. (*Riches* [1936], p. 178)

If you find that you have been for some time in an organization called "the church," and that such organization teaches that which is contrary to God's Word of truth, then you will have to choose whether you will remain in accord with that so-called "church" organization and its teachings or will forsake the same and rely upon the Word of God. . . . Ask the God of all wisdom and comfort to let you see the truth. (*Riches* [1936], pp. 178-179.)

Paradoxically, the Witnesses—who pride themselves on being champions of truth—are very afraid of finding out what the truth about the organization really is. I had found out what the truth about the organization is. My research had proven to me that the organization's authority is not of God. I could now clearly see how the Society employs many of the mind control techniques cultlike groups use in attracting and holding onto their members. And my therapist had helped me understand the role my personal psychology had played in making the struggle to leave the organization so difficult.

As a child, I had no real options to escape the abuse that I suffered. As an adult abused by the organization, I had carried over those feelings of helplessness from my childhood and still felt that I had no options; the Society's inculcating its members with the thought that only two choices exist—either obey the organization's rules and have a chance of surviving Armageddon, or leave the organization and die at Armageddon—confirmed those feelings.

And the Society continually impressed on everyone's mind that "There is nowhere else to go." Although complaining is forbidden, still many times during my long association with the organization I had heard small groups of Witnesses murmuring their disagreements with the Society; these conversations always had the same ending—frustrated voices would sigh, "But there is nowhere else to go." So thoroughly indoctrinated were the congregation members with this mindset that no other options existed, that rare was the person who challenged it. Now I was ready for the challenge. Now I could see things differently and knew that other options did exist; being outside the organization did not mean I would die. That God wanted me to acquiesce quietly to the Society and follow its rules—even though its rules hurt people and didn't make sense—I wanted to deny that vision of God before it punished me. I had had enough of letting the organization threaten me with its power; I knew if I did not make the decision to leave it, that eventually the elders would catch me in a disagreement with the Society and disfellowship me for apostasy.

I learned through my therapy how people leave the organization has much to do with how they were raised as children. The environment in which a person grows up affects how that person comes to view the world, which in turn affects how he or she handles leaving a group like the Watchtower Society. If the person were raised to be an independent thinker with good self-esteem and self-confidence, he or she will likely be the one who will easily and readily take a stand for what they believe and disassociate him- or herself. Others may be able to simply walk away, go on to lead the life they choose, and give no credence whatsoever to what the Witnesses think or if the elders disfellowship them, and never look back. Still others will choose to fade away instead of taking such a stand, to retain friendships and to avoid the trauma of being publicly shunned.

Knowing the organization allows no honorable way out, I was faced with the decision of whether to publicly leave under my own volition, or to try to fade away and go on with my life in whatever way I chose and hope nobody noticed—which would mean living under the constant fear that someone would notice and turn me in to the elders. The latter did not seem to be the wisest choice, because being the wife of an elder made me somewhat of a spectacle in this circumstance. I knew I would be under surveillance by the servants of the congregation; they were anxious to catch me in some act of "apostasy"—i.e., going into a church, reading literature that exposes the organization, speaking critically to anyone about the organization, contacting anyone who had left the organization, going into a Christian bookstore, and the like. I was aware that my husband had already been repeatedly interrogated by the other elders as to who my friends were, where I went, what activities I was involved in, what sort of reading materials I had, what kinds of things I talked about, and if I had attended a church.

Relating all of this to my therapist, he discussed with me the psychological difference between my making the decision to leave the organization of my own free will, versus being thrown out by the organization. He cautioned, "There will be a big difference in your self-esteem if you proactively choose to leave the organization. Waiting until they disfellowship you will make you feel still tied to them as the parent who says, 'You're a bad kid!' And you'll carry that feeling, and you'll never be truly free." My therapist pointed out that every decision has an effect; leaving the organization would have serious consequences in my life, but staying in it would have serious consequences, too. Life in the organization had come to be like living in a toxic cocoon—it was suffocating my spirit, my individuality, and my respect for myself. Living my life in the organization had ultimately become even more painful than leaving it.

My therapist helped me to understand that subconsciously, I wanted to go back to my childhood and confront my abusive mother; although she was no longer there, the organization was now playing the same role.

I could stand up to my abusive mother now by taking action to separate myself from the organization. I made the choice to voluntarily disassociate myself from the organization of Jehovah's Witnesses. Disassociating myself was important to me because it meant that I was in control of my life, instead of allowing the elders and the organization to wield control and be the authority over me. It meant that I was protecting myself from further victimization and spiritual abuse. I wanted to write a detailed letter to the elders outlining my reasons for leaving the organization, but I knew they would only use my letter as ammunition against me to disfellowship me for apostasy. I was finally at the point where I felt I didn't need this fight; it was time to go on, to walk away from the fight. On my desk laid four worn pages I had torn from my desk calendar the previous year; I now drew strength from their inscriptions:

- I can stop allowing myself to be so controlled by others, and start being true to myself.
- I can choose my own course of action.
- I am not a victim. I can walk away. I can stand up for myself. I can refuse to let others control or manipulate me.

- Today, I will refuse to think, talk, speak, or act like a victim; instead, I will claim my power and take responsibility for myself.

My letter, which I delivered to the homes of each of the elders on March 2, 1993, was a simple statement that gave them no basis upon which they could disfellowship me. "This letter is to inform you that I have voluntarily disassociated myself from The Watchtower Society's organization of Jehovah's Witnesses." As I dropped my letter into the elders' mailboxes, I whispered: *"You'll never hurt me again!"*

Leaving the organization resulted in a mixture of emotions:

- *I felt scared* because of not knowing what lay in the future; I felt as if I had let go of the trapeze bar I had held onto for dear life and was now flying through midair alone; I no longer had "all the answers"—in fact, I wasn't even sure if I had any of them.
- *I felt apprehension* at the prospect of having to make entirely new friends at this stage of my life, and of figuring out what the truth about life really is.
- *I felt sad* that the few Witnesses I really enjoyed would not allow themselves to be friends with me any longer; and I felt a certain sadness about leaving a way of life I had embraced for nearly half of my life.
- *I felt disappointed* that the organization was much different than it professed to be.
- *I felt angry* that the Witnesses' constant preparation for the end of the world left us so unprepared to be alive in it. And I felt angry about the way the Society cheated me and others out of our lives through its denial of death. Believing the Society's teaching that I lived in the unique time of "The End," and that my generation overlapped that of the special "marked generation" that would never have to experience death was a grand belief; but, in this denial of death there was a price paid—living was put off until some uncertain future. Nearly all available time was spent warning others about the end of this present system. Careers, education, relationships, and enjoyment of life were put on hold, postponed until after the realization of the new system on the Earth; that belief robbed me and others of making the most of each precious day, of living our lives more fully. As for my generation being a part of "the marked generation of 1914" that will live to see Armageddon—that is just another prophecy to add to the Society's long list of failed prophecies.
- *I felt rage* because of being so deceived and betrayed by the organization

I had trusted. The one that had promised protection and a safe refuge from the abusive world had instead become the abuser. While I know that holding onto the anger I feel toward the Watchtower Society only shackles me to it as a prisoner, the process of releasing that anger and moving on is not an easy one—and it remains an ongoing process for me. Because the Watchtower Society has not demonstrated repentance nor begged forgiveness for all its errors that have caused great injury to others, I cannot pardon it. I am not sure that forgiveness is possible or even necessary, as what evidence does the Bible give that even God forgives unrepentant sinners, or those who take the lives of others without remorse?

- *I felt relief* at being able to take off the mask I had worn for so long, and to start living a life free of pretense.
- *I felt hopeful*, recalling my therapist's encouragement that "Crisis and chaos is the time of opportunity."
- *I felt excited* about having the freedom to choose a way of life that genuinely feels like the truth. Having to go through the process of figuring out what I believe is better than continuing to live a false faith. And I have learned that instead of the Society's rigid black-or-white rules, there is freedom in shades of gray.
- *I felt joy* for having been released from bondage and slavery to the dictates of men.
- *I felt triumphant* for having reclaimed my mind and my life.

As my therapist once told me:

> Part of the struggle in life is to become as free as you can as an adult, and to realize that you don't always know the right answers. But by evaluating information, and learning from your mistakes, and making choices that feel right, you live the truth as you feel it by choosing the path that feels right, and following that path with integrity. How hard it is to have integrity without the rules and to try to live a life that really is disciplined and makes sense and your beliefs really stand-up for something and you live them. Life is not about having all the answers; it's about feeling okay about being on the path.

TWENTY-FIVE

CONCLUSION

As one would struggle to free oneself from a twisted, tangled briar patch, its sharp thorns inflicting pain and suffering with every attempt to escape from the gnarled prison—so I struggled to free myself from the Watchtower Society's twisted, tangled thinking patterns and doctrines, their threats, punishments, and implanted phobias inflicting pain and suffering with every attempt to escape from their convoluted psychological prison.

As stinging wounds from thornpricks heal, and those from penetrating lacerations produce scars that remain, so heals the emotional pain caused by my involvement with Jehovah's Witnesses—though the scars may long be with me.

As roses rising above tangled vines, the blossoming of life—the growth to development of one's full potential—can occur when one is finally freed of the oppression of the Watchtower Society's organization of Jehovah's Witnesses.

EPILOGUE

The Witnesses who knew me were shocked when the elder read my disassociation letter to the congregation. All Jehovah's Witnesses continue to shun me. At times when I was running errands with my husband, Witnesses came up to us, but acknowledged my husband only—complete with hearty backslapping, enthusiastic handshakes, and friendly smiles. They completely ignored me, looking through me as though I were not even present.

The friendships I had within the organization were superficial when compared with the deeper, more meaningful and satisfying friendships I have developed since I left the organization. I have not become involved in any other religious group; I am allowing time to pass to get some distance on my Watchtower experience, as I know from my research those who were once involved in a cultlike group are at risk to be lured into another such group. I do, however, hold a firm belief in Jesus. Occasionally I visit Christian churches and enjoy the spiritually uplifting, contemporary music offered there.

I maintain a close relationship with both of my children. My daughter is now 29, single, owns a prosperous business, and has a very positive outlook on life. Although she does not have a particular religious affiliation at this time, she occasionally visits various Christian churches. My son is now in his thirties, has a successful business, and is happily remarried after escaping an abusive marriage to a Witness. He has not been actively involved with the Witnesses for quite some time.

After I disassociated myself, the elders instructed my husband never to pray with me, nor talk with me about God or spiritual matters. As curious as my husband at times seemed to be about what I spent so much time writing as I was compiling this book, he still has not read this work. Like an ostrich that hides its head in a hole in the sand, my husband denies the evidence that my research has produced by looking the other way and pretending not to notice, or by finding a multitude of ways to discount it.

My husband and I march to the beats of different drummers. Choosing two very different paths regarding this religion has recently led to our traveling separate paths in life as well.

AUTHOR
RECOMMENDED READING

Arterburn, Stephen, and Jack Felton. *Toxic Faith*. Nashville, Tenn.: Oliver-Nelson Books, 1991.

Barefoot, Darek. *Jehovah's Witnesses and the Hour of Darkness*. Grand Junction, Colo.: Grand Valley Press, 1992.

Beattie, Melody. *Codependent No More*. San Francisco: Harper & Row, 1987.

Bergman, Jerry. *Blood Transfusions*. Clayton, Calif.: Witness Inc., 1994.

———. *Jehovah's Witnesses and the Problem of Mental Illness*. Clayton, Calif.: Witness Inc., 1992.

Botting, Heather, and Gary Botting. *The Orwellian World of Jehovah's Witnesses*. Toronto: University of Toronto Press, 1984.

DesRoches, Brian. *Reclaiming Your Self*. New York: Dell Publishing, 1990.

Enroth, Ronald M. *Churches That Abuse*. Grand Rapids, Mich.: Zondervan Publishing House, 1992.

Farmer, Steven. *Adult Children of Abusive Parents*. New York: Ballantine Books, 1989.

Franz, Raymond. *Crisis of Conscience*. Atlanta, Ga.: Commentary Press, 1983.

———. *In Search of Christian Freedom*. Atlanta, Ga.: Commentary Press, 1991.

Gil, Eliana. *Outgrowing The Pain*. New York: Dell Publishing, 1983.

Hassan, Steven. *Combatting Cult Mind Control*. Rochester, Vt.: Park Street Press, 1990.

Johnson, David, and Jeff VanVonderen. *The Subtle Power of Spiritual Abuse*. Minneapolis, Minn.: Bethany House Publishers, 1991.

Langone, Michael D. *Recovery From Cults*. New York: W. W. Norton & Company, 1993.

Penton, M. James. *Apocalypse Delayed*. Toronto: University of Toronto Press, 1985.

Reed, David. *Blood on the Altar*. Amherst, N.Y.: Prometheus Books, 1996.

————. *Behind The Watchtower Curtain.* Southbridge, Mass.: Crowne Publications, 1989.

Tobias, Madeleine L., and Janja Lalich. *Captive Hearts, Captive Minds.* Alameda, Calif.: Hunter House, 1994.

WHY COULDN'T SHE JUST LEAVE?

Jerry Bergman, Ph.D., MSBS, L.P.C.C.

Persons who were raised in the Watchtower or who have studied the Watchtower will be able to follow Diane's story without problems. Other readers will no doubt find much of her story baffling. "Why not just leave the Watchtower and go on with your life?" many will ask. This brief appendix will help these readers to understand Diane's life and why she made the decisions that she did.

BRIEF HISTORY OF THE WATCHTOWER

The modern-day movement now known as Jehovah's Witnesses was founded in 1879 by Charles Taze Russell (1852–1916). In July of that year he began his journal, *The Watchtower and Herald of Christ's Presence*, a semimonthly magazine. *The Watchtower* is still published today. The first issue had a printing of 6,000 copies; as of the year 2000, it is published in 130 languages with an average printing of 22,328,000 copies. Russell was involved with the Second Adventists, a church related to the modern Seventh-Day Adventist church; when he started his own church, he borrowed many Adventist doctrines, which explains the many similarities that still exist between the two denominations. The organization that Russell founded in 1879 has distanced itself greatly from the viewpoints of the original founders.

Once called "Bible Students," Jehovah's Witnesses is the name chosen in 1931 by Joseph Franklin Rutherford, the former leader of the movement who succeeded Russell, to distinguish it from the many schisms from the group originally founded by Russell.

Rutherford was succeeded as president by Nathan Homer Knorr (1905–1977) in 1942 and was president until 1977 when he died of a brain tumor.

Fred Franz (1893–1992) then became president; he was considered the Watchtower's chief theologian even under the presidency of Knorr. Franz was a college student at the University of Cincinnati until he was contacted by several Russellites in 1914. The teaching then was that the end of this system of things (meaning the end of this old world) would come in 1914, so Franz left college and he soon ended up at the Watchtower world headquarters. As one of the better educated Witnesses then, he rose up the ranks rapidly. A member of the editorial staff in 1926, he became vice president in 1945. He died in 1992 of a heart attack at age 99. In 1992 Milton G. Henschel was appointed to take Franz's place.

The power of the first two presidents was absolute, but as the Watchtower grew, one person could no longer control the Watchtower as before. As a result, the power of later presidents was diminished when a "Governing Body" (a group of about twelve to sixteen men) was established at the world headquarters in New York; the Governing Body became the composite leader, formulating doctrine and policy. For active Witnesses, the headquarters is shrouded with clouds of mystery and an aura of Godhead. Witnesses are required to believe that the Watchtower is God's organization, the only group that God is working through today. It is only through it that truth can be had, they believe, and all persons outside of it are condemned forever to the second (meaning eternal) death. In fact, the president still retains a great deal of power but many decisions are now voted on (a practice which does not square with their belief that the Watchtower is directed by God and is the only organization today that has that status).

The Watchtower Society world headquarters has been in Brooklyn, New York, since 1909. The Watchtower is now becoming very wealthy. They own a large number of expensive properties in New York and a 670-acre, $50,000,000 retreat center at Patterson, New Jersey; their property reportedly includes such luxuries as million dollar chandeliers and billions in real estate.

Why Do People Join the Watchtower?

The Witness community offers a high degree of security, and both an immense amount of emotional and social support, as well as practical aid at times. In order to gain these benefits, however, one has to sacrifice a great deal of time and adhere to a rigid belief system and a strict set of moral rules. Their major appeal is community, and converts often join to fill a void in this area.

Several major reasons exist why persons become a part of an organization such as the Jehovah's Witnesses:

1. They were born into a family or have a parent who is a member, and have learned from a young age to accept its beliefs as both normal and correct.
2. They become Witnesses through acquaintances. If a friend, neighbor, relative, workmate, or spouse is a Witness, through their association one will often become involved, and in time will to some extent view the world as a Witness.
3. The organization tends to be a home for the socially maladjusted. One involved with the Witnesses soon discovers their high level of acceptance of the downtrodden, poor, minorities, and others. Individuals who are somewhat different, eccentric, lonely, lacking friends or social contacts are most often highly accepted in the Witness community, providing only that they can conform to the Witness belief and behavioral requirements, and are not extremely deviant in most areas of life. People with problems often accept the Witnesses' friendship, which is customarily offered in spite of one's problems. Once community is presented, the path to conversion has begun, and the convert soon begins to see the world in a different light. The original exposure produces an attraction which soon begins to solidify; in a short time, often less than a year, the person becomes enmeshed in the Witness belief structure. After a person becomes a baptized Witness, the pressure to conform becomes greater. The congregation usually will put up with nonconformists and deviant or neurotic behavior only for so long. When one is no longer seen as a new Witness, one is expected to have towed the line or solved one's problems, and if one doesn't, he or she may be forced to leave. Nonetheless, the Witnesses tend to attract a large number of people, and their holding power is quite strong, especially after the initial stages of conversion.
4. Unemployment, crime in the cities and suburbs, war without end, massive starvation in Ethiopia and other parts of the Third World, floods, hurricanes, tornadoes and earthquakes in all parts of the world cause all but the most callous of individuals to die a little each time they hear of

the latest catastrophe; involvement in the Witnesses helps make the pain a little easier to endure. For them, the ever-deteriorating conditions in the world foretell of the imminence of Armageddon, when Satan and all his followers will be destroyed forever and God's kingdom will finally bring lasting blessings to mankind on Earth.

5. Witness theology often appeals to the deprived, the poor, the discouraged, and the disappointed. By stressing better conditions soon to come, and by constantly pointing out just how bad the current social system really is, a vivid contrast is provided to their community. Another attraction is they are repeatedly told that racism does not exist in the New World Society. Equally important, the cognitive filter inculcated by the Society's culture building processes enables racial injustices experienced in the secular world to be reinterpreted as signs that point to the approaching end of this present evil system.

6. The potential convert is often at a crisis point in life, e.g., he is dissatisfied with his current life, possibly drugs have taken their physical and mental toll, his life is disrupted and disjointed and he needs a supportive community. Or perhaps he has just experienced the trauma of divorce or the death of a loved one. The convert is often at a point of decision—he has quit (or been expelled from) school, lost his job, and so forth. At this point, the meeting of the proselytizer and the convert is the beginning of induction into the movement.

7. Involvement with the Witnesses offers a valid sense of purpose if one can buy into their theology.

8. Many emotional needs are met through Witness involvement:

   • Being shielded from the troubles of the secular world in the microcosm of the organization
   • A large supply of instant friends, so that one does not have to work at finding persons with whom to develop relationships
   • Security by being protected by God in life, not to mention at the future end times calamity often called Armageddon
   • Instant "family" (especially appealing to people who have no or an alienated real family)
   • Having decisions for nearly every thing major (and often even minor areas) made for you (an advantage for people who have trouble making decisions). If a situation comes up that is not directly covered by Watchtower rules, the elders are usually ready and willing to help make the decision for the Witness.
   • Never having to worry about falling into the ranks of the "homeless."

The congregation never would let one of their dedicated, active members live on the street. Congregation members usually will take in a Witness who suddenly found him or herself homeless, and help would be given to get them back on their own.

- Association with only other Witnesses helps keep one's children on the straight and narrow, and out of the common trouble that plagues so many youths today.
- Feeling special
- The feeling that the organization offers "prescreened" marriage partners, i.e., all the rules Witnesses must follow makes for a desirable husband or wife; all one has to do is choose a mate from among Witnesses in good standing—certain qualities are automatically there (i.e., they are often hardworking, free of drugs, drunkenness, smoking, etc.)

9. The Witness culture gives men the opportunity for positions of power and authority. Only men have the possibility to become leaders in the group, and even men with minimal education can work their way up through the ranks to positions held in high esteem by congregation members.

The Witness Mindset

Each Witness has as his or her first priority achieving the Watchtower's goals, even to the extent of giving up family, career, education, or other "selfish" pursuits. The "Kingdom" must be first in one's life. Frantic activity devoted to spreading the Watchtower word before God destroys "this system of things" is foremost in their minds.

Marriage and having children were strongly eschewed for decades, and even today career advancement, education, hobbies, and even overtime work are all strongly discouraged. Pressures in these directions are due to Satan's "evil machinations" to be overcome in order to achieve that all important and divine goal of "preaching the good news of God's Kingdom to the entire inhabited Earth," and serving "God's people." Each Witness believes that he is a part of God's organization which was established by God Himself to carry out His will, and thus everyone must cooperate in order to achieve the laudable divine goals which God has assigned to it.

The role of the male as being assertive and head of the house is constantly emphasized; Witnesses believe the husband has the scriptural right to make all final decisions for the family. A very rigid division exists between the sexes, and all adult females are to take a decidedly inferior role—that the woman is inferior even to a man who is "inferior" according to "male standards," i.e., that the best woman is below the worst man. Constant emphasis is put upon insuring that females remain in a clearly secondary role. Females are not allowed to assume any formal teaching role in the congregation (ministerial servants, elder, etc.). Especially are the intelligent, better-educated females continually counseled against asserting themselves or displaying their knowledge in an ostentatious way. All of these activities are discouraged because they amount to endeavoring to "usurp the headship of males."

Witnesses are totally focused on "the end" of the world as we know it, and the idea is taught that those who are not Witnesses are not only wrong, but evil as well; nevertheless, Witnesses are also taught to be friendly with everyone—not only other Witnesses but also non-Witnesses, primarily in order to promote a positive image of the Watchtower and to encourage converts. Appearances are important to Witnesses because it facilitates selling their belief structure. Since each Witness is a reflection of the validity of their beliefs, as a group they endeavor to put on a good show in order to impress outsiders. Witnesses almost always interact with others with their "hidden agenda," the covert desire to steer the conversation to the "last days," how bad the world is, the need to join the Watchtower Society—in short, to proselytize the person.

The Witnesses' most controversial beliefs include their conclusion that the Watchtower Society is God's organization, and it is only through this that salvation can be achieved. All of those who are not part of this "ark of salvation" will be destroyed in the Battle of Armageddon, which they expect will come very soon. All other churches, therefore, as they are not in support of God's organization, are viewed to be in opposition to it. The Witnesses are particularly hostile toward those religions with belief systems that compete directly with their own, concluding that they are being used by Satan to deliberately mislead people into everlasting destruction. They believe that all the religious ships are sinking except one—the Watchtower Society—and that all other religions that tell their members they are saved are actually deceiving them to their everlasting death.

Witnesses are to be very careful as to their conduct with each other out of fear of "stumbling someone," i.e. causing a person to leave the Watchtower organization because of poor conduct by its members. Witnesses are taught that a person who is "stumbled" will lose out on everlasting life if he/she does not die first. If a person dies before Armageddon as a non-Witness, the belief is that that person will probably be resurrected and will then have a chance to accept Watchtower theology—a step that the Watchtower teaches will be much easier in the New World because all in authority will be Witnesses, and the influence of other religions will be nonexistent. This doctrine is called "the second chance doctrine." The stumbler, however, will lose his or her life forever at Armageddon; this functions as a strong deterrent that serves to reduce interpersonal conflicts.

Psychologically many, but certainly not all Witnesses, at some level believe that they are in the organization by God's will—and even when they are totally unhappy with being a Witness, they tend to feel that something is wrong with them, not the Watchtower. Faithful Witnesses rarely blame failure on the Society; if they have a problem, it is somehow part of God's purpose, or a personal failure of one or more of the individuals involved.

Why do People Stay so Long?

Many Witnesses sincerely believe that the Watchtower Society is God's organization, and that He is directing it; thus, even if things the organization does are wrong—such as their past erroneous teachings—they are done for a purpose. No matter what good or bad the organization does, they come to believe it is all part of God's purpose. Others even feel that the past tragic teachings, such as condemning vaccinations and organ transplants, do not matter since loss of life is now somewhat like having to go on a long vacation—a faithful person will be resurrected anyway, thus what does it matter? A common reason many stay is because they have given their life to this organization, e.g., they did not marry, they feel they are too old to begin a career, etc., thus they feel they may as well stay involved in the organization. Many have a "crisis of conscience" and feel that they can no longer support an organization that they no longer believe in, but stay because of family.

Leaving the organization is not uncommonly severely traumatic. Many Witnesses have various fears or even phobias about leaving, such as Jehovah will destroy them at Armageddon if they leave, or that they will lose all control and self-destruct if they leave; both beliefs—even though irrational—are nonetheless common, and therefore prevent them from leaving. The Watchtower often tells stories of what happens to those who leave, such as they become involved in drugs, immorality, and their marriage falls apart. And these happenings are not uncommonly true. Most Witnesses know of someone who has left, and many throw the baby out with the bath water.

Many lose their moral bearing and are determined to do exactly what the Watchtower condemns. They may start to regularly get drunk, and some even turn to crime as a reaction to their Watchtower involvement. Many at the least will grow a beard—which is condemned in the Watchtower—or start attending college, which was also condemned for years.

Also, Witnesses hear years of lambasting of all other churches and find it very difficult to replace what they have with the Watchtower, so they stay. It takes years to overcome the intense indoctrination against all religions, and many ex-Witnesses never do bring themselves to join another church or even join a church related group such as the YMCA. It is common for ex-Witnesses to refuse blood transfusions years after they leave, so effective is the indoctrination.

Leaving Is No Easy Matter

The trauma of leaving the organization is great, whether voluntary or forced. Even when they become mature Witnesses it is typically very difficult to leave, although many eventually do—such is the power of community and the effectiveness of the Witness indoctrination. When people become Witnesses, they are slowly indoctrinated into a belief structure which requires them to give up their friends—often even their family—and adopt a new family, that of the Watchtower. After they have been Witnesses for a few years, most all have only Witness friends. Leaving means virtually every one of their friends—and often their family, if they are Witnesses—will cut off all meaningful association with them.

Those who are expelled or who leave voluntarily are to be treated as if dead. If it is determined that a Witness has not steadfastly complied with this shunning rule, he or she will likely also be disfellowshipped. Common are stories of children who left the Watchtower and, as a result, all communication between parents and the children ended. Consequently, many find leaving extremely traumatic even after they are fully convinced the Watchtower is wrong. For this reason many elect to stay, trudging along to Watchtower meetings and hearing and saying things that they themselves disagree with. Eventually the conflict may become too great, and they conclude they must resign, giving up family, friends, and their whole previous life.

The Watchtower Society often infers that all those who leave do so because of their personal inability to desist from immoral behavior. They also tend to color all those who slowly drift away with the same brushstroke of immorality. Interviews that I have conducted with the leading four dozen or so contemporary anti-Watchtower activists, however, found that not a single one severed their relationship with the Society because of disagreements over their moral teachings. The reason most left is because of sincere questions about specific Watchtower doctrines which the Society had not been able to answer; they leave because they can no longer consciously accept and proclaim certain dogmatic teachings of the Society that lack biblical support. Those who leave are often spiritually in most every way the cream of those who have a scripturally trained conscience; when it is violated by the Society, they must make a choice between the Scriptures and the Watchtower. They are not unlike those in Nazi Germany who concluded that Hitler was wrong, and must buck the tide whatever the cost— and leaving the Witnesses often has horrible costs, such as loss of friends, family, and one's business.

Those who once embraced the faith and then left are hated traitors in the full sense of the word (see *WT* 7-15-92, pp. 12–13). Witnesses are also often vicious toward those who leave partly because this event often causes doubts about the Watchtower in their own minds. They believe that one who leaves is the "worst sort of all men" and commonly save their greatest hatred for these persons. Even a Witness who starts to drift away is threatening to the faithful Witnesses, causing them to be quite antagonistic. This treatment also tends to keep many weak Witnesses firmly in the fold.

Many people, especially those who are psychologically innner-directed, look to themselves as the source of many of their problems and not others, such as an organization. Persons who are other-directed tend to blame their troubles on their life situation or on those persons around them. Many people are governed by both of these coping styles, and consequently they react accordingly. The more inner-directed the person, often the more difficult it is to leave. This coping style is a fundamental part of the personality; and for this reason, even in the face of good reasons, it is often difficult to leave the organization.

I have worked with people who still clung to the Watchtower long after most everyone else in their family and many of their Witness friends had left it. On the other hand, many people leave for rather trivial reasons, such as an elder snubs them one too many times. These people leave and never look back, while the inner-directed person may look back with mixed feelings long after they have left, sometimes even years after they have left.

Many active Jehovah's Witnesses strongly believe that they are Witnesses by choice, fully as a result of their own free will—yet some of these people find it very difficult to leave. It is as if they in fact do not have a choice about leaving. Some of these people do not have family in the Watchtower, and therefore not being able to leave is not due to a fear of losing their family; something greater is involved, often the nagging fear that the Watchtower just may be correct. They may reason, "What if I am wrong about my suspicions and they are in fact the truth? What if they are correct and I am just a faultfinder and do not know the whole story as the brothers claim?" If one is in the Watchtower by conscious choice, the person should be able to leave by choice, but the doubts about one's own objections can be paralyzing.

The mental and emotional agony that goes on with the internal psychological struggle that Witnesses can experience often belies the common assumption that they are in the Watchtower fully by choice. In fact, they are often locked in an intense personal struggle with their doubts. If they come to the point that they have absolutely no question that the Watchtower is wrong, leaving is often not as difficult, but until they resolve their doubts, they will be torn between leaving and staying. And resolving their doubts can take years, and in some cases decades. This is especially true of persons who become Witnesses by choice and are fully committed to the Watchtower theology. For those who were, as Witnesses say, "raised around the Truth," leaving is far less traumatic.

The Way Out

Most Witnesses are able to accept one or two conflicts, even three or four, and still believe that the Society is God's organization. The Society is often unwilling to objectively reason about its doctrine and policies and therefore cannot even begin to adequately respond to the many questions that typically surface. This forces many thinking Witnesses to conclude that they are set in their ways and determined to adhere to the "traditions of men" as opposed to the Word of God. When a religious organization begins to develop, it is usually fairly flexible and amenable to Scriptural counsel; time often results in rigidity, however, and it then follows only its own traditions.

Some Witnesses who become disillusioned with the organization believe, at some point in their sojourn, that the organization will change; however, in time they come to realize that the Society has simply far too many changes to make. Added to that is the fact they come to learn that the Society is adamant in resisting almost all input from others, no matter how well researched or valuable it is. Most discouraged Witnesses are far past the point where they feel that the Society can be reformed.

Fortunately, some do find the way out. While many become agnostics or atheists, hating God and all attempts to understand and reach Him, some are fortunate in that through intensive Bible study, they come to realize that the Watchtower is based on a misunderstanding of the Bible and a mis-reading of many select "proof texts." These persons realize a firm faith does exist that is not based on the shifting sands of a man-made organization that is directed by individuals who are often scripturally illiterate and ill-informed about historical Christianity—or even modern biblical research—and whose publications are riddled with errors of fact and logic. These people are able to look back at their experience in the Watchtower as one that can be used to help others.

The path of leaving the Witnesses usually starts with growing doubts about certain teachings. This does not in itself usually create problems, but the Watchtower Society's response to sincere questions often does cause problems. Once questions are voiced, the questioner is all too often told that he or she is to accept whatever the Society teaches and is not to "reason" about it, but must blindly and dogmatically fully accept whatever is taught. The individual's reason, they stress, is "human reasoning," but the Watchtower's reasoning is "God's reasoning." If one does not blindly accept all that is taught—however foolish—often their spirituality is impugned, even for sincere and honest questions. One then learns that questions are not to be voiced. This is usually the first step out of the orga-nization. Once the alienation begins, it tends to find its own fuel, often causing a raging fire, and eventually the abandonment of an organization which one formerly passionately defended, in many cases for decades.

Many Witnesses depart quietly by simply fading away; but some, partly because their disappointment is so immense, feel that they must openly respond to what they conclude are the gross sins and injustices committed by the Watchtower by exposing them through the printed page.

Dissident Witnesses resemble Blacks living in the American South who perceived that the system was wrong and defiantly state, "I will not move to the back of the bus." And so they refused to bow to injustice and the existing inhumane laws and traditions. Likewise, the dissident ex-Wit-nesses of today refuse to bow to the inhumanity being perpetuated by an organization they once fully trusted and were loyal to, giving it their all for years, even decades. To betray someone's trust is a serious matter. The con-cern and goal of the ex-Witness movement is to let the world know the Watchtower's grievous wrongs. They are not content to be the "silent majority," but feel it is their duty to speak out for what they believe is true.

Blind religious faith has caused untold tragedy in the past and also our modern era. Many examples exist of the evil that resulted from believing that what one personally happens to conclude is of God, and that those who disagree with this are listening to the words of demons. Faith is simultaneously both a wonderful and a tragic thing which must be tempered with a reasonableness which comes from a valid awareness of both sides. Conclusions in religion, as in all other areas, require an impartial examination of a wide variety of evidence.

Few of us have the time to examine many of these areas in much depth—even those who make their living in scholarly pursuits achieve an exhaustive knowledge in, at best, only a very few small areas of a field of knowledge. Realizing this should help one to be humble about what one believes, neither lightly giving up one's beliefs, nor incredulously adhering to ideas which one accepts because they were told to us when we were young, or by someone that we trust—or simply because they were repeated so often that they became part of our mental schemata.

The Watchtower Society is a complex ever-growing and changing organization about which this appendix has only briefly touched on some relevant points that relate to Diane's story. The reader is encouraged to peruse one or more of the following references which go into much more depth on the history and psychology of the Witness movement. For an extensive list of almost 10,000 references, see my book, *Jehovah's Witnesses, A Comprehensive and Selectively Annotated Bibliography* (Westport, Conn.: Greenwood Press, 1999).

References

Alston, John P. "Congregational Size and the Decline of Sectarian Commitment: The Case of the Jehovah's Witnesses in South and North America." *Sociological* 40, no. 1 (spring 1979): 63–70.

———. "Jehovah's Witnesses: A Study in Cognitive Dissonance," *Universitas* 92 (September 1973): 103–105.

Beckford, James A. *The Trumpet of Prophecy: A Sociological Study of Jehovah's Witnesses*. Oxford: Basil Blackwell, 1975.

———. "Organization, Ideology and Recruitment: The Structure of the Watchtower Movement," *The Sociological Review* 23, no. 4 (November 1975).

———. "Sociological Stereotypes of the Religious Sect," *The Sociological Review* 26, no. 1 (February 1978).

———. "Structural Dependence in Religious Organizations: From 'Skid-Row' to Watchtower," *Journal for the Scientific Study of Religion* 15, no. 2 (June 1976).

Cooper, Lee. "Publish or Perish" Negro Jehovah's Witnesses; Adaptation in the Ghetto *Religious Movements in Contemporary America.* Ed. by Irving Zaretsley. Princeton, N.J.: Princeton University Press, 1974.

Gruss, Edmond Charles. *The Jehovah's Witnesses and Prophetic Speculation.* Nutley, N.J.: Presbyterian and Reform Publishing Co., 1978, rev. ed.

Harrison, Barbara. *Visions of Glory: A History and a Memory of Jehovah's Witnesses.* New York: Simon and Schuster, 1978.

Hickman, Richard. *The Psychology of Jehovah's Witnesses: Reflections of Twenty-Five Years.* Worthville, Ky.: Love Agape Ministries Press, 1984. Rev. ed., 1985.

Montague, Havor. "The Pessimistic Sect's Influence on the Mental Health of Its Members: The Case of Jehovah's Witnesses," *Social Compass* 24, no. 1 (1977): 135–47.

Penton, M. James. *Jehovah's Witnesses in Canada.* Toronto: Macmillan, 1976.

Spencer, John. "The Mental Health of Jehovah's Witnesses," *British Journal of Psychiatry* 126 (1975): 556–59.

Sterling, Chandler. *The Witnesses: One God, One Victory.* Chicago: Henry Regnery Co., 1975.

Stevens, Leondard. *Salute! The Case of the Bible vs. the Flag.* New York: Coward, McCann and Geohegan, Inc. 1973.

White, Timothy. *A People for His Name.* New York: Vantage Press, 1967.

———. *Religious Sects.* London: World University Library, 1970.

———. *Religion in Sociological Perspective.* Oxford: Oxford University Press, 1982.

Zygmunt, Joseph. "Prophetic Failure and Chiliastic Identity: The Case of Jehovah's Witnesses," *American Journal of Sociology* 75, no. 6 (May 1970): 926–48.

APPENDIX B

DISCUSSION OF WATCHTOWER BELIEFS

Jerry Bergman, Ph.D., MSBS, L.P.C.C.

CLOSED BELIEF STRUCTURE

The five hours of formal indoctrination and the six hours of study required each week serve to insure that the Witnesses' belief structure is firmly internalized. Once the Witness is socialized into the New World Society model, he or she can explain or account for almost everything—even clear contradictions—because the Watchtower beliefs are what is called a "closed belief structure." This term means that a person either accepts the entire set of beliefs or rejects the set, and includes the idea that the set as a package can justify or rationalize almost everything, even clear contradictions. Each idea is not considered as an entity by itself, but as part of the set which must be accepted as a package. It is uncanny to listen to Witnesses use the same reasons to explain contradictory events, i.e., both persecution and favor from outsiders alike are proof of God's blessing; thus, no matter what events occur, they can be used as "proof" of God's blessing and favor.

COMMUNITY AND ISOLATION

It is repeatedly stressed that "bad associations spoil useful habits" and "one should not be unevenly yoked with unbelievers," or anyone of the world. It is the Witness belief that the world is corrupt because Satan has 'spiritual jurisdiction over it.' Witnesses may even find it hard to relate to "the world," and it is a rare Witness that seeks attention or counsel from the world. They are taught that all of those of the world are evil, and even though worldly people may appear to be kind, this is one of Satan's tactics to lure people out of God's organization.

Witnesses attempt to isolate themselves from the community as a whole; therefore, their primary socialization is predominantly from individuals who avoid not only what is socially accepted as deviant behavior, but also much which is socially approved. Examples include celebration of holidays, acceptance of blood transfusions, involvement in career and occupational pursuits beyond what is necessary to make a living, and saluting the flag. In time, they come to accept these activities as clearly wrong and perceive this view as normal and natural. When this acceptance occurs, viewing all non-Witnesses with either sorrow or disapproval is natural, solidifying the "we-they" dichotomy and forcing them to rely heavily on other Witnesses for social and other needs. The pressure imposed upon members for isolation from non-Witnesses is so complete that it places a heavy strain on family memberships, especially if the entire family is not fully committed to the Watchtower.

The Watchtower publications constantly, both overtly and covertly, endeavor to shape the Witnesses into a united worldwide caring family, one community with one major goal, to push forward the building of the New World Society. They try to remove any factor which may cause division within that community, whether caused by differences in income, status, socioeconomic class, race, ability, and even position in the congregation. They are fond of quoting Paul's words found at 1 Corinthians 1:10-17 which, in summary, says that "There are not to be divisions among you, you are one body, all serving Christ." Involvement in community always involves a trade-off to obtain its benefits. Many sacrifices are required including higher education, career advancement, avoidance of secular politics, and strict adherence to their rigid belief system. The organization defines separation from the world as requiring avoidance of an extremely long list of activities which include saluting the flag, becoming part of the armed forces, running for office, any patriotic display, membership in organizations such as civic groups, the Boy or Girl Scouts, and even participating in extracurricular school activities including sports.

The love and fellowship Witnesses give one another is clearly conditional, based primarily on intellectual, emotional, and physical loyalty to the Society, its organization, and the persons it has placed in leadership positions.

DISFELLOWSHIPPING

For Witnesses whose behavior is interpreted as rebellious, especially if they question the belief that the Watchtower is God's organization or indulge in complaining, not putting forth the effort necessary to attend all of the meetings, study, prepare for the meetings, engage in Bible study with others, go from door-to-door, and the like, counseling communication may take the form of condemnation or criticism instead of positive help to change what is viewed as improper.

The ultimate sin of a Witness is disagreeing with the organization; it—not God—must be obeyed without question in all areas. Adherence to the Society teachings, even doctrines that they know to be wrong, is imperative; Witnesses are condemned even if they advocate a doctrine that the Watchtower later teaches is correct. The authority structure of the Witness organization and the reasons behind the harshness of the total ban upon those who openly discuss differing exegetical positions, is an important doctrine.

Hunting out heretics is a major Watchtower preoccupation, and large numbers of Witnesses are forced out due to what are often minor faith differences with the Society. One is to unquestioningly accept all of the teachings of the Watchtower Society without exception, and all members are required to report to the Watchtower authorities any person who is wavering in Watchtower loyalty.

When questions by Witnesses develop over the Society's ever-changing doctrine, the Watchtower Society tends to ignore the members' concerns. If they feel the questions are too damaging, they will stop them by the Witnesses' expulsion. Once the Watchtower makes an adverse judgment, which is the rule if a Witness espouses a non-Society idea, even in minor areas, or question any of the Society's doctrines, the Witness is expelled—disfellowshipped. This means that Witness can no longer have any normal fellowship whatsoever with any friends or family who are still Witnesses. And once this occurs, generally no recourse exists: the elders are all-powerful.

Witnesses are not to be individualistic, but are always to live their life in harmony with the rules and goals of the organization. Actually, the typical Witnesses' entire life is wrapped around the organization, so much so that it makes many life decisions for them. Witnesses can decide whether or not they have eggs or cereal for breakfast, but issues such as going to college, working wives, celebrating holidays, or working overtime, for years were decided for them in the negative. The Society has an elaborate set of rules by which each person is to abide, and Witnesses are pressured or forced to conform under pain of disfellowshipping. The Watchtower prohibitions have reached into virtually every area of life and cover minutia to the extreme.

One is not to "speculate," but rely on Jehovah because all knowledge comes through His organization. Arriving at a conclusion contrary to the Society's teaching is being presumptuous, or endeavoring to "run ahead of Jehovah's organization," and can be punished by expulsion. Even reading literature critical of the organization is a disfellowshipping offense.

The Society does not feel in the final analysis that the way to truth is by logic, reason, or science, but by authority. They consider their way correct, and any logic used to tear down their system is considered "the wisdom of this world"; thus, they are encouraged to avoid higher education, reading of secular materials, the less practical sciences, and reflective thinking in general.

Witnesses do not view this conformity as being forced, but rather view the Society as a loving parent helping them to "do what is right." All Witnesses come out of the same mold of indoctrination and therefore conform highly, even in small areas. Those who do not respond fully to indoctrination or social pressure, disapproval or formal punishment (being talked to by the elders or given public reproof), are disfellowshipped.

Excommunication has historically been one of the most effective means of social control because in its extreme forms it amounts to almost total social isolation, and the Witnesses practice one of the most severe forms of this isolation. One can be disfellowshipped for many vague sins such as "rebellion" or "conduct unbecoming a Christian." A major reason Witnesses are disfellowshipped is due to refusing to accept the full authority of the Watchtower, and guilt of any charge depends on one's attitude as judged by the elders. There are few rules to guide their system of "justice."

What does one do when one's individual conscience conflicts with an organization's dictates, be it state, church, or business? Who shall he or she obey? This issue has been of concern time and time again throughout history. Many conclude that they are constrained to obey the organization; others feel that they must do what they sincerely believe to be correct and, in view of the fact that the Witnesses require rigid adherence to the teachings that they espouse (even though their teachings change, and some are poorly researched and thought out), much room for conflict exists.

Watchtower leaders are regularly accused by their detractors of brainwashing, specifically because they attempt to rigidly control all of the information that members receive. Reading literature critical of the Witnesses is a disfellowshipping offense. Witnesses are to unquestioningly accept all of the central teachings of the Watchtower Society without exception. They are even strongly discouraged from reading any religious literature aside from that printed by the Watchtower Society.

Disfellowshipping admittedly has some positive affects for the organization—it helps to insure that the members walk the moral straight and narrow. The control that disfellowshipping gives insures that the organization is unified and dissonants are effectively and quickly purged out. To do this, though, the organization's welfare is put above individual concerns. Even writing books in favor of the Society is discouraged; many of the few active Witnesses who wrote books supportive of the Society were eventually disfellowshipped.

THEOCRATIC WARFARE

Theocratic warfare is another controversial doctrine. This teaching concludes that it is appropriate for Witnesses to withhold information from those they feel could use it to harm the Watchtower Society. This doctrine specifically teaches that it is not necessary to reveal the truth to those who have no right to know it, such as where Witness activities are circumscribed. Therefore, "in time of spiritual warfare it is proper to misdirect the enemy by hiding the truth." (*WT* 5-1-57, p. 286) "She was not a liar. Rather, she was using theocratic war strategy, hiding the truth by action and word for the sake of the ministry." (*WT* 5-1-57, p. 285; see also *AW* 2-8-2000, p. 21)

While ostensibly condemning lying, the doctrine approves behavior which is legally lying, i.e., the court requirement that one tell "the whole truth and nothing but the truth." They thus not uncommonly openly "lie" in court, inferring or directly stating that practices which the Watchtower Society condemns are permissible, such as blood transfusions or intimate association with outsiders. The doctrine is a major teaching which has often been elucidated in their publications. One booklet prepared for Witnesses involved in child custody cases even openly advises Witnesses to deceive the court relative to their faith and practice. (See Jerry Bergman, *The Theocratic War Doctrine: Why Jehovah's Witnesses Lie in Court* [Clayton, Calif.: Witness Inc., 1998]).

WHY JEHOVAH'S WITNESSES HAVE MENTAL PROBLEMS

Having myself worked with almost one hundred active Witnesses who were mentally ill, I have repeatedly experienced their revealing significant doubts, troubles, and fears—and then a short time later, while attempting to proselytize their neighbors, claim that Jehovah's Witnesses are the happiest people on Earth.

Numerous reasons exist for the mental health problems among Witnesses, but research has determined the following often are among the most important:

1. *Change in policy.* The Watchtower is in a perpetual state of doctrinal change, often flip-flopping as many as three or four times on a single issue. Nowhere has this been so tragic as in their antimedical teachings; deaths due to obedience to these teachings are especially traumatic if the doctrine changes, and what was once condemned becomes approved. When Witnesses read the earlier Watchtower publications, most agree that much which was once taught is absolute foolishness.

2. *Prophecy failure.* Those who are not part of the Watchtower often do not understand the critical significance Watchtower failed prophecy and erroneous teachings have in the lives of Witnesses. Witnesses as a whole firmly believe—at least they must verbalize they firmly believe—that the Watchtower is God's *only* organization and is directed by Him; for this reason, the many changed teachings are of no small importance. Watchtower publications are not simply books and magazines written by humans to try and explain Scripture, but they are viewed as quasi-inspired, almost like a new Bible chapter that arrives each week. False prophecy vividly tells the Witness they devoted much of their life to a false religious organization. Dealing with this reality is enormously traumatic, can take years to adjust to, and can bring on psychological as well as somatic symptoms. Thus, many Witnesses' responses to these prophetic failures often involve an initial disappointment, then puzzlement and chagrin, and finally an adjustment involving explaining away the failure—or regressing to an attitude of watchful waiting for the yet unfulfilled prophesies to in some way yet occur.

Those Witnesses who were openly critical of the Watchtower's prediction that Armageddon would come in 1975 were often forced out of the organization, even though history has proved them right and the

Watchtower wrong. Rather than welcoming them back with open arms and apologizing for their error, the Society insisted that these persons are to remain disfellowshipped unless they repent, serve penance, and again rigidly follow the Watchtower. The Watchtower teaches that even Witnesses who advocate teachings that are later acknowledged by the Watchtower to be correct may be destroyed by God because unity is more important than truth. If the Watchtower is indeed wrong, they believe that God will eventually cause the Watchtower to change, and individual Witnesses are not to be influential in this process.

3. *An unhealthy subordination to the authority of the sect.* Jehovah's Witnesses must rigidly follow the organization; they are taught that *no one* except the very top Watchtower leaders can discern God's will through Bible study alone. Only by being part of God's organization, the Watchtower Society, can one be saved. The key is not being saved in the Christian sense or even being good, but being in the Watchtower organization— although they also teach that *even this* does not guarantee salvation.

The Watchtower policy of requiring Witness professionals such as lawyers, doctors, or psychologists to report information to the elders relative to Watchtower defined wrong-doing has created much controversy. I recently received a copy of an agreement form, a Waiver of Confidentiality, which a Witness psychologist requires all of his Witness patients to sign before he will work with them. It is appalling that any licensed therapist would indulge in the highly unethical practice of using an agreement which requires them to "report" to the elders their patient's behavior that the Watchtower considers wrong. Given the large number of offenses that the Watchtower disfellowships for, it is probably a rare psychiatric client that has not committed some of them. This form almost guarantees that the client will not be free and open with a counselor— but rather will be extremely guarded, fearful that what they say will be used against them later. I cannot imagine a poorer situation in which to do counseling. The whole point of therapy is to lay bare one's soul so that the therapist can work with clients to help them build a better life.

Of course, the client could elect to reveal damning information and face the consequences—a situation which in most cases is hardly very conducive to helping the person deal with his or her problems which are the basis for whatever sin may have occurred. Even if the judicial committee elects not to disfellowship, the fear that one could be thrown out of the congregation and be rejected by one's counselor during this difficult time can work against helping the client. The counselor is clearly saying with this statement, "You and your needs are not as important as strictly obeying the dictates of the Watchtower." And, "If, in the elders' opinion, you violate these dictates, I, as your counselor, who once endeavored to unconditionally accept you and help you with your problems, will also toss you out, and will no longer help you."

As has been well-documented, the elders tend to feel that the solution to every problem is to pray, study more, and trust in Jehovah; they feel the guilt over whatever emotional problems one is suffering from is likely due to some sin or shortcoming on that person's part. In my experience, the elders often do more harm than good, which is what we would expect: putting people who have not only no training, but also a false view of humanity and a distorted perception of reality, in charge of an emotionally disturbed person could well be lethal—as it sometimes is.

Discouraged from many normal means of self-fulfillment, Witnesses slavishly devote their time and energy to serving an organization that does not care about them as individuals. Many feel they are trapped in a way of life in which virtually every alternative is undesirable. Many thus plod along for years, hoping that Armageddon will come soon to rescue them from their plight. In the meantime, their depression and hopelessness colors everything they do, even though they ostensibly may appear to be "happy serving Jehovah."

The attractions that originally pulled many people to the Watchtower often do not last much beyond baptism. Their associates who were once very supportive and tolerant of their lack of doctrinal conformity soon insist that they rigidly teach and believe all Watchtower policy. They are now considered mature and must rigidly follow every whim of the Watchtower. Once they are trapped, the easy-going tolerance that lured them into the Watchtower is no longer manifested. They are thus successfully pressured into doing things they had first resisted, sometimes tremendously. The hope of the new world just around the corner becomes more and more in the future until many wonder if this often delayed promise will ever come.

Most Witnesses who leave consistently report that involvement in the Watchtower, while usually positive at first, in time often causes much emotional turmoil for months or even years. After one has adjusted to the outside world, most ex-Witnesses do not regret leaving, and many conclude that their involvement seriously adversely affected their mental health. An examination of the many available case histories reveals a clear pattern of progressive mental health deterioration caused by the conflicts Witnesses have with the world, the demands that the Society's belief structure makes upon them, the practices, the doubts that some members have relative to the validity of the Watchtower's various teachings, and the environment that the Watchtower produces.

WITNESS JARGON

The sense of community and isolation from the outside world is heightened by an extensive Witness jargon. Witnesses know the specific meaning the Society gives to terms such as New World Society, Brooklyn, Governing Body, placement, publisher, auxiliary pioneer, field overseer, secretary, luck, disfellowshipping, etc. It is fairly easy to determine whether or not a person is an active, involved Witness by evaluating one's familiarity with the current terminology.

Regular changes in terminology are an effective means to insure that those who are active in the Witness community can be distinguished from those who are either less committed or are impostors. The Witnesses are very sensitive to a wide variety of subtle cues which not only distinguishes the "in" from the "out" group, but also the various levels of commitment of the "in" group—and they are trained specifically to use this means to test strangers who claim to be Witnesses; if they pass, they are treated as close friends, i.e., "brothers." Their training, much of it informal, includes listening to what fellow Witnesses tend to talk about and assessing their attitudes toward a wide variety of things. Witnesses are keenly attuned especially to evidence indicating lack of respect for the Society, the Witness organization, and its doctrines and beliefs. This contributes to the Witnesses' feeling of unity, oneness of purpose and goals. This commitment is necessary for one to give the level of time and money resources to the movement that one is often pressured to give.

GLOSSARY

Anointed   A group of 144,000 Witnesses chosen by God to rule in Heaven with Jesus after they die on Earth.

Armageddon   God's war to rid the Earth of wickedness and to save faithful Jehovah's Witnesses.

Assembly   Many congregations gathering for an all-day meeting, usually held twice each year under the direction of the Society.

Baptism   Water immersion of an individual by a brother in good standing, symbolizing dedication to Jehovah through a commitment to the Watchtower Society and their organization. A requirement to become one of Jehovah's Witnesses, and to survive Armageddon.

Bethel   The world headquarters of the Watchtower Society in New York City, and main printing factory for the Society's literature.

Bible Study   Regular one-on-one meetings at the home of a person who wants to learn the teachings of Jehovah's Witnesses. A study of the Watchtower Society's interpretations of the Bible, using Watchtower literature and taught by a Witness.

Bloodguilty   The state of being responsible for the loss of one or more human lives.

Brother   A male baptized Jehovah's Witness.

Brothers (The)   Male baptized Jehovah's Witnesses collectively. Also a term that is sometimes used when referring to the elder body, or the leaders in the organization.

Christian   Jehovah's Witnesses exclusively.

Christendom   All religions that profess to be Christian (excluding Jehovah's Witnesses); the Society views these as false Christianity.

Circuit   A group of congregations designated by the Society.

Circuit Overseer A traveling elder who is appointed by the Society to supervise a circuit.

Committee   (See "Judicial Committee")

Congregation   A group of Witnesses who regularly meet together under the leadership of one or more elders, under the direction of the Watchtower Society.

Convention   A large Witness gathering of several circuits lasting from three to seven days, held yearly under the direction of the Society.

Demons   Angels who chose to follow Satan the Devil; the Devil and the demons were ousted from heaven in 1914 down to the vicinity of the Earth.

Disassociation   Voluntary removal of oneself as one of Jehovah's Witnesses. Viewed by Witnesses as "suicide," as they believe Jehovah will forever destroy disassociated persons at Armageddon. Viewed also as "turning one's back on Jehovah" and choosing the Devil's side, hence Witnesses are required to shun disassociated persons.

Disfellowship   Involuntary, forced removal by the elders of a person from the organization (excommunication) for biblical wrongdoing or violation of the organization's rules. Viewed by Witnesses as a "death sentence" if the person does not repent and return to the organization. Witnesses are required to shun disfellowshipped persons.

Elder	A "Scripturally qualified" brother appointed by the Society to a position of leadership in a congregation. An elder is following the recommendations of the local body of elders. In actuality, friendship and family networks are often important in this process (similar to a pastor in a church). There is no limit to the number of elders a congregation may have.
Elder Body	All of the elders in a congregation.
Emblems	The unleavened bread and wine, symbolizing Jesus' body and blood, that are circulated among the congregation members during the celebration of The Memorial.
End, The	Armageddon, bringing the end to the world as we know it.
Evil Slave (The)	Former Witnesses who openly oppose the Watchtower Society.
Faithful and Discreet Slave/Servant	The Society's interpretation of Matthew 24:45, meaning that Jesus predicted that God would establish a special "servant" or "slave" on the Earth, having the sole spiritual authority to represent Him, and acting as the sole interpreter of the Bible. The Watchtower Society, as represented by the Governing Body, applies this designation to itself.
Field Service	Jehovah's Witnesses' house-to-house preaching, distribution of Watchtower literature, and conducting of home Bible studies with interested persons who are not Jehovah's Witnesses.
Goat	A person opposed to the message of Jehovah's Witnesses.
Governing Body	A group varying from approximately eleven to seventeen anointed Witness men residing at the Watchtower headquarters in New York City, claiming to be enlightened by Jehovah God, the sole interpreter of the Bible, and the only channel of communication between God and all humankind. The Governing Body makes the rules all Witnesses are required to believe and obey.

Great Crowd   Persons surviving Armageddon into the new system on Earth.

Great Tribulation Time of great trouble and anguish on the Earth directly preceding Armageddon, marked by the world's governments—led by the United Nations—attack on Jehovah's Witnesses.

Jehovah   The name of the only true God; the Father of Jesus Christ.

Jehovah's Witness Baptized member of the Watchtower Society's organization of Jehovah's Witnesses.

Jehovah's Witnesses Adherents to the tenants of the Watchtower Society, believing themselves to be God's chosen servants and the only true Christians on Earth.

Judicial Committee A meeting of three elders appointed to conduct a hearing (or a trial) with a Witness who is accused of breaking the Society's rules, or of committing a biblical wrongdoing.

Kingdom Hall   The building used for the meetings of Jehovah's Witnesses.

"Marked"   A label applied to Witnesses who are guilty of disobeying the Society's rules, but not seriously enough to warrant disfellowshipping. Witnesses who are marked are socially ostracized.

Marked Generation People living in the time period from 1914 onward. This time period is "marked" in that some of the people born in 1914 will live to experience Armageddon.

Memorial   The mandatory yearly observance of the Lord's Evening Meal (similar to "communion" in many churches). Only Witnesses of the elite anointed class of 144,000 may partake of the bread and wine, while others in attendance simply observe.

Ministerial Servant A brother appointed by the elder body to assist the elders. The scriptural requirements for ministerial servant are fewer than those for elders.

New Light New information or insights regarding Witness doctrines that Witnesses believe to be channeled from God to the Society's Governing Body, and presented through the Society's literature or speakers at Watchtower Society conventions or assemblies.

New System (The) The paradise that God will restore to Earth after Armageddon, where obedient humankind will live forever under God's rule as administered on Earth through the Watchtower Society.

NWT *New World Translation of the Holy Scriptures*, the Watchtower Society's own translation of the Bible.

Organization (The) The organization of the Watchtower Society, including all the congregations of Jehovah's Witnesses, its leaders, its headquarters and branch offices, and its printing facilities. It lays claim to being God's sole organization and the only true religion on Earth.

Overseer Term formerly used in reference to an exemplary brother chosen by the Society to lead, supervise, and shepherd a congregation (similar to a pastor in a church); this arrangement was later replaced by a body of elders. Term still used to describe the positions of leadership over assemblies, conventions, circuits, districts, and branches.

Pioneer An exemplary Witness whose field service is regularly 100 hours a month (later lowered to 90 hours a month).

Placements Watchtower Society literature given to a non-Witness, or left at homes or public places for people to read.

Platform The stage in the Kingdom Hall from which brothers deliver lectures or address the congregation. One must be in good standing in the congregation to use the platform. Comments that brothers make from the platform carry great weight of importance.

Presiding Overseer The elder who is the chairman of the elder body in a congregation.

Publisher A Witness who shares Watchtower literature and doctrine with non-Witnesses, participating in the Witness preaching activity.

Reinstatement The elder body's reacceptance back into the organization of a person who had been disfellowshipped or who had disassociated himself.

Remnant A collective name given to those living who claim to be part of the anointed group of 144,000 who will inherit heavenly life when they die.

Satan the Devil Spirit creature who is the adversary of God, believed to be misleading the entire inhabited Earth, particularly since 1914 when he was cast out of Heaven.

Servant A brother who has been assigned responsibility in the congregation as an elder or ministerial servant.

Service Meeting An hourly (later changed to 45 minutes) meeting held weekly at the Kingdom Hall, primarily focused on teaching and recruiting methods to be used when preaching to outsiders.

Service Report A monthly report every active Witness is required to turn in, indicating how many hours he or she spent in the preaching work, how many magazines and books were placed with non-Witnesses, how many follow-up visits were made, and how many Bible studies the Witness conducted that month.

Sheep A person interested in the message of Jehovah's Witnesses.

Sister A baptized female Jehovah's Witness.

Society (The) The Watchtower Bible and Tract Society, consisting of the Governing Body and the various committees they have selected to assist them. The Society's headquarters are in New York City. Responsible for overseeing publication of all Witness literature. All Witnesses must submit to the Society's authority completely.

Spiritual Food	Doctrines, scriptural interpretations, literature, Kingdom Hall meetings, assemblies, and conventions emanating from the Watchtower Society.
Stumble	To cause a person to leave the organization because of poor conduct by a Witness.
Territory	The geographical area assigned to each congregation to cover in the preaching work. Attending a congregation outside one's territory is viewed as spiritual weakness, unless the Society instructs one to do so for a special or specific purpose.
This System of Things	The world as we now know it.
Theocratic	A word describing a person or event adhering to all of the Society's rules.
Theocratic Ministry School	A meeting which is held for about an hour weekly at the Kingdom Hall. This school teaches Witnesses communication and speaking skills through giving short talks to the congregation, to equip them for the Witness house-to-house evangelizing work. All Witnesses are expected to participate.
Truth	The teachings of the Watchtower Society at any given moment, believed to be the only and absolute truth from God.
Untheocratic	A word describing a person or an event that does not adhere to all of the Society's rules.
World, The	Life outside of the organization.
Worldly	A word describing people who are not Jehovah's Witnesses, or to describe Witnesses who have untheocratic attitudes.
Yearbook	A book the Society publishes yearly depicting Witness activities in various parts of the world.

LIST OF PERIODICALS

The following publications, from which I have quoted in this work, were all written and published by the Watchtower Society.

Aid to Bible Understanding. A 1,696 page Bible encyclopedia completed in 1971, covering Bible topics from the viewpoint of the Watchtower Society.

AW (Awake!). The magazine that replaced *Consolation* in 1946; published twice monthly containing short articles on a variety of subjects appealing to the general public, written from the perspective of the Watchtower Society. It is a more secular journal, designed to proselytize more discreetly than the *Watchtower* magazine.

Blood, Medicine, and The Law of God. A 62-page booklet published in 1961 wherein the Society attempts to justify their position against blood transfusions.

Children. A 382-page book published in 1941, which is a theology text for young people; this is the book that discouraged young Witnesses from marrying.

Consolation. A magazine which replaced the *Golden Age* in 1937, and was renamed *Awake!* in 1946.

Face the Facts. A 64-page booklet published in 1938, a diatribe against the Catholic and other churches.

Finished Mystery, The. A 608-page book published in 1917 as vol. VII of the *Studies in the Scriptures* series, featuring a discussion of the Bible books of Revelation and Ezekiel. This work was banned by the American and Canadian governments because of statements which were viewed as critical of the war effort. As a compromise, the Society agreed to ask its members to tear out pages 247–58, and thus many copies of this book lack these pages.

315

From Paradise Lost to Paradise Regained. A 256-page book published in 1958, which is a text of basic theology designed for children, covering basic Witness doctrine and focusing on end of the world theology.

GA (Golden Age, The). A magazine published from 1919 to 1937, at which time it was renamed *Consolation.*

Harp of God, The. A 384-page book published in 1921 and extensively revised in 1928, covering basic doctrine including creation, Jesus, the ransom, and Christ's return.

How Can Blood Save Your Life? A 32-page booklet published in 1990, attempting to convince readers that blood transfusions are against the law of God and often medically harmful.

Informant. A monthly newsletter 2 to 4 pages long.

Insight on the Scriptures. Two volumes, 1,278 pages each, published in 1988; a Bible dictionary covering Witness doctrine.

Is This Life All There Is? A 192-page book published in 1974, including the Watchtower teaching on the afterlife, hell, heaven, and life in the "new world."

Judge Rutherford Uncovers Fifth Column. A 32-page booklet by J. F. Rutherford, second president of the Watchtower Society; basically a diatribe against the Catholic Church, written to answer a newspaper's questions.

KM (Kingdom Ministry). A 4- to 8-page monthly bulletin for baptized Witnesses in good standing, containing programs for Service Meetings. At times contains inserts with information for Witnesses only—information that the Society does not want to be made public.

Let God Be True. A 320-page book published in 1946 and revised in 1952, covering the topics of hell, the trinity, the end of the world, the new world, the resurrection, and Satan.

Life Everlasting—in Freedom of the Sons of God. A 416-page book published in 1966 containing Witness doctrine, featuring a chart of significant dates from the creation of man, pointing to the year 1975 as the likely date for God's Kingdom to begin ruling over the Earth.

Make Sure of All Things: Hold Fast to What Is Fine. A 512-page book published in 1965 which was a reference book used primarily as an aid to Witnesses while participating in the door-to-door preaching work, as it is a reference book of scriptures listed under topics to support Witness doctrine. Many Witnesses had this book bound into the back of their Bibles for discreet use.

Man's Salvation Out of World Distress At Hand! A 382-page book published in 1975 containing Bible prophecy and the "last days," and much about the enemies of God's people.

Messenger, The. A report related to the Society's conventions

Millions Now Living Will Never Die. A 128-page book published in 1920 that includes the prophecy that the year 1925 will witness the return to life on Earth of Abraham, Isaac, Jacob, and other faithful prophets of the Bible.

NIV *(New International Version).* A translation of the Bible.

New World, The. A 384-page book published in 1942, containing doctrines related
to death, resurrection, and judgment.

NWT (*New World Translation of the Holy Scriptures*). The Watchtower Society's own
Bible translation, completed in 1960. Witnesses believe this to be the most
accurate Bible translation in the world, as it was produced by the Society, who
they believe to be "divinely directed" by Jehovah God. Published for years
with a green cover, this translation has drawn much criticism, primarily
because of its "slanted" rendering of various Scriptures that relate to major
Christian doctrines.

Organization for Kingdom-Preaching and Disciple-Making. A 192-page book published in 1972 for Witnesses; it outlines the Society's policies on the preaching
work, organizational structure, Kingdom Hall meetings, how the organization
is financed, and the necessity of turning-in to the elders any Witness who
breaks the Society's rules.

Organized to Accomplish Our Ministry. A 224-page book published in 1983; essentially an update of *Organization for Kingdom-Preaching and Disciple-Making*

Pastor Russell's Sermons. An 804-page book published in 1917; a choice collection
of the most important discourses on all phases of Christian doctrine given by
the Watchtower's first president, Charles Taze Russell.

Prophecy. A 358-page book published in 1929, featuring doctrine on Satan versus
God's organization.

Qualified to be Ministers. A 384-page book published in 1955 and revised in 1967,
designed for use in the Society's Theocratic Ministry School.

Reasoning from the Scriptures. A 445-page book published in 1985 and revised in
1989; replaced the *Make Sure of All Things* book as an aid to Witnesses while
participating in the door-to-door preaching work, as it is a reference book
ofscriptures listed under topics to support Witness doctrine. Witnesses commonly had this book bound into the back of their Bibles for discreet use.

Religion. A 384-page book published in 1940; an exposé of religion, all of which
the Society teaches are corrupt except for their own.

Reprints. Watchtower Society magazines from 1879–1919, collected after the death
of the Society's first president and published by the Society as bound volumes.

Revelation—The Grand Climax at Hand! A 320-page book published in 1988; a
commentary on the Bible book of Revelation, the prophecies and symbols of
which are interpreted as referring primarily to Jehovah's Witnesses and their
history.

Riches. A 386-page book published in 1936 on Watchtower theology.

School and Jehovah's Witnesses. A 32-page booklet published in 1983, written for
Witness parents of school-age children to share with public school teachers. It
covers many Witness prohibitions that may conflict with school activities, and
why they exist.

Time Is at Hand, The. A 366-page book published in 1888, revised in 1889 to 387
pages; vol. II in the *Studies in the Scriptures* series, covering Bible chronology.

This Means Everlasting Life. A 318-page book published in 1950 dealing with salvation through Jesus Christ.

Three Worlds, The. A 197-page book published in 1877, featuring chronology and arguing for the presence—not coming—of Christ. Also discusses God's plan of redemption.

Thy Kingdom Come. A 426-page book published in 1891 as vol. III in the *Studies in the Scriptures* series, discussing God's Kingdom and the time of the end. Features an entire section about Egypt's great pyramid of Gizeh, claiming the pyramid teaches an outline of the plan of God—past, present, and future.

Truth That Leads to Eternal Life, The. A 190-page book published in 1968, containing basic doctrine text used as the teaching tool for conducting home Bible studies with interested outsiders through 1981. Witnesses commonly referred to it affectionately as "the little blue bomb." The Society claims that it quickly became an all-time "best seller," with no other book in the Western world besides the Bible exceeding its circulation (*AW* 9-22-73, p. 8). What the Society doesn't mention is that the book cost only twenty-five cents for years, and that many were even given away for free.

United in Worship of the Only True God. A 192-page book published in 1983, reviewing the Society's social and moral teachings; stresses the need to follow God's organization on Earth, i.e., the Watchtower Society.

WT (*Watchtower, The*). Magazine published twice monthly; required reading for all Witnesses, and the primary vehicle through which "new light" from Jehovah is revealed.

Watchtower Publications Index. An index, published every few years in book or magazine form, arranged according to subject, to serve as a guide to finding the Society's viewpoints on a vast array of topics in Watchtower literature. Also contains a Scripture index, listing those Scriptures on which the Society has commented, and which Watchtower publications contain those comments.

Way to Paradise, The. A 256-page book published in 1924, reviewing Watchtower theology for young people; much on the creation account and the fall and restoration of humankind.

Yearbook of Jehovah's Witnesses. A book of roughly 260 pages published annually, discussing the worldwide witnessing work.

You Can Live Forever in Paradise on Earth. A 256-page book published in 1982 and revised in 1989, containing basic doctrine text; replaced *The Truth That Leads to Eternal Life* as the teaching tool for conducting home Bible studies with interested outsiders.

Your Will Be Done on Earth. A 384-page book published in 1958, which presents a history of God's dealings with humans, and concludes that God's earthly Kingdom will soon be established.

INDEX

abuse
  by Watchtower Society. *See also* Discipline
  of children, 81
  through public humiliation, 232
  by blaming the Witnesses, 81–83
  like an addiction, 130
  through doctrines 214
  through elders, 62
  in childhood
    by mother, 17–18
    leads to codependency, 226, 228, 230
    psychological effects of, 114, 225–27, 272
angels, 24, 34, 61,154
anointed, 70–71, 105, 192
apostasy, apostates, 239, 245–46, 273
appearances, 69, 70, 288
"ark of salvation," 23, 288
Armageddon
  casualties of
    for not heeding the warning, 32
    all non-Witnesses, 78
    children of non-believers, 107
    disfellowshipped Witnesses, 254
    outsiders, 288

    Witnesses who leave the organization, 289
  definition of, 20, 22, 72
  fear of, 43,72, 97
  predictions of, 22, 84, 157–58
  requirements for survival of
    baptism, 40
    be a Witness, 20
    Kingdom Hall attendance, 27
    obedience to Watchtower Society, 70
    participate in witnessing work, 32
    put on new personality, 29
assemblies
  counsel given at, 38, 59, 61, 65–66, 94
  talks given at, 78, 80, 172, 236
authority
  of men, 36
  of Watchtower Society, 55, 213, 217, 224, 303

bad associates, 103, 297. *See also* isolation
baptism, 40–43, 92
beards, forbidden, 43
behavior control, 232–33

319